Has Devolution Delivered?

Has Devolution Delivered?

Edited by Catherine Bromley, John Curtice,
David McCrone and Alison Park

Edinburgh University Press

Editorial arrangement © Catherine Bromley, John Curtice, David McCrone
and Alison Park, 2006. Other material © the contributors, 2006.

Edinburgh University Press Ltd
22 George Square, Edinburgh

Typeset in Goudy Old Style by
Iolaire Typesetting, Newtonmore, and
printed and bound in Great Britain by
Biddles Ltd, King's Lynn, Norfolk

A CIP record for this book is available from the British Library

ISBN-10 0 7486 2246 2 (paperback)
ISBN-13 978 0 7486 2246 7 (paperback)

 **Scottish Centre for
Social Research**

Published with the support of the Edinburgh University Scholarly
Publishing Initiatives Fund.

Contents

Tables

Notes on the Contributors

Ross Bond is Lecturer in Sociology at the University of Edinburgh.

Catherine Bromley is a Research Director at the Scottish Centre for Social Research.

John Curtice is Research Consultant to the Scottish Centre for Social Research and is Professor of Politics at the University of Strathclyde.

Asifa Hussain is Lecturer in Public Sector Management and Human Resource Management at the University of Glasgow.

David McCrone is Professor of Sociology and Director of the Institute of Governance at the University of Edinburgh.

William Miller is Edward Caird Professor of Politics at the University of Glasgow.

Alison Park is a Research Director at the National Centre for Social Research.

Lindsay Paterson is Professor of Educational Policy at the University of Edinburgh.

Michael Rosie is Lecturer in the Sociology of Scotland at the University of Edinburgh.

Paula Surridge is Lecturer in Sociology at the University of Bristol.

CHAPTER I

Introduction

INTRODUCTION

Devolution has transformed the way Scotland is governed. No longer is policy on such key domestic matters as health, education and law and order formally made by the UK government in concert with the House of Commons. Instead, it is settled by a Scottish Executive and a Scottish Parliament located in Edinburgh.

For its advocates, this new arrangement has two key advantages (Paterson 1998). First, it recognises and expresses the distinctive sense of nationhood felt by most Scots. While the Treaty of Union in 1707 had guaranteed recognition of the separate legal system and religious settlement north of the border, it meant that Scotland no longer had its own autonomous political institutions. The devolution settlement, in contrast, acknowledged the nationalist sentiment that any nation should have its own political institutions (Gellner 1983), a sentiment fuelled by the fact that the Conservatives had been able to run Scotland between 1979 and 1997 even though they failed to win a majority of the country's parliamentary seats. However, unlike the option of independence, the devolution settlement acknowledged this nationalist sentiment within the framework of the Union. Indeed, by demonstrating that it is possible to develop a quasi-federal territorial settlement that accommodates Scots' distinctive national sentiment, many advocates of devolution hoped that the creation of the Scottish Parliament would actually help to strengthen support for the Union (Aughey 2001: chapter 7; Bogdanor 1999; Friedrich 1968; Mackintosh 1998; Stepan 1999).

The second key advantage commonly claimed for devolution is that it makes government more accessible and accountable (see also Courchene 1995). Instead of being run by a small group of ministers shuttling between London and Edinburgh and a Westminster parliament for whom Scottish affairs were a peripheral concern, Scotland now has some two dozen ministers located in Edinburgh answerable to a parliament for whom domestic Scottish affairs constitute its only concern. The governance of Scotland is given the attention and scrutiny it deserves, while ministers and politicians are geographically accessible to those who wish to lobby and persuade them (Scottish Constitutional Convention 1995). Indeed, this strand of thinking was particularly prominent in the work of the Consultative Steering Group that was established to develop the initial working rules of the parliament (Scottish Office 1999). Accountability and accessibility together with 'sharing power' and 'equal opportunities' were two of the four principles to which the group argued the parliament should adhere. These were expressed, for example, in proposals that the parliament should have a relatively powerful system of committees, enable the public to influence its work through a system of public petitions, and more generally move away from the remote confrontational style of politics associated with Westminster. As a result, it was argued, devolution would help to 'engage' a public that had become increasingly disenchanted with the way it was governed (Curtice and Jowell 1997; Dewar 1998).

However, the devolution settlement was not without its doubters. Far from strengthening the Union, it was suggested that the creation of a separate Scottish Parliament that symbolised Scottish rather than British national identity would simply fuel nationalist sentiment yet further (Thatcher 1998). Devolution would set Scotland on the 'slippery slope' to independence (Dalyell 1977). Moreover, despite the claims of the SNP leadership that all who lived in Scotland should have the right to become citizens of Scotland, devolution could unleash a 'narrow nationalism' that was intolerant of those who were not regarded as 'real Scots' on account of their birth, ancestry or accent. Far from making government more accountable and accessible, the parliament and its committees would be at the mercy of every lobby group imaginable and would certainly be subject to the dictates and demands of party politics in just the same way as politics is at Westminster (Bradbury and Mitchell 2001). Instead of helping to engage voters in the political process, sub-state institutions run the risk that their elections are regarded as unimportant affairs that are not thought worth participating in. Meanwhile, by requiring that the parliament be elected by a system of proportional representation, the devolution settlement more or less guaranteed that the country would be run by coalition, thereby making it more difficult for those voters who did bother to go to the polls to know whom to hold accountable when things go wrong.

Whatever the merits of these various arguments, one crucial point emerges. The ability of devolution to deliver on its promises depends on the response it receives from the public. For example, its ability to help restore the emotional glue that might be thought to help hold the Union together depends on whether ordinary Scots become more or less willing to acknowledge a sense of British national identity. Their willingness to support the maintenance of the Union can be expected to depend too on whether they feel that devolution has demonstrated the ability of the Union in practice to accommodate the distinctive needs, interests and aspirations of the people of Scotland. Meanwhile, devolution could only help to 'engage' people in their nation's political life if they felt it gave them more influence and if they wanted to participate in its work. Devolution will only ensure that Scotland's politicians are held accountable for their successes and failures if the public takes cognisance of these when deciding how to vote in Scottish Parliament elections. Equally, whether devolution un-leashes a 'narrow nationalism' depends on how ordinary Scots interpret and reinterpret what it means to be Scottish.

This book assesses how the public has reacted to its initial experience of devolution now that two Scottish parliamentary elections have taken place. In particular, it asks whether the public's reaction has been in tune with the expectations of the advocates of devolution or whether instead develop-ments have realised the fears of its critics. This task is undertaken in three parts. In Part 1, comprising Chapters 2 to 4, we ask what impact devolution has had on support for the maintenance of the Union and how well Scots feel they are being governed. This includes an assessment of what has happened in the wake of devolution to the pattern of support for the principal advocates of the break-up of the Union, the SNP. In Part 2, Chapters 5 to 8, we examine the impact of devolution on the health of the nation's democracy by looking at how the public has behaved in the two elections to the Scottish Parliament that have been held so far. It examines who votes in those elections and why, how far voters use them to hold the parliament's politicians accountable, and how the public has responded to and used the more proportional electoral system. Finally, in Part 3, Chapters 9 and 10, we look at trends in and patterns of national identity. In particular, we examine whether Scottish national identity is an open 'civic' identity to which all those living in Scotland are thought to have a valid claim, or whether there are signs of a narrow ethnic nationalism that questions, for example, the right of those with an English or Pakistani background to play a full role in the life of the nation.

Our evidence comes from a series of high-quality social surveys. With the advent of devolution in 1999, the Scottish Centre for Social Research, part of the National Centre for Social Research, instigated the *Scottish Social Attitudes* survey. Its aim is to facilitate the academic study of public opinion in post-devolution Scotland and to chart public attitudes towards the nation's policy agenda. Each year, it asks a representative sample of around 1,500 adults their views about a wide range of social and political issues (Paterson et al. 2001; Curtice et al. 2002; Bromley et al. 2003). In the first five years of the survey from 1999 to 2003, many of the questions were about attitudes towards devolution, national identity and the Union. In both 1999 and 2003, particular attention was paid to how people voted in the Scottish Parliament elections of that year and why. Meanwhile, the 2003 survey paid particular attention to who was thought to be Scottish and to attitudes towards Scotland's English and Pakistani minorities. This means that the survey is uniquely well placed to assess how public opinion in Scotland has developed since the advent of devolution.

However, if we are to understand the impact of devolution on public opinion, we need to be able to do more than chart developments since 1999. We also need to have measures of public opinion prior to the creation of the Scottish Parliament. Fortunately, we have access to three surveys, similar in design to the Scottish Social Attitudes survey, that provide us with such measures. Two of these were conducted immediately after the 1992 and 1997 UK general elections as part of the *Scottish Election Study* series (Bennie et al. 1997; Brown et al. 1999), while a third, the *Scottish Referendum Study*, was undertaken immediately after the September 1997 referendum (Taylor and Thomson 1999). Many of the key questions about devolution, the Union and national identity that have been included in the Scottish Social Attitudes series since 1999 were in fact first asked in one or more of these earlier surveys. This means that we can compare directly what people in Scotland think today with how they felt in the years immediately before devolution.[1]

The early years of devolution have not been without their trials and tribulations. The people of Scotland gave strong backing to the creation of a Scottish Parliament in the referendum held on 11 September 1997: on a 60 per cent turnout, 74 per cent voted in favour of establishing the parliament, while 64 per cent also agreed that the new body should have the ability to vary the basic rate of income tax by up to three pence in the pound. Yet they have not shown an equivalent enthusiasm when it came to participating in elections to the new body. At the first election in 1999, when the election campaign was overshadowed by the outbreak of war in Kosovo, no more than 58 per cent voted, well down on the 71 per cent who had participated in the last UK general election just two years earlier. True, turnout appeared to be on the slide at all elections, as confirmed by the outcome of the 2001 UK general election, in which again only 58 per cent participated. Perhaps the parliament simply had the misfortune to have been established at a time when all political institutions were being greeted by a wave of apathy. But, in the second Scottish Parliament election in 2003, which also took place under the shadow of war, this time in Iraq, even fewer made it to the polls. A little under half (49 per cent) voted after a campaign that, in the eyes of many commentators, suggested there were few serious differences between the parties in how they wanted to run the country over the next four years (Allardyce 2004). In contrast, the 2005 election to the UK parliament recorded a marginal increase in turnout to 61 per cent. It seems as though the parliament has been struggling to maintain the interest and attention of the public it seeks to serve.

The parliament has also found itself mired in controversy. From its inception, it was pilloried in sections of the media for its preoccupation with the level of expenses that should be paid to different kinds of MSPs. It was faced, too, with allegations that a lobbying firm had undue access to the Executive, not least because it had previously employed the Finance Minister, Jack McConnell. Rather than leaving the sins of Westminster behind, it appeared that the new institution was equally vulnerable to allegations of sleaze. More serious, however, was the controversy that in the autumn of 2001 engulfed Henry McLeish, who had succeeded the 'father of devolution', Donald Dewar, as First Minister following Mr Dewar's un-timely death the previous year. It emerged that Mr McLeish had been charging the Commons' authorities the cost of space in his constituency offices that had in fact been commercially let. When it emerged that a statement purporting to give full details of the organisations that had at some time been tenants of his offices was less than complete, he succumbed to intense pressure to resign. Although the row concerned his role as an MP at Westminster rather than his work as an MSP at Holyrood, and arguably helped demonstrate the greater transparency of the Scottish Parliament's financial procedures, inevitably his forced resignation was widely regarded as a serious own goal for the parliament.

But the most serious public relations problem for the parliament was the story of its new home. When the UK government put forward its plans for devolution in a white paper in July 1997 (Scottish Office 1997), the cost of building a new home for the parliament was estimated publicly at just £40 million. Four years later, the cost eventually topped £400 million, while the date for completion was repeatedly postponed. In truth, as revealed by the official enquiry into what happened (Fraser of Carmyllie 2005), much of the responsibility for the increased cost did not lie with the parliament, while the validity of the original £40 million estimate was highly question-able. But the train of events enabled critics to argue that the parliament was unable to run its own affairs let alone the country, while repeated media stories along the lines that escalating demands were being made on the taxpayer simply in order to make life comfortable for politicians hardly made for a favourable public image. Indeed, research conducted for the parliament itself suggested that the story of the building became the one and perhaps only feature of the parliament which everyone in Scotland felt willing and able to discuss (Scottish Parliament 2001).

Still, the parliament did also have some achievements to its name. Between 1999 and 2003, it passed no fewer than sixty-two bills, thereby seemingly demonstrating how Scotland needed its own legislature in order for its affairs to receive proper attention. Moreover, not all of this legislation emerged from the Executive; nine were private members' bills, while three were initiated by one of the parliament's committees. But much of the legislation was detailed and technical and did not easily command public interest. Meanwhile, Westminster still played a greater role in legislating about Scotland's domestic affairs than many of its advocates had antici- pated; no fewer than forty-eight 'Sewel motions', allowing Westminster to legislate about a devolved matter, were passed, though most were uncon- tentious (Cairney and Keating 2004). Although the public petitions pro- cedure did have some impact (Jones 2004), the Executive initiated many a consultation; and, while committees regularly took evidence from interest groups and experts, it proved difficult – as the parliament's own Procedures Committee acknowledged – to draw into the policy-making process the kind of person who had not previously been involved in the policy process (Scottish Parliament Procedures Committee 2003).

Some policies did, however, attract public attention if not necessarily approval. University students in Scotland were absolved of the need to pay tuition fees while they were studying. Older people in need of long-term personal care were to have their care costs met irrespective of their financial circumstances. In both cases, the Executive and the Parliament were departing from recently developed UK government policy, thereby sym- bolically demonstrating that devolution could make a difference. On the other hand, one of the earliest decisions made by the Executive – to repeal, in tandem with similar moves by the UK government, legislation that barred local authorities (and thus their schools) from promoting homo- sexuality – produced a torrent of controversy, not least from the Catholic Church, and a well-funded opposition campaign financed by the business- man Brian Souter. This incident left many a minister rather bruised, and it perhaps inclined them thereafter to exercise caution in their pronounce- ments on social and moral issues.

But, whatever the difficulties that devolution faced in its early years, one potential strain in the Union appears to have been avoided – serious conflict between Holyrood and Westminster. Most potential conflict has, it seemed, been negotiated away by civil servants or by informal contacts between UK and Scottish ministers (Trench 2004). This was made possible by the existence of a favourable political and fiscal climate. Although the use of a proportional-representation system did indeed result in coalition government in Edinburgh, it was still a coalition led by Labour, together with Liberal Democrat partners with whom for the most part good relations were maintained. Thus, with Labour being re-elected at Westminster in 2001, the loyalties and networks of party could be used to sustain relations between the two administrations. Meanwhile, in 1999, the UK government embarked on a substantial expansion of public expenditure, not least in areas such as health and education, in which increases in the money made available to departments in England automatically trigger, under the terms of the 'Barnett formula', increases in the block grant assigned to Edinburgh. Overall, the Scottish Executive budget increased from £16.8 billion in 1999–2000 to £22.8 billion in 2003–4 (Jones 2004). Such largesse meant that London could hardly be blamed for denying Edinburgh the resources to do what it wanted. It also meant that, while the SNP campaigned in the 1999 election in favour of using the parliament's tax-varying power in order to reverse a one-penny cut in income tax that had been announced that spring by the Chancellor, in 2003 none of the main political parties was suggesting that it should be used.

However, while the political character of the administrations in Edinburgh and London largely resembled each other, the political composition of the Scottish Parliament as a whole was very different from that of the delegation of Scottish MPs at Westminster. Scotland's representation at Westminster was dominated by Labour while, after 1997, the Conservatives struggled to secure any representation at all. In contrast, as can be seen in Table 1.1, there has not only been significant Conservative representation at Holyrood but also a substantial phalanx of nationalist MPs, giving the nationalists the status of Scotland's main opposition party. Meanwhile, after the 2003 election at least, two parties which have never secured representation at Westminster, the Greens and the Scottish Socialist Party, also emerged with significant representation.

In part, the very different outcomes of UK and Scottish Parliament general elections are simply the result of the use of different rules for the allocation of seats. Whereas in UK general elections all seats are allocated using single-member plurality, in Scottish Parliamentary elections such constituency seats are supplemented by fifty-six additional regional seats allocated in order to make the overall outcome as proportional as posible. But this is not the only reason for the difference. As can also be seen from Table 1.1, voters appear to be more inclined to vote for the SNP and less

Table 1.1 Outcome of Westminster and Scottish Parliament elections in Scotland, 1997–2005

a) Scottish Parliament elections 1999–2003

1999	Constituency vote	List vote	Constituency seats	List seats	Total seats
	%	%			
Labour	38.8	33.6	53	3	56
SNP	28.7	27.3	7	28	35
Conservatives	15.6	15.4	0	18	18
Liberal Democrats	14.2	12.4	12	5	17
Greens	–	3.6	0	1	1
Scottish Socialist Party	1.0	2.0	0	1	1
Others	1.7	5.7	1	0	1

2003	Constituency vote	List vote	Constituency seats	List seats	Total seats
	%	%			
Labour	34.6	29.3	46	4	50
SNP	23.8	20.9	9	18	27
Conservatives	16.6	15.5	3	15	18
Liberal Democrats	15.4	11.8	13	4	17
Greens	–	6.9	0	7	7
Scottish Socialist Party	6.2	6.7	0	6	6
Others	3.4	8.5	2	2	4

b) UK Parliament elections in Scotland, 1997–2005

	1997		2001		2005	
	% vote	seats	% vote	seats	% vote	seats
Labour	45.6	56	43.9	56	39.5	41
SNP	22.1	6	20.1	5	17.7	6
Conservatives	17.5	0	15.6	1	15.8	1
Liberal Democrats	13.0	10	16.4	10	22.6	11
Others	1.9	0	4.0	0	4.4	0

Note: The Speaker is included in the Labour total in 2001 and 2005. The total number of UK Parliament seats in Scotland was reduced from 72 to 59 in 2005.
Sources: Rallings and Thrasher 2000; Electoral Commission 2003; Butler and Kavanagh 2001; Kavanagh and Butler 2005.

inclined to vote Labour in Scottish Parliament elections than they are in elections to the House of Commons. Meanwhile, smaller parties win more support in Scottish Parliament elections too. This at least suggests the possibility that voters vote differently in the two kinds of elections because they recognise that the Scottish Parliament is dealing with different issues, and that Scottish Parliament elections give MSPs a mandate that is independent of that enjoyed by their colleagues at Westminster.

The record of the early years of devolution has thus been a mixture of apparent successes and disappointments. It is unwise at the best of times to attempt to read the tenor of public opinion from the flow of events. It would appear impossible to do so in the case of the early years of devolution in Scotland. We have instead to ask the people themselves. Just how they reacted to the experience of the early years of devolution is the story we now attempt to tell.

Note

1. Unless otherwise stated, all of the analyses reported in this book come from either the Scottish Social Attitudes series or one of these three earlier surveys. Further technical details about how each of these surveys was conducted can be found in the Technical Appendix at the end of the book.

Acknowledgements

This project has incurred many debts. The biggest is to the 1,500 people who freely gave of their time to answer the questions on the 2003 Scottish Social Attitudes survey, together with all those who participated in the earlier surveys on which we have drawn. No survey can be conducted at all without the willingness of its interviewers to go out in all weathers and all times of the day and to encourage our respondents to take part. In doing so, they, and the researchers, have been admirably supported by the Scottish/ National Centre for Social Research's administrative staff. The funds required to undertake the survey work reported in this book were generously provided by the Economic and Social Research Council (ESRC) as part of its Devolution and Constitutional Change research programme, the Leverhulme Trust under its Nations and Regions research programme, the Nuffield Foundation and the Joseph Rowntree Charitable Trust. Brian Taylor of BBC Scotland kindly gave freely of his time to chair the conference held in February 2004 at which initial versions of the chapters in this book were presented. Finally, we are grateful to Ann Mair of the Social Statistics Laboratory at the University of Strathclyde for her careful and detailed work in preparing the datasets on which we have so heavily relied.

References

Allardyce, J. (2004), 'Scotland 2003: the election campaign and the political outcome', in M. Spicer (ed.), *The Scotsman Guide to Scottish Politics*, Edinburgh: Scotsman Publications.

Aughey, A. (2001), *Nationalism, Devolution and the Challenge to the United Kingdom State*, London: Pluto Press.

Bennie, L., Brand, J. and Mitchell, J. (1997), *How Scotland Votes: Scottish Parties and Elections*, Manchester: Manchester University Press.

Bogdanor, V. (1999), *Devolution in the United Kingdom*, Oxford: Oxford University Press.

Bradbury, J. and Mitchell, J. (2001), 'Devolution: new politics for old?', *Parliamentary Affairs*, 54: 254–75.

Bromley, C., Curtice, J., Hinds, K. and Park, A. (2003), *Devolution – Scottish Answers to Scottish Questions?*, Edinburgh: Edinburgh University Press.

Brown, A., McCrone, D., Paterson, L. and Surridge, P. (1999), *The Scottish Electorate: The 1997 General Election and Beyond*, London: Macmillan.

Butler, D. and Kavanagh, D. (2001), *The British General Election of 2001*, London: Palgrave.

Cairney, P. and Keating, M. (2004), 'Sewel motions in the Scottish Parliament', *Scottish Affairs*, 47: 115–34.

Courchene, T. (1995), 'Glocalization: the regional/international interface', *Canadian Journal of Regional Science*, 18: 1–20.

Curtice, J. and Jowell, R. (1997), 'Trust in the political system', in R. Jowell, J. Curtice, A. Park, L. Brook, K. Thomson and C. Bryson (eds), *British Social Attitudes: The 14th Report – The End of Conservative Values?*, Aldershot: Ashgate.

Curtice, J., McCrone, D., Park, A. and Paterson, L. (eds.) (2002), *New Scotland, New Society? Are Social and Political Ties Fragmenting?*, Edinburgh: Polygon.

Dalyell, T. (1977), *Devolution – The End of Britain?*, London: Jonathan Cape.

Dewar, D. (1998), 'The Scottish Parliament', *Scottish Affairs: Special Issue on Understanding Constitutional Change*, pp. 4–12.

Electoral Commission (2003), *Scottish Elections 2003*, London: Electoral Commission.

Fraser of Carmyllie (2005), *The Holyrood Inquiry*, Edinburgh: Scottish Parliament.

Friedrich, C. (1968), *Trends of Federalism in Theory and Practice*, London: Pall Mall Press.

Gellner, E. (1983), *Nations and Nationalism*, Oxford: Blackwell.

Jones, P. (2004), 'The first term of the Scottish Parliament: big change and big sameness', in G. Hassan and D. Fraser (eds), *The Political Guide to Modern Scotland*, London: Politico's.

Kavanagh, D. and Butler, D. (2005), *The British General Election of 2005*, London: Palgrave.

Mackintosh, J. (1998), 'A Parliament for Scotland', reprinted in L. Paterson (ed.), *A Diverse Assembly: The Debate on the Scottish Parliament*, Edinburgh: Edinburgh University Press.

Paterson, L. (ed.) (1998) *A Diverse Assembly: The Debate on the Scottish Parliament.* Edinburgh: Edinburgh University Press.

Paterson, L., Brown, A., Curtice, J., Hinds, K., McCrone, D., Park, A., Sproston, K. and Surridge, P. (2001), *New Scotland, New Politics?*, Edinburgh: Polygon.

Rallings, C. and Thrasher, M. (2000), *British Electoral Facts 1832–1999*, Aldershot: Ashgate.

Scottish Constitutional Convention (1995), *Scotland's Parliament: Scotland's Right*, Edinburgh: COSLA.

Scottish Office (1997), *Scotland's Parliament*, Cm 3658, Edinburgh: Stationery Office.

Scottish Office (1999), *Shaping Scotland's Parliament: Report of the Consultative Steering Group on Scotland's Parliament*, Edinburgh: Stationery Office.

Scottish Parliament (2001), *Scottish Parliament Procedures Committee Official Report, Meeting 9 2001*, Edinburgh: Scottish Parliament.

Scottish Parliament Procedures Committee (2003), *Third Report 2003: The Founding Principles of the Scottish Parliament*, SP Paper 818, Edinburgh: Scottish Parliament.

Stepan, A. (1999), 'Federalism and democracy: beyond the US model', *Journal of Democracy*, 10: 19–34.

Taylor, B. and Thomson, K. (eds) (1999), *Scotland and Wales – Nations Again?*, Cardiff: University of Wales Press.

Thatcher, M. (1998), 'Don't wreck the heritage we all share', reprinted in L. Paterson (ed.), *A Diverse Assembly: The Debate on the Scottish Parliament*, Edinburgh: Edinburgh University Press.

Trench, A. (2004), 'The more things change the more they stay the same: intergovernmental relations four years on', in A. Trench (ed.), *Has Devolution Made a Difference? The State of the Nations 2004*, Exeter: Imprint Academic.

PART I

Devolution and Independence

CHAPTER 2

The Devolution Conundrum?

Alison Park and David McCrone

INTRODUCTION

What do the Scottish public make of devolution so far? If one relied simply on newspaper accounts, we might assume a fairly negative verdict to date. To be sure, the fact that less than half of the electorate turned out to vote at the parliamentary elections in May 2003 would suggest that devolution has been something of a disappointment for many people. Moreover, the mounting costs of the Holyrood building project, and the fact that its completion was around two years overdue, have drawn considerable adverse comment. Relying on press reports, however, is hardly the most systematic way of gathering evidence about public opinion. In this chapter, we draw instead upon survey evidence collected between 1997 and 2003 and examine what this more systematic source tells us about the public's attitude towards devolution and how it has changed during the parliament's lifetime. In particular, we examine whether the apparently critical reaction received to date by the work of the Scottish Parliament has undermined support for the principle of devolution, or whether instead support for devolution has been robust in the face of any disappointment with devolution to date.

CONSTITUTIONAL PREFERENCES

Much was made in the 1980s and 1990s of the 'slippery slope' to independence that devolution would help to create (to the alarm of Conservatives and the delight of Nationalists). So, we begin by considering the extent to which people support devolution, as opposed either to wanting a return to the arrangements that preceded it or to complete independence from the United Kingdom. As Table 2.1 shows, devolution along the lines that currently operate (that is, involving a parliament with tax-varying powers) has consistently been the most popular constitutional option since the first of our surveys conducted after the May 1997 general election. Thereafter, its popularity increased markedly between the second survey undertaken in September 1997 (that is, immediately after the referendum, when issues of constitutional change might have been especially salient in voters' minds) and the third carried out after the first elections to the Scottish Parliament in 1999. Although there have been some fluctuations in support since then (most notably in 2002, when it dipped to 44 per cent), just under a half now choose this as their preferred way of governing Scotland. By contrast, support for independence appeared to peak, at 37 per cent, immediately after the referendum in September 1997; since then, it has consistently attracted the support of just over a quarter of people.

Table 2.1 Constitutional preferences, 1997–2003

	May 1997	Sept. 1997	1999	2000	2001	2002	2003
	%	%	%	%	%	%	%
Devolution, tax-varying powers	42	32	50	47	54	44	48
Devolution, no tax-varying powers	9	9	8	8	6	8	7
Independence	26	37	27	30	27	30	26
No devolution	17	17	10	12	10	13	13
Sample size	882	676	1,482	1,663	1,605	1,665	1,508

The fact that devolution has *not* fuelled an increased desire for independence appears to be recognised by the Scottish public (see Table 2.2). In 1999, over one-third thought that devolution would make independence more likely; by 2003, only a quarter did. There is little sign here that people expect devolution to lead to independence as a matter of course.

Table 2.2 Has devolution made independence more likely? (1999–2003)

	1999	2000	2001	2003
	%	%	%	%
More likely	37	27	28	25
No difference	27	43	41	39
Less likely	30	25	27	31
Sample size	1,482	1,663	1,605	1,508

RUNNING SCOTLAND

Devolution has created, of course, a balance of powers between Holyrood and Westminster. How do people think this is working? And which of the two is perceived to have more influence over the way Scotland is run? To assess this, we asked:

> Which of the following do you think has most influence over the way Scotland is run? The Scottish Parliament, the UK government, local councils, or the European Union?

Ever since we first asked this question in 2000, consistently around two-thirds have said the UK government has most influence, while only around 15 per cent have reckoned that the Scottish Parliament did (see Table 2.3). This was in stark contrast to people's expectations in 1999 when we asked them which body they thought *would* have most influence. Then, in fact, slightly more people anticipated that the parliament would be the more influential body than believed the UK government would be.

One might ask: does this really matter? Surely devolution implies a division of powers between different levels of government in which the higher tier retains the greater influence? This, however, is not how most people in Scotland see things. For, as Table 2.3 also shows, most think that it is the Scottish Parliament that *ought* to have most influence over the way the country is run. Although the proportion who take this view fell somewhat between 2001 and 2003, even on the more recent reading no less than two-thirds think that the Scottish Parliament should have primacy. Evidently, people do not accept the constitutional hierarchy of legislatures as laid down in the Scotland Act.[1]

So, even though, as we saw in Table 2.1, devolution along its current lines is the most popular constitutional preference, the marked imbalance between the influence that people think the parliament has in reality and

Table 2.3 How much influence does the parliament have? How much should it have? (1999–2003)

	1999	2000	2001	2003
	%	%	%	%
Parliament has (1999: will have) most influence	41	13	15	17
Parliament should have most influence	74	72	74	66
Sample size	1,482	1,663	1,605	1,508

that which they would like it to have suggests there might be support for the parliament having more power than at present. This indeed proves to be the case. When we ask people whether they agree or disagree with the statement 'the Scottish Parliament should be given more powers', nearly six in ten (59 per cent) agree. Although this 2003 figure is lower than the 68 per cent registered in response to the same question in 2001, there is evidently still a substantial demand for the devolution settlement to be taken further. Indeed, even among those whose constitutional preference is devolution as it currently exists, nearly two-thirds would like the parliament to have more powers (63 per cent). Evidently, as the former Secretary of State for Wales, Ron Davies, once famously said, devolution is a process rather than an event.

But there are perhaps two rather different possible interpretations of the demand for more powers. The first is to take this wish at face value; the Scottish public would like their parliament to have more powers. The second possibility, however, is that this desire reflects a disenchantment with the performance of the parliament to date. Rather than a desire for the parliament to have *new* powers, it signifies a wish for it to use its *existing* powers better. However, the former explanation sits better with the fact that the desire for the parliament to have greater powers is highest among those who would like Scotland to be independent and is lowest among those who would like to return to life before devolution. Moreover, when we examine people's perceptions of the parliament's performance to date, it emerges that the desire for the parliament to have more powers is highest among those with the most positive evaluations of the parliament's performance. For example, 73 per cent of those who think that the parliament has improved education in Scotland think that it should be given more powers, compared with just 39 per cent of those who think that the parliament has had a negative impact on education (Bromley et al. 2005). Together, this evidence suggests that the desire for the parliament to have more powers does, indeed, reflect a wish for it to be more powerful, particularly in its relationship with the UK parliament at Westminster.

EVALUATING PERFORMANCE

So far, we have been looking at attitudes to the principle of devolution and the powers of the parliament. Now we turn to examine the perceived impact in practice of the parliament to date upon policy and governance in Scotland. We begin by assessing how people's views about the impact of the parliament on life in Scotland have changed as devolution has evolved. To do this, we examine a series of questions, asked regularly since 1997, that focus upon the impact of the parliament on three areas: education, Scotland's relationship with the rest of the UK, and the relationship between people in Scotland and those who govern them. Up to and including 2000, we asked people about the impact they envisaged devolution *would* have in these areas; since 2001, we have asked about the impact devolution is perceived actually to have had.

Table 2.4 Perceived impact of the Scottish Parliament upon life in Scotland, 1997–2003

% say having a Scottish Parliament is . . .	1997 Sept.	1999	2000	2001	2002	2003
giving ordinary people more say in how Scotland is governed	79	64	44	38	31	39
increasing the standard of education in Scotland	71	56	43	27	25	23
giving Scotland a stronger voice in the United Kingdom	70	70	52	52	39	49
Sample size	676	1,482	1,663	1,605	1,665	1,508

Note: The question wording in each year was:
1997 and 1999: 'Will a Scottish Parliament give/increase . . .?'
2000: 'Do you think that having a Scottish parliament is going to give/increase . . .?'
2001–3: 'Do you think that having a Scottish Parliament is giving/increasing . . .?'

Table 2.4 shows the proportion each year that has expressed the view that having the Scottish Parliament is improving (or will improve) each area. It clearly shows that something of the shine has been taken off devolution as time has passed. Perhaps this was always likely to happen, as hard policy choices had to be made and party-political life made itself felt. Certainly, the years immediately before devolution, and its early days, appear to have been something of a honeymoon period. At the time of the 1997 referendum, for instance, as many as eight out of ten people thought that having a Scottish Parliament would give ordinary people more say in how Scotland is governed; by 2003, this had more than halved. The fall in optimism was especially steep in the early years of devolution, such that, by the time the parliament was actually up and running in 2000, less than half thought that it was going to give people more say, while a majority (51 per cent) said it would make no difference. The perceived impact of the parliament on educational standards has fallen yet further below expectations; in 1997, 71 per cent thought it would improve standards, whereas by 2003 only 23 per cent thought it had actually done so. Here, though, the decline appears to have levelled off since 2001. Moreover, few think the parliament has actually made educational matters worse; only 7 per cent said that it has *reduced* educational standards in Scotland. Rather, as in the case of giving ordinary people more say, the majority (59 per cent) simply think that it is not making any difference. Meanwhile, evaluations of the impact of the parliament upon Scotland's relationship with the UK are more positive. Around a half think that Scotland now has a stronger voice in the UK as a result of devolution, though even this figure represents a decline of 20 percentage points as compared with expectations in 1997.

We can also assess the apparent impact of the parliament in the eyes of the public by looking at the answers people gave when in 2003 they were simply asked whether each of the standard of the NHS, the quality of education, and general living standards, had got better or worse since 1999. As Table 2.5 shows, pessimists outnumber optimists so far as changes in the NHS and education since 1999 are concerned. Pessimists are, however, outnumbered by optimists when it comes to the trend in living standards since 1999; around a third think they have increased since then, while only a quarter think they have declined.

Table 2.5 Perceived trends in education, NHS and standard of living in Scotland, 1999–2003

		Increased	Stayed the same	Fallen	Don't Know	Sample size
Standard of the health service	%	20	25	46	8	1,508
Quality of education	%	25	27	29	19	1,508
General standard of living	%	33	36	24	7	1,508

Of course, people may not hold the Scottish Parliament responsible for the perceived decline in educational and NHS standards since 1999. After all, in our commentary on Table 2.4, we noted that few think the existence of the parliament has brought about declining standards in education. At the same time, while education and health are formally prime responsibilities of the Scottish Parliament, Scotland's 'standard of living' is arguably something for which Westminster (which has responsibility for taxation policy and macro-economic affairs) is mainly responsible. So, we also have to consider to *whom* people attribute responsibility for developments since 1999. To assess this, after asking respondents what they thought had happened to health, education and living standards between 1999 and 2003, we asked in each case:

What do you think this has been mainly the result of? Please choose an answer from the card.

Mainly the result of the UK government's policies at Westminster
Mainly the result of the Scottish Executive's policies
For some other reason.

In each case, those who felt there had been a change (whether in a positive or negative direction) were more likely to give the credit or the blame to Westminster than to Holyrood. As we anticipated, this is particularly true of the standard of living, for which 46 per cent lay responsibility at Westminster's door, twice the proportion who say Holyrood is responsible. Yet the figures, 42 per cent and 25 per cent respectively, are much the same for health. Only in the case of educational standards does the picture look somewhat different; but, even on this, 38 per cent attribute responsibility to Westminster and only 33 per cent to Holyrood. In the light of these figures, it is perhaps little wonder that most people think Westminster has more influence on how Scotland is run than Holyrood does.

But who gets the brickbats and who the bouquets? Is one institution more likely than the other to be blamed by those who think that standards are declining? Here we encounter an intriguing finding which helps to make sense of the apparent contradiction that, while people are critical of the parliament's performance to date, they still would like it to have more powers. We find a kind of reverse symmetry. Take standards of education, for example. As Table 2.6 shows, those who think that standards have *declined* are more likely to blame the UK government (45 per cent doing so) than they are to regard the Scottish Executive as responsible (25 per cent). However, among those who think that standards have *improved*, the reverse is true; more credit the Scottish Executive (43 per cent) for this than they do the UK government (31 per cent). Evidently then, people who think education standards have improved are more likely to give the credit to the devolved institution, whereas those who think they have deteriorated are more likely to blame the UK government at Westminster.

A similar pattern exists with regard to standards in the NHS. Those who think they have gone down tend to blame Westminster (48 per cent) rather than the Scottish Executive (16 per cent), while those who think the NHS has improved are inclined to give the credit to the Scottish Executive (46 per cent) rather than Westminster (30 per cent). Meanwhile, even in the case of living standards, pessimists firmly believe that the UK government (60 per cent) is responsible rather than the devolved institution (12 per cent). In contrast, optimists are fairly evenly divided as to whom they regard as responsible (36 and 31 per cent respectively). It would appear that the reason why disappointment with devolution has been greeted with a demand for more devolution is that Westminster is blamed for the perceived lack of achievement, and that rather more might be achieved if the Scottish Parliament had a larger role in the life of the nation.

Table 2.6 Perceived responsibility for changes in educational standards between 1999 and 2003

	Educational standards since 1999 have . . .		
% assign responsibility to	gone up	stayed the same	gone down
UK government	31	35	45
Scottish Executive	43	25	25
Sample size	365	406	434

We cannot conclude our examination of people's evaluations of the parliament to date without considering their reactions to the parliament building. To assess this, we asked people to choose one of three responses: that the building 'should never have been built in the first place', that it 'needed to be built but should never have cost so much', or that 'building it will be worth it in the end'. An overwhelming majority opt for one of the first two critical statements. Nearly half (46 per cent) think that the building should never have been built, while 45 per cent think it should never have cost as much. Only 7 per cent take the more generous view that it will be worth it in the end.

Even the most enthusiastic supporters of devolution tend to be critical of the parliament building. Over a third (38 per cent) of those who would like the parliament to have more powers think that the building should never have been built, while a half (51 per cent) think it was necessary but cost too much. Only one in ten of this group think that it will be worth it in the end. Evidently, however, their criticism of the handling of the parliament building has not been enough to destroy their faith in devolution itself.

Trust and bias

Still, the trials and tribulations of the parliament building might have helped undermine people's trust in the Scottish Parliament. The degree of trust that people have in the parliament is discussed more fully in Chapter 3. Here, we can simply note that, while the proportion who think that the

Scottish Parliament can be trusted to look after Scotland's interests 'just about always' or 'most of the time' has fallen from 81 per cent in 1999 to 63 per cent in 2003, the latter figure is still far higher than the 21 per cent who express the same level of trust in the UK government. Meanwhile, there is a strong relationship between trust in the Scottish Parliament and the belief that the Scottish Parliament should have the most influence over Scottish affairs, with seven in ten of those who trust the parliament thinking it should have most influence. There is also a relationship between trust and the desire for the Scottish Parliament to have more powers, with 66 per cent of those who trust the parliament wanting it to have more powers (compared with only 21 per cent of those who do not trust it).

The trust placed in the Scottish Parliament to work in Scotland's long-term interests seems to be widely shared across Scottish society and can be considered one of its major successes. Even among those groups who are least trusting – such as Conservative supporters and those living in the south of Scotland – more have faith in the Scottish Parliament to work in Scotland's long-term interests than have faith in the UK government.

This does not mean, however, that the parliament is seen to be completely even-handed. We asked:

Would you say the Scottish Parliament looks after the interests of all parts of Scotland more or less equally, or would you say that it looks after some parts of Scotland more than others?

Those who gave the latter response were then asked which part of Scotland they thought the parliament looked after more: Edinburgh, the central belt as a whole, or the rest of Scotland? As Table 2.7 shows, in every part of Scotland only a minority think that the parliament looks after the interests of all parts of Scotland equally.[2] This is particularly true of those in the north, only 16 per cent of whom take that view. Rather, they are particularly likely to think that the Scottish Parliament is a central-belt affair.

However, there is little association between overall trust in the parliament to do what is right for Scotland, and whether or not it is also seen to be biased in favour of particular areas. For example, while the north of Scotland perceives that the parliament operates in central-belt interests, it also evinces the highest amount of trust in the parliament to operate in Scotland's long-term interests. This would simply seem to reinforce the argument that the Scottish Parliament has managed to lay down high levels of trust in a relatively short career.

Table 2.7 Perceptions of regional bias in the Scottish Parliament by region, 2003

	Region				
% say looks after	South	West Central	East Central	Central	North
All parts equally	28	29	30	28	16
Edinburgh more	22	32	18	18	12
Central Belt more	35	19	33	37	64
Sample size	429	259	284	298	238

PERFORMANCE AND PRINCIPLE

We have uncovered a core conundrum in post-devolution Scotland. On the one hand, there appears to be some disappointment with, or at best muted enthusiasm for, what the Scottish Parliament has achieved to date, with the building saga acting as something of a lightning-conductor for its ills. On the other hand, devolution with tax-varying powers, albeit never activated, is undoubtedly the 'settled will' of the people of Scotland. Home rule shows no signs of being the slippery slope to independence, or a fillip to the SNP, or such a disappointment that people want to revert to the status quo ante. Indeed, there is consistent support for the view that the parliament should have more powers, not fewer. As we have found, if there are perceived failings in particular policy areas, the parliament does not appear to attract the blame. Meanwhile, the Scottish Parliament is far more likely to be trusted to look after Scotland's long-term interests than is Westminster. Evidently, neither simple condemnation of the failings of the parliament, nor blind-eyed support for it come what may, captures the nuances and complexities with which people view devolution to date. In this final section, we explore this conundrum further.

How do views about devolution relate to evaluations of the performance of the parliament? Put simply, there are two options. On the one hand, evaluations of performance, such as in areas like health, education, economic well-being or greater democratic accountability, might be driving enthusiasm (or lack of it) for devolution as a constitutional position. Thus, one might expect views about devolution to ebb and flow in line with people's evaluations. However, on the other hand, causality might be operating the other way round; constitutional preferences might be shaping people's evaluations of the parliament. If this is true, one might expect to find that those who favour devolution are more positive in their views about the parliament's performance and are less likely than other groups to have become disgruntled over time.

Let us first of all review people's assessments over time to provide some benchmarks. If we compare the trend in support for devolution with tax-varying powers in Table 2.1 with that in evaluations of the performance of the parliament in Table 2.4, there seems little connection between the two. After all, more people now support devolution than did so in the autumn of 1997, despite the fact that perceptions about what the parliament has achieved have plummeted.

However, if we ignore the early years of devolution (when people had little on which to base their assessments), there are hints that there *is* a relationship between devolution and assessments of performance, at least with regard both to the parliament giving Scotland a stronger voice in the UK, and to whether it is giving ordinary Scots more say. Support for devolution was at its lowest in 2002, when evaluations of its performance in these two areas were very low, only to increase by 2003 as evaluations became more positive. Moreover, when we use multivariate analysis techniques to predict support for devolution in 2003, those who think that the parliament has given ordinary Scots more say in government are significantly more likely than those who disagree to opt for devolution as their constitutional preference.

We turn now to examine whether there is any evidence that people's evaluations of the parliament reflect their existing constitutional preferences. Do those who support devolution, for instance, have a rose-tinted view of the parliament's performance to date? Or have their evaluations changed as the parliament has evolved? We assess this in Table 2.8, which divides people in each of four years into three groups: those who support devolution as we have it; those who support independence; and those who either want a return to the status quo ante or would rather have devolution with no tax-varying powers. As the table shows, those who favour devolution do indeed have more positive evaluations than those who prefer a weaker form of devolution, or no devolution at all. On the other hand, their evaluations are matched (and at times exceeded) by the views of those who would rather have an independent Scotland. Moreover, there was a substantial fall in the evaluations of *all* groups between 1997 and 2001. This applies as much to those who support devolution as to any other group, suggesting that this support has done little to 'protect' them from falling levels of satisfaction with the parliament's performance. However, the largest proportionate decline in positive evaluations has taken place among those who would rather there was not any devolution at all, or at least merely a weak form, suggesting that people's constitutional preferences might provide some form of prism through which to judge the parliament's performance.

Table 2.8 Evaluations of the Scottish Parliament by constitutional preference, 1997–2003

% parliament will give/ is giving people more say	Sept. 1997	Sample size	1999	Sample size	2001	Sample size	2003	Sample size
Constitutional preference								
Pro-devolution with tax powers	87	227	68	753	42	851	45	730
Pro-independence	91	232	77	395	44	431	47	387
Other	53	118	40	259	14	236	19	296
% parliament will give/is improving educational standards								
Constitutional preference								
Pro-devolution with tax powers	83	227	62	753	29	851	26	730
Pro-independence	89	232	65	395	35	431	30	387
Other	40	118	32	259	12	236	11	296

We can adopt the same approach to studying the relationship between people's constitutional preferences and whether or not they trust the parliament to work in Scotland's long-term interests. Is there any evidence that the two move up and down in tandem? Or do we find that it is those who did *not* support devolution in the first place whose trust in the parliament has been undermined?

The first possibility can be dismissed fairly quickly. Earlier, we saw that there has been a decline in the proportion that trust the parliament at least 'most of the time', from 81 per cent in 1999 to 63 per cent in 2003. Yet, as we have seen, this has not been accompanied by a decline in support for devolution per se. This is despite the fact that multivariate analysis confirms that support for devolution is most common among those who have high levels of trust in the Scottish Parliament, even when other factors such as party support are taken into account. However, support for devolution does seem to make a difference to levels of trust. Unlike evaluations of the parliament's performance, there are marked differences between the levels of trust shown by those who favour devolution and those who would rather have independence. As Table 2.9 shows, trust in the parliament is strongest among those who favour devolution, followed by those who want independence, and is weakest among those opposed to devolution or who want a weaker version of it. Moreover, while levels of trust have declined among all three groups since 1999, the decline has been least marked among those who favour devolution.

Table 2.9   Trust in the Scottish Parliament by constitutional preference, 1999–2003

% trust Scottish Parliament just about always/most of the time	1999	Sample size	2001	Sample size	2003	Sample size
Constitutional preference						
Pro-devolution	84	753	72	851	72	387
Pro-independence	89	395	66	451	63	730
Other	68	259	42	236	48	296

So, when we look at the relationship between attitudes towards devolution and both evaluations of what it has achieved and levels of trust in the parliament, there is some evidence to suggest that evaluations and trust might affect support for devolution. But there is also considerable evidence that attitudes towards devolution affect evaluations and trust. Here is another important clue as to why disappointment with devolution appears not to have undermined faith in the principle.

CONCLUSIONS

In the light of the parliament's first session from 1999 to 2003, what are we to make of its performance? On the one hand, we find greater pessimism about, even disappointment with, what it has achieved in key policy areas, especially when we compare people's assessments with the expectations they had in the heady days of the late 1990s. Moreover, there has been some fall in trust in its ability to look after Scotland's long-term interests, while almost half think the new parliament should not have been built. On the other hand, there is continued consistent support for devolution as the preferred constitutional option for Scotland, while most people want the parliament to have more powers. Moreover, the parliament is three times more likely than Westminster to be trusted with Scotland's long-term interests.

How do we explain this conundrum? Part of the reason appears to be that, where there is disappointment about its achievements (notably in health, education and people's standard of living more generally), it is Westminster rather than Holyrood that is blamed for shortcomings, and the latter which gets any credit going. People in Scotland may grumble but are, as yet, willing to give the Scottish Parliament the benefit of the doubt. At the same time, it appears that support for the principle of devolution may not rest heavily on its perceived performance to date; indeed, perceptions of its performance are in part influenced by people's attitudes towards the principle of devolution. Although far from being uncritical, those in favour of devolution are least likely to feel that progress to date has not matched their positive expectations.

In trying to make sense of Scottish politics, commentators have developed a liking for the quote in Walter Scott's novel, *Heart of Midlothian*, where Mrs Howden complains: 'I ken, when we had a King, and a chancellor and Parliament – men o' our ain, we could aye peeble them wi' stanes when they werena gude bairns – But naebody's nails can reach the length o' Lunnon.' Scott's character was complaining that she and her neighbours did not have the satisfaction of witnessing the hanging of Captain Porteous, whose soldiers had fired on the Edinburgh mob. Scotland's MSPs do not, thankfully, have to run the risk of physical assault but there is an immediacy and an intimacy about the Holyrood Parliament which encourages critical comment, especially at a time in the western world where politics is something of a degraded trade, and where political trust is a weak currency. Plainly, devolution is here to stay. It is the most popular arrangement for governing Scotland, and there is little evidence either that it will lead to independence in the short term, or that people want the whole thing abolished. In general terms, people are far less trusting in 2003 than they were in 1997, but the trust differential between Holyrood and Westminster is huge. People may be critical of Holyrood, but at least they think of it as their own.

NOTES

1. It is also intriguing to compare these responses to similar questions asked in Wales. This shows that people in Wales are slightly *more* likely than those in Scotland to think that their devolved body has most influence over the way the country is run (21 and 17 per cent respectively), despite the fact that the powers of the National Assembly for Wales are considerably more limited than those of the Scottish parliament.

2. The regions used for this analysis were defined as follows:

   South: Borders; Dumfries & Galloway; North, East and South Ayrshire; South Lanarkshire

   West Central: West and East Dunbartonshire; Glasgow; Inverclyde; Renfrewshire

   South Central: East, West and Mid Lothian; Edinburgh; Falkirk; North Lanarkshire

   Central: Angus; Argyll & Bute; Clackmannanshire; Dundee; Fife; Perth & Kinross; Stirling

   North: Aberdeen; Aberdeenshire; Highland; Moray

REFERENCE

Bromley, C., Curtice, J. and Given, L. (2005), *Public Attitudes to Devolution: The First Four Years*, London: National Centre for Social Research.

CHAPTER 3

A Better Union?

Paula Surridge

INTRODUCTION

There was a range of official and unofficial motivations for the creation of the Scottish Parliament in 1999, but it is clear that not least among those motivations was the aim of keeping Scotland within the United Kingdom. The extent to which this has been achieved has certainly been a recurrent theme in research on the impact of devolution (see, for example, Paterson et al. 2001; Curtice and Seyd 2001). This chapter also looks at attitudes to the Union in post-devolution Scotland, but in so doing it adopts a broader conception of the Union than is usually taken. As well as considering Scots' constitutional preferences, it also examines how well they think the Union is working and the degree of emotional attachment that Scots exhibit towards the United Kingdom.

These three aspects of attitudes towards the Union can be labelled the cognitive, the evaluative and the affective. Firstly and most straightforwardly, we can chart the level of cognitive support for the institutions of government that are now to be found in the Union. Do people support or oppose the existence of devolved institutions within the framework of the Union? Or would they prefer to dissolve the Union entirely? Secondly, we can examine people's evaluations of how well the Union is working. How well do they think the political system of the United Kingdom is working now that devolution is in place? How much trust do they have in the political institutions of the post-devolution Union, and how well is it thought to be working economically? Finally, we can consider one of the crucial affective underpinnings of the Union, national identity. To what extent do Scots identify themselves as 'British'? And how much pride do they have in some of the symbols of 'Britishness' such as the British flag?

In taking this broad look at Scots' attachment to the Union, we can move beyond charting dissatisfaction with particular political parties, policies or processes in post-devolution Scotland and examine whether there is a deeper attachment to the Union north of the border. Moreover, by examining how the strength of these three aspects of attachment to the Union has changed since the advent of devolution, we can analyse whether the establishment of the Scottish Parliament has strengthened or weakened public support for the Union.

Attitudes to the Union

One of the simplest and most prevalent ways of measuring cognitive attitudes towards the Union is to ask people which constitutional arrangement they prefer. In the 2003 Scottish Social Attitudes survey, this question took the form:

> *Which of these statements comes closest to your view?*
> Scotland should become independent, separate from the UK and the European Union
> Scotland should become independent, separate from the UK but part of the European Union
> Scotland should remain part of the UK, with its own elected parliament which has some taxation powers
> Scotland should remain part of the UK, with its own elected parliament which has no taxation powers
> Scotland should remain part of the UK without an elected parliament.

This question has been asked in exactly the same way since 1997, before the Scottish Parliament was created. As can be seen from Table 2.1 in Chapter 2, the responses to this question have been remarkably stable over time. The proportion whose preferred option for Scotland is some form of independence from the UK has remained static at a little over one in four. There is no evidence that devolution has fostered a desire for independence or that it has helped quell existing levels of support. Equally, some form of Scottish Parliament has consistently been the preferred option of most Scots.

However, a substantial shift in the balance of opinion occurred among those in favour of devolution after the referendum had taken place and the form the parliament would take had been settled. After the general election in May 1997, of the 51 per cent who wished to see a Scottish Parliament, over half preferred this to be a parliament *without* tax-varying powers. But, after the establishment of the Scottish Parliament, complete with its tax-varying powers, a large majority of those in favour of a devolved Scottish Parliament wished it to have tax-varying powers. So, while there was broad support for the creation of a Scottish Parliament before the September 1997 referendum, it was only after the referendum had been held and the parliament was up and running that the 'settled will' of Scots was in line with actual institutional arrangements.

We can probe a little further the degree to which the details of the current devolution settlement are in fact in tune with Scots' constitutional preferences. Respondents to both our 1999 and 2003 surveys were asked whether they agreed or disagreed that 'The Scottish Parliament should be given more powers'. The responses given to this question, broken down by people's constitutional preferences, are shown in Table 3.1.[1]

Table 3.1   More powers for the Scottish Parliament by constitutional preference, 1999 and 2003

% agree Scottish Parliament should have more powers	Constitutional preference			
	Independence	Parliament with tax-varying powers	Parliament without tax-varying powers	No parliament
1999	84	52	41	15
2003	84	63	25	14
Sample size 1999	395	395	395	395
Sample size 2003	387	387	387	387

As we might anticipate, in both years, very large majorities (over four-fifths) of those in favour of independence want the parliament to have more powers. Those who want to see an independent Scotland are evidently keen to use the Scottish Parliament as a stepping stone on the road to independence. Of greater interest, however, are the views of those who support devolution. Among those whose preferred option is a parliament with tax-varying powers, a majority (just over half in 1999 and over three in five in 2003) wish to see the parliament have its powers extended. These figures clearly suggest that, while there is some agreement on the broad form the parliament should take, there is also potential for pressure for further powers to be vested in the Scottish Parliament. This is a slightly mixed message for the 'Union'. On the one hand, there is widespread support for a more powerful Scottish Parliament, suggesting some continued unhappiness with the degree of influence exercised in Scotland's affairs by the United Kingdom government. On the other hand, this unhappiness has not translated into an increase in popular support for complete independence.

Evaluations of the Political System

We now look at how people evaluate the performance of the Union. Has the creation of the Scottish Parliament had any impact on how well the political system of the United Kingdom operates? Is devolution thought to offer a 'better Union' or not? Our first clues come from the responses to a question that was first asked in survey work conducted for the Royal Commission on the Constitution in 1970.

> *Which of these statements best describes your opinion on the present system of governing Britain?*
> *Works extremely well and could not be improved*
> *Could be improved in small ways but mainly works well*
> *Could be improved quite a lot*
> *Needs a great deal of improvement.*

The answers to this question may of course be influenced by a host of other issues such as attitudes towards the electoral system, the House of Lords or even the current party system. Nevertheless, if the creation of the Scottish Parliament is thought to have had a positive impact on the way the United Kingdom is governed, responses should be more favourable now than they were before devolution. In fact, the proportion of Scots saying that the system of government 'needs a great deal of improvement' almost doubled between 1997 and 2003 from 8 per cent to 15 per cent.[2]

However, respondents to our surveys were also asked more directly whether they thought creating the Scottish Parliament had improved the way Britain is governed. They were asked:

> *Do you think that so far creating the Scottish Parliament has improved the way Britain is governed, made it worse, or has it made no difference?*
> *Improved it a lot*
> *Improved it a little*
> *Made no difference*
> *Made it a little worse*
> *Made it a lot worse.*

In fact, over half (56 per cent) simply say that the creation of the Scottish Parliament has not made any difference. Indeed, this has been the most popular response ever since the question was first asked a year into the parliament's life in 2000. It is apparently not an attitude that has evolved over the life of the parliament in response to specific policies and events but rather is something more deeply rooted in attitudes towards devolution. However, at least on this measure, it does not appear that the creation of the Scottish Parliament itself has actually had a negative impact on how well people think they are being governed; only 9 per cent say that it has made the way that Britain is governed worse, while 30 per cent feel it has made it better.

But, even if Scots feel that the Scottish Parliament has not made much difference to how well Britain is governed in general, perhaps they do feel it has improved how the political system works in particular ways or that it has had a positive impact on policy outcomes. As discussed in Chapter 2, the 2003 survey included a range of questions that were designed to tap this possibility. However, as shown there, only in one instance – that is, whether or not people believed that having a Scottish Parliament was giving Scotland a stronger voice in the United Kingdom – do a plurality feel that devolution has had a positive impact. No fewer than 49 per cent took that view in 2003. On the other two measures, that is, whether the Scottish Parliament gives people more say in government and whether the Scottish Parliament has improved standards in education, the majority of respondents in 2003 believed that it had made no difference. Moreover, in each case, the perceived reality has been well short of the expectations people had at the time they voted in favour of having a parliament in 1997 (see also Bromley and Curtice 2003; Surridge 2002; Paterson et al. 2001).

One further possibility, however, is that perhaps people now feel more efficacious about the way in which they are governed, that is, they feel that the political system is more likely to respond to their wishes and demands. Two specific measures of this have been included on the surveys since 1997. Respondents were asked whether they agreed or disagreed that:

Generally speaking, those we elect as MPs lose touch with people pretty quickly

and

Parties are only interested in people's votes, not in their opinions.

Table 3.2 shows, however, that neither of these measures provides any evidence that the creation of the Scottish Parliament has encouraged Scots to feel more politically efficacious. Rather, they appear to feel less efficacious now. On both questions, there has actually been an increase in the proportion of Scots who agree with the statement. However, it would be wrong to assign responsibility for this to the creation of the Scottish

Parliament. Two further factors must be considered. Firstly, evidence published elsewhere over a longer time series suggests that political efficacy was relatively high immediately after the general election in 1997 (Bromley et al. 2001). This means that our starting point may not be representative of the longer-term position. Secondly, the position in Scotland still looks more favourable than it does in the rest of the UK. Whereas one in five Scots agreed with our statements in 2003, the equivalent figure in England is no less than one in four. Moreover, this difference exists despite the fact that, prior to the advent of devolution, levels of political efficacy were similar on both sides of the border. This suggests that the creation of the Scottish Parliament may at least have helped stem north of the border a tide of growing disillusionment that has been sweeping across the whole of the UK.

Table 3.2 Political efficacy, 1997–2003

	May 1997	Sept. 1997	1999	2001	2003
	%	%	%	%	%
MPs soon lose touch					
Strongly agree	n/a	11	14	22	20
Agree	n/a	48	52	50	51
Neither agree nor disagree	n/a	24	17	12	15
Disagree	n/a	13	15	14	12
Strongly disagree	n/a	1	*	1	*
Parties only interested in votes					
Strongly agree	16	12	14	21	20
Agree	48	45	50	53	53
Neither agree nor disagree	17	19	15	11	12
Disagree	18	19	19	15	15
Strongly disagree	1	2	1	1	1
Sample size	882	676	1,482	1,605	1,508

n/a = not asked; * Less than 0.5 per cent.

Trust in the institutions of the Union

A further element of Scots' faith in the political system is the extent to which they trust political institutions to work in their interests. Do they trust the UK government and the Scottish Parliament to work in Scotland's interests, and has the experience of devolution made any difference to their perceptions?

Table 3.3 shows how people responded to two questions that have been asked regularly since the 1997 referendum:

How much do you trust the UK government to work in Scotland's best long-term interest?

How much do you trust the Scottish Parliament to work in Scotland's best interests?

Table 3.3   Trust in the UK government and the Scottish Parliament to work in Scotland's interests, 1997–2003

% trust to work in Scotland's interest	Sept. 1997	1999	2001	2003
UK government				
Just about always	4	3	2	2
Most of the time	30	29	20	19
Only some of the time	52	52	55	58
Almost never	10	14	22	20
Scottish Parliament				
Just about always	35	26	13	10
Most of the time	47	55	52	52
Only some of the time	12	14	28	31
Almost never	3	2	4	4
Sample size	676	1,482	1,605	1,508

Scots are much more likely to trust the Scottish Parliament to work in Scotland's interests than they are the UK government. Indeed, this lack of trust appears to be an important motivation for supporting the existence of a relatively powerful body in Edinburgh. Among those who trust the UK government 'almost always' or 'most of the time', just under half believe that the Scottish Parliament should be given more powers. However, among those who trust the UK government 'only some of the time', 60 per cent wish to see the parliament have more powers, while among those who trust the UK government 'almost never', this figure rises to almost seven in ten. Moreover trust in the UK government has actually declined since 1997 to the point where no fewer than four-fifths of Scots trust the UK government 'only some of the time' or 'almost never'. However, there has been a similar drop in trust in the Scottish Parliament too. As a result, it is impossible here to disaggregate the effects of a generalised fall in trust in politicians from any impact that devolution might have had.

Economic evaluations

So far, we have found it difficult to find any consistent evidence that the political system of the United Kingdom is thought by Scots to be working more effectively following the creation of the Scottish Parliament. But perhaps people's constitutional preferences and attitudes towards the Union are driven by other concerns. The initial Treaty of Union of 1707 has been described as 'a settlement between two patrician classes for economic gain and political gains' (Brown et al. 1998: 40). Perhaps the economic gains of the Union are perceived as outweighing any political difficulties that are thought still to exist. The 2003 Scottish Social Attitudes survey asked two questions that enable us to gauge attitudes to the economic consequences of the Union for Scotland:

> *Would you say that, compared with other parts of the United Kingdom, Scotland gets **pretty much** its fair share of government spending, **more** than its fair share, or **less** than its fair share of government spending?*
>   *Much more than its fair share of government spending*
>   *A little more than its fair share of government spending*
>   *Pretty much its fair share of government spending*
>   *A little less than its fair share of government spending*
>   *Much less than its fair share of government spending.*

> *On the whole, do you think that England's economy benefits more from having Scotland in the UK, or that Scotland's economy benefits more from being part of the UK, or is it about equal?*
>   *England benefits more*
>   *Scotland benefits more*
>   *Equal.*

Many people in Scotland suspect that their country does not get a fair share of government spending. Just under half say that Scotland gets less than its fair share. Only one in ten believe that it gets more than its fair share. There is little evidence here that Scotland is thought to gain financially from the post-devolution Union.

However, a look at our second measure, which has been asked on a regular basis since 1992, suggests that the creation of the Scottish Parliament has helped change attitudes towards the economic costs and benefits of the Union. Table 3.4 shows that, up to and including the referendum in September 1997, around half of Scots felt that England's economy benefited more from the Union, while no more than one in seven thought that Scotland's economy benefited more. But, since 1999, the picture has looked increasingly different. By 2003, only 30 per cent thought that England's economy benefited more, only six points higher than the 24 per cent who thought Scotland's economy did. Both figures are less than the two in five who think that the two economies benefit equally. While Scots may still feel short-changed from the Union in terms of government spending, there is evidently no longer a clear perception that Scotland's economy loses out from the Union.

Table 3.4 Perceptions of which economy benefits more from the Union, 1992–2003

	1992	May 1997	Sept. 1997	1999	2001	2003
	%	%	%	%	%	%
England's	49	50	48	36	38	30
Scotland's	14	11	14	22	18	24
Both equally	32	31	32	36	39	40
Sample size	*957*	*882*	*676*	*1,482*	*1,605*	*1,508*

Conflict with England

The political institutions and economic consequences of the Union are perhaps its most visible elements, but the Union also brings together two potentially different societies. While much has been written about Scottish society itself and about the troubled relationship between nation, state and society in a Scotland that is part of the United Kingdom (see for example McCrone 2001), relatively little attention has been paid to possible sources of conflict between Scots and the English (although see McIntosh et al. 2004 for a different approach to this issue). However, we might expect attachment to an idea of the Union to be manifested in a perception that the two countries are in fact part of a shared society. An indication of how far this might be the case is given by answers to a question that asked people how much conflict they thought there was between Scots and the English (leaving aside sport). Just one in four think there is 'very' or 'fairly' serious conflict between the two. This figure is actually lower than the 30 per cent who took that view when a similar question was asked in 1992, although on that occasion respondents were not explicitly invited to leave aside any conflict on the sporting field. While only 8 per cent would say that there is no conflict at all, no fewer than two-thirds say that there is 'not very serious' conflict. It appears that there are few social pressures for the break-up of the Union based on a perception that there are irresolvable differences between its peoples.

ATTACHMENT TO THE UNION

The third and final aspect we need to consider is the extent to which Scots feel an affective bond with the Union, expressed through a sense of pride in Great Britain and a sense of British identity. The character of Scottish national identity in particular is examined fully in Chapter 9. Our interest here, in contrast, is in the impact that devolution may have had on a sense of 'Britishness' among people living in Scotland. In this, we need to bear in mind that people do not necessarily feel British instead of feeling Scottish. Rather, they may feel British as well as feeling Scottish. One measure of national identity that captures this possible sense of dual identity is the 'Moreno' question (Moreno 1988). Rather than forcing people to choose one national identity rather than another, this question invites them to indicate their balance of feeling between two identities, in this case feeling Scottish and feeling British.

Table 3.5   Moreno national identity, 1992–2003

	1992	May 1997	Sept. 1997	1999	2001	2003
	%	%	%	%	%	%
Scottish, not British	19	23	32	32	36	31
More Scottish than British	40	38	32	35	30	34
Equally Scottish and British	33	27	28	22	24	22
More British than Scottish	3	4	3	3	3	4
British, not Scottish	3	4	3	4	3	4
Sample size	957	882	676	1,482	1,605	1,508

Table 3.5 shows that, throughout the last decade, a large majority of people in Scotland have placed themselves in one of two predominantly Scottish categories, that is 'Scottish, not British' or 'more Scottish than British'. To that degree, the sense of 'Britishness' in Scotland was already relatively weak prior to devolution. However, it has consistently appeared even weaker since the September 1997 referendum. Immediately after the 1997 general election, only 24 per cent of respondents said they were 'Scottish, not British'. But later that year, after the referendum vote, this figure had risen to 32 per cent. It has stabilised at around one in three ever since.

It is worthy of note that, unlike the change in perceptions of the economic benefits of the Union, this apparent decline in Britishness occurred as soon as devolution was set in train and not after the parliament was up and running. We should not be surprised by this. Billig (1995) has described national identity as 'banal', in other words that it is largely an implicit and taken-for-granted identity driven by everyday encounters with national symbols. This suggests that people were more likely to feel Scottish once the devolution process had started, as they were more likely to meet discussion in the media and elsewhere of 'Scottish' issues and symbols. However, we should stress that, despite the rise in the proportion saying they are not British, nearly two in three Scots still express some form of British identity, in most cases together with some form of Scottish identity too.

A not dissimilar picture is obtained if we look at the degree to which people feel proud of being Scottish or British. No fewer than 70 per cent say they are 'very proud' of being Scottish, while only 23 per cent say the same about being British. Nevertheless, another 41 per cent say that they are at least 'somewhat proud' of being British. Again, it appears that a strong sense of identification with Scotland need not rule out some degree of identification with Britain. Indeed, no fewer than 70 per cent of those who said they were 'very proud' of being Scottish also claimed that they were very or somewhat proud of being British.

A final way to measure attachment to the Union is to examine how people say they feel about the visual symbolism of the Union, and in particular the Union Jack. In the 2003 survey, respondents were shown pictures of the Union Jack together with the Saltire and were asked whether they felt proud or hostile towards them. Three-quarters (76 per cent) expressed pride in the Saltire. In contrast, over half of people in Scotland (55 per cent) felt indifferent about the Union Jack, though only 7 per cent actually felt hostile towards it. Scots may not love this symbol of the Union, but at least they are not openly hostile towards it.

Most Scots do, then, feel some degree of emotional attachment to the Union. Most acknowledge some kind of British identity and some degree of pride in being British. This attachment is weaker than the sense of being Scottish, but is capable of living alongside it. There is, however, no sign that it has been strengthened since the advent of the Scottish Parliament; indeed, if anything, the opposite is true.

WHO SUPPORTS THE UNION?

So far, we have said relatively little about who in Scotland supports the Union. Does support have its roots in particular social groups, such as the young or those with higher educational qualifications? To answer this question, we examine the pattern of responses to a question that is designed to tap both cognitive and affective support for the Union together. This questions reads as follows:

If in the future Scotland were to become independent and leave the UK, would you be sorry, pleased, or neither pleased nor sorry?
Sorry
Pleased
Neither pleased nor sorry

In 2003, almost half (48 per cent) said they would be sorry if Scotland left the UK, with nearly one in four (24 per cent) saying they would be pleased. The remainder said that they would be neither pleased nor sorry. Table 3.6 shows the proportion of various social groups who say they would be pleased to see Scotland leave the Union.

Table 3.6 Pleased to see Scotland leave the Union (by various social characteristics)

	% Pleased to see Scotland leave the Union	Sample size		% Pleased to see Scotland leave the Union	Sample size
Religion			**Education**		
No religion	26	649	Degree	19	243
Roman Catholic	31	193	Higher education below degree	30	230
Church of Scotland	19	479	Higher Grade	20	254
Other	21	175	Standard Grade	24	390
			No qualifications	26	367
Gender					
Male	26	684	**Social class**		
Female	23	825	Managerial and professional	19	487
			Intermediate	17	144
Age group			Small employers	26	109
18–30	26	272	Lower supervisory	30	205
31–44	27	425	Semi-skilled and routine		
45–59	25	400	occupations	28	416
60+	19	408			

There are a few notable differences. Roman Catholics are more likely than any other group to express pleasure at the prospect of Scotland leaving the UK. As many as 31 per cent say they would be pleased if this happened. In contrast, and in line with earlier work on religion in Scotland (Seawright 1999; Bruce and Glendinning 2003), only 19 per cent of those who belong to the Church of Scotland would be pleased. There are also some social-class differences; those in semi-routine and routine occupations are more likely to feel pleased than those in professional, managerial or intermediate occupations. Meanwhile, those aged over 65 are also rather less likely to be pleased. None of these differences is large however, and for the most part what is more remarkable about Table 3.6 is the similarity of attitudes across the various social groups. For the most part, it appears that support for or opposition to the Union is not the particular preserve of any one social group.

Understanding attachment to the Union

The chapter has so far considered a number of different aspects of support for the Union in Scotland but has not, so far, tried to see which may be the most important. In this section, we attempt to examine which is of most import by undertaking a logistic regression of whether a respondent would feel pleased if Scotland left the UK (for further details about regression, see the Technical Appendix). Included as potential explanations of this attitude are measures associated with all three aspects of support for the Union, together with various social characteristics, though we have excluded respondents' constitutional preference because it is too close to what we are trying to explain. The results are summarised in Table 3.7, while full details of the results of the model are found at Table 3A.1.

The variable most strongly associated with feelings towards the prospect of Scotland leaving the Union is national identity. Those who feel Scottish and not British are very much more likely to feel pleased if Scotland left the UK than are those who feel equally Scottish and British. But, in addition to this affective component, we find that evaluations of the political system, as measured by perceptions of how well the system of government in Britain is working, and evaluations of the economic benefits of the Union also make a difference. Those who think the system is not working well and those who think that England's economy benefits more from the Union are more likely to say they would be pleased if Scotland left the United Kingdom. In addition, one cognitive component, support for the Scottish Parliament having more powers, is also associated with pleasure at the prospect of Scotland leaving the Union. In contrast, people's age, gender, education and social class make little or no difference, as do perceptions of conflict between Scots and the English.

This suggests two important points. First, patterns of national identity are important to the maintenance of the Union. It seems unlikely that support for the Union would be maintained in the face of a substantial increase in the proportion who denied that they were British at all. Secondly, those who wish to advocate support for independence are unlikely to enhance their cause by trying to appeal to specific social groups as opposed to influencing perceptions of how the Union is or is not working among Scots as a whole. But, at the same time, it looks as though there would be little mileage to be gained from attempting to appeal to such hostility towards the English as does exist in Scotland.

Table 3.7 Summary of regression model of those pleased to see Scotland leave the Union

Variable	Category	Significance
Gender (Male)		
	Female	ns
Age (18–30)		
	31–44	ns
	45–59	ns
	60+	ns
Social class (Semi-skilled and routine occupations)		
	Managerial and professional	ns
	Intermediate	–
	Small employers	ns
	Lower supervisory	ns
Education (No qualifications)		
	Degree	ns
	Higher education below degree	+ +
	Higher Grade	ns
	Standard Grade	ns
National identity (Equally Scottish and British)		
	Scottish, not British	+ +
	Scottish more than British	+ +
	British more than Scottish	ns
	British, not Scottish	ns
Economic benefits (Both equally)		
	England benefits more	+ +
	Scotland benefits more	–
Parliament should have more powers (Neither)		
	Agree	+ +
	Disagree	– –
System of government works well (Improved a lot/a great deal)		
	Works extremely well/improved in small ways	– –
Scottish/English conflict (No conflict)		
	Very serious	ns
	Fairly serious	ns
	Not very serious	ns

For each independent variable, the reference category is shown in brackets.
+   significant positive coefficient at 5 per cent level
+ +   significant positive coefficient at 1 per cent level
–   significant negative coefficient at 5 per cent level
– –   significant negative coefficient at 1 per cent level
ns   coefficient not significant

Conclusions

The constitutional preferences of the Scottish people have remained stable in the period since devolution. But there are some warning signs about Scotland's relationship with the Union. Firstly, there is a sense that in many areas (notably whether the Scottish Parliament has given people more say in government and whether the Scottish Parliament has improved the system of government) the creation of the Scottish Parliament has not had much impact on political evaluations of the Union. At the same time, the advent of devolution has not immunised Scotland from an apparent UK-wide growth in disillusion with politics and politicians that may yet be a cause for concern for supporters of the Union.

Despite these warning signs for the Union, and the failure of devolution in many respects to persuade Scots that they are being better governed, the Union is at least thought now to be in better health. After the 1997 referendum, 59 per cent believed that Scotland was 'very' likely or 'quite' likely to become independent in the next twenty years. By 2003, this figure had fallen to 28 per cent. Not only do the majority of Scots continue not to wish to see independence, they do not expect it to happen either. Meanwhile, in two important areas, Scotland's position in the Union is now thought to be stronger. Nearly half believe that the parliament has given Scotland a stronger voice in the UK, while Scotland is now far less likely to be thought to be losing out from the Union. Devolution may not have lived up to all the expectations that were heaped upon it, but it does at least seem to have strengthened Scotland's place in the Union by helping to foster a perception that the Union is now more responsive to Scotland's needs.

Appendix: Modelling support for the Union

Table 3A.1 shows the results of a logistic-regression model of whether or not a respondent would be pleased to see Scotland leave the Union. Those who would be pleased were coded 1, those who would be sorry or neither pleased nor sorry, 0.

Table 3A.1 Logistic regression of whether people would be pleased if Scotland left the union

Variable	Category	Coefficient	Standard error
Gender (Male)			
	Female	−0.230	0.173
Age (18–30)			
	31–44	−0.378	0.262
	45–59	−0.085	0.270
	60+	−0.507	0.299
Social class (Semi-skilled and routine occupations)			
	Managerial and professional	−0.390	0.255
	Intermediate	−0.624	0.310
	Small employers	−0.107	0.349
	Lower supervisory	0.122	0.245
Education (No qualifications)			
	Degree	0.559	0.360
	Higher education below degree	0.868	0.306
	Post-compulsory; below HE	0.089	0.304
	School	0.026	0.234
National identity (Equally Scottish and British)			
	Scottish, not British	2.123	0.295
	Scottish more than British	1.255	0.297
	British more than Scottish	−1.491	1.358
	British, not Scottish	−0.729	0.855
Economic benefits (Both equally)			
	England benefits more	0.816	0.183
	Scotland benefits more	−0.510	0.262
Parliament should have more powers (Neither)			
	Agree	1.167	0.256
	Disagree	−1.072	0.420
System of government works well (Improved a lot/a great deal)			
	Works extremely well/improved in small ways	−0.513	0.181
Scottish/English conflict (No conflict)			
	Very serious	0.224	0.452
	Fairly serious	−0.227	0.370
	Not very serious	−0.206	0.332

For each independent variable, the reference category is shown in brackets.

NOTES

1. For the purposes of this comparison, those who wish to see an independent Scotland, whether within or outside the European Union, are collapsed into a single category.

2. It is worth noting that Scots are slightly more positive about the system of government than people in England. In 2003, 22 per cent of people in England responded that the system 'needs a great deal of improvement', compared with 15 per cent of Scots. It would, therefore, be misleading to assume that the problems that people in Scotland perceive with the system of government in Britain are necessarily anything to do with Scotland's place within it.

References

Billig, M. (1995), *Banal Nationalism*, London: Sage.

Bromley, C. and Curtice, J. (2003), 'Devolution: scorecard and prospects', in C. Bromley, J. Curtice, K. Hinds and A. Park (eds), *Devolution – Scottish Answers to Scottish Questions?*, Edinburgh: Edinburgh University Press.

Bromley, C., Curtice, J. and Seyd, B. (2001), 'Political engagement, trust and constitutional reform', in A. Park, J. Curtice, K. Thomson, L. Jarvis and C. Bromley (eds), *British Social Attitudes: The 18th Report: Public Policy, Social Ties*, London: Sage.

Brown, A., McCrone, D. and Paterson, L. (1998), *Politics and Society in Scotland*, 2nd. edn, London: Macmillan.

Bruce, S. and Glendinning, T. (2003), 'Religious beliefs and differences', in C. Bromley, J. Curtice, K. Hinds and A. Park (eds), *Devolution – Scottish Answers to Scottish Questions?*, Edinburgh: Edinburgh University Press.

Curtice, J. and Seyd, B. (2001), 'Is devolution strengthening or weakening the UK?', in A. Park, J. Curtice, K. Thomson, L. Jarvis and C. Bromley (eds), *British Attitudes: The 18th Report: Public Policy, Social Ties*, London: Sage.

McCrone, D. (2001), *Understanding Scotland: The Sociology of a Nation*, 2nd edn, London: Routledge.

McIntosh, I., Sim, D. and Robertson, D. (2004), ' "We hate the English, except for you, cos you're our pal": identification of the "English" in Scotland', *Sociology*, 38: 43–59.

Moreno, L. (1988), 'Scotland and Catalonia: the path to home rule', in D. McCrone and A. Brown (eds), *The Scottish Government Yearbook 1988*, Edinburgh: Unit for the Study of Government in Scotland.

Paterson, L., Brown, A., Curtice, J., Hinds, K., McCrone, D., Park, A., Sproston, K. and Surridge, P. (2001). *New Scotland, New Politics?*, Edinburgh: Polygon.

Seawright, D. (1999), *An Important Matter of Principle: The Decline of the Scottish Conservative and Unionist Party*, Aldershot: Ashgate.

Surridge, P. (2002), 'Society and democracy: the new Scotland', in J. Curtice, D. McCrone, A. Park and L. Paterson (eds), *New Scotland, New Society? Are Social and Political Ties Fragmenting?*, Edinburgh: Polygon.

CHAPTER 4

Sources of Support for the SNP

Lindsay Paterson

INTRODUCTION

The Scottish National Party is in an odd position. On the one hand, it has achieved more in the last eight years than in the previous sixty: a parliament is now well established in Edinburgh, the party has been confirmed in two elections as the main challenger to Labour, and independence is now a serious option for Scotland. There is something approaching a consensus for strengthening the parliament's powers, and a growing although still minority support for separate statehood (McCrone and Paterson 2002). And yet the party seems becalmed. It, like Labour, has fallen victim to Scotland's new multi-party politics, such that its performance at the elections of 2003 and 1999 – and at the UK general elections of 2001 and 2005 – was judged to be rather disappointing by most disinterested observers. The party has seemed to be reluctant to claim the setting up of a home rule parliament as any kind of victory, so totemic is its preference for independence. Unlike its counterparts in Catalonia or Quebec, it has yet to learn to live with mere devolution.

The fortunes of individual parties may seem to be of rather arcane interest, but that of the SNP cannot but command attention for at least two reasons. One is simply that it is indeed Scotland's opposition party, still the only one capable of beating Labour across all its heartlands. If there is ever to be any alternation of power in Scotland, then the fate of the SNP will be central to that – either as the core of a new government, or as the reason why no other party seems likely to be in a position to provide such a focus. That reason to be interested in the party would be common to any multi-party system; but there is a second reason peculiar to Scotland. The SNP has, historically, been the main motor of the debate about Scotland's constitution, however much its opponents might like to pretend otherwise. Its enthusiastic participation in the referendum of 1997 was the main reason why such a clear majority was achieved: its supporters voted by no less than

76 to 1 in favour, ahead of Labour's 66 to 7 and the Liberal Democrats' 45 to 32 (Surridge and McCrone 1999: 43). It was the SNP's revival in the mid-1980s that began to focus Labour minds again on a Scottish assembly, although Donald Dewar himself did not need such prodding (Dewar 1988). It was SNP success in 1973–4 that persuaded the Wilson government to legislate on a Scottish assembly, and it was the party's winning of the Hamilton by-election of 1967 that persuaded Wilson to set up the Royal Commission on the Constitution whose report remained influential on the settlement we now have (Paterson 1998: 226). Throughout the period from its founding in 1934 until 1996, the party's ephemeral electoral successes also nudged Conservative and Labour governments into strengthening the administrative powers of the old Scottish Office (Finlay 1994, 1997; Kellas 1984; Lynch 2002). The SNP's capacity to attract votes from elsewhere has always concentrated the minds of other parties' leaders.

Nevertheless, despite that, the Scotland of the early twenty-first century is a very different place from the country which the SNP seemed to be about to take by storm thirty years ago. Some of these changes might have been expected to have favoured the party, given what is known about its social base in the 1970s (Kendrick 1983; McCrone 1992: 146–73). Scotland is now more affluent and better educated, and has an economy based on services rather than manufacturing. All these changes entailed a relative growth in those social groups which provided the core of the party's support in 1974: it benefited from the same kinds of social change that underpinned the success of Thatcher's Conservatives in England. But the ideological difference between these parties also points in a paradoxical direction for the SNP. It moved left while the country was becoming more middle-class. That in itself would not necessarily have been an ideological obstacle: the growing Scottish middle class remained quite firmly social democratic, rather more akin to its counterparts in Scandinavia than to the middle class in southern England (Paterson 2002a, 2002b). But its ideology was a cautious communitarianism, which Labour has been adept at leading, and which the leftist rhetoric of some leading strands of opinion in the SNP has rather missed.

During the 2004 leadership contest in the SNP, there was much public discussion of the party's immediate prospects and current sources of support. This chapter stands back from the fray and examines changes in the party's base over a long time-scale, in some respects since the 1970s and, in greater detail, since the pivotal year of 1997. There are four main sections. The first examines the social base of SNP support from 1974 until 2003: why has social change apparently not strengthened the party's support? The second looks briefly at the relationship between support for the party and people's views about Scotland's constitution: why has the party not benefited from the strengthening popular belief that Scotland needed a parliament, and indeed a parliament with more substantial powers than it currently has? The third section concentrates on the party's capacity to build up a core of loyal supporters: how far is the SNP from commanding the kind of heartland loyalty which underpins Labour's dominance of Scottish political preferences? The fourth section then looks at the SNP's effectiveness at translating vague support into votes: in particular, did the advent of the Scottish Parliament allow the party to recover the capacity it famously had in the early 1970s for mobilising people behind a national crusade?

Social base of SNP support

The first three sections are about broad support (or party identification) for the party,[1] the overall trend of which is shown in the first row of Table 4.1. The party's level of support remained remarkably constant at around one in five of the whole population (except in 1979), even though its vote at parliamentary elections fell from 30 per cent in October 1974 to 17 per cent in 1979, recovered to just under that peak in the first Scottish parliamentary election in 1999 but then fell again in 2003.[2]

Five major developments in the social base of SNP support may be detected within this apparent stability. There are two reasons for examining this. One is to assess simply whether the SNP has shifted its social base: for example, does it still manage to command the enthusiasm of young people in the way that it undoubtedly did in the 1970s? The other is to investigate the question, noted in the introduction, of why the SNP has apparently not benefited from the relative expansion of social groups in which it used to do well (for example, people who have been upwardly mobile in social-class terms).

The first development in the social basis of SNP support concerns age, shown in the second segment of Table 4.1. Older people (aged 65 and over) have always tended to give lower support to the party than younger groups. But whereas in the 1970s those aged below 35 clearly gave the strongest support, that has not been the case since the early 1990s. Indeed, there is some evidence here that, as the young people of the 1970s have aged, they have taken quite high levels of support for the SNP with them, while new generations of young people have been somewhat more sceptical of the party. Thus the level of support in the age groups 45 and older was higher in the recent surveys than in 1974, whereas in the younger age groups it was clearly lower. Another way of expressing this is that the average age of SNP

Table 4.1 Support for the SNP by class, gender and age, 1974–2003

	1974		1979		1992		1997		1999		2001		2003	
	%	N	%	N	%	N	%	N	%	N	%	N	%	N
Age														
18–24	34	148	15	55	27	118	20	85	28	95	10	136	11	101
25–34	27	240	14	155	20	183	22	170	25	305	17	275	20	244
35–44	18	208	11	132	26	172	18	153	22	259	15	320	18	307
45–54	19	168	8	119	24	162	20	148	23	247	16	254	19	247
55–64	13	188	5	93	12	137	15	125	16	209	22	219	19	260
65 +	10	182	10	138	9	171	8	192	11	356	13	400	13	346
Gender														
Men	24	543	11	350	21	445	20	376	24	667	16	645	15	659
Women	16	593	10	375	18	512	15	506	17	815	15	960	18	849
Class[*]														
Professional	16	37	7	45	9	22	6	34	16	57	5	77	10	85
Intermediate	21	85	12	78	12	204	14	189	18	387	12	397	13	363
Routine non-manual	16	98	10	62	20	229	17	205	15	280	19	320	15	303
Skilled manual	18	191	12	92	23	199	22	169	27	272	16	252	24	305
Semi-skilled manual	30	227	14	155	24	185	19	141	25	228	15	280	21	224
Unskilled manual	18	208	7	102	24	81	22	89	29	120	16	118	20	89
All	20	1,175	10	729	19	957	17	882	20	1,482	15	1,605	17	1,508

[*] Class measured by Registrar General scheme, 1992–2003, and by social grade in 1974 and 1979.
All main cell entries show percentage of those in that group supporting the SNP.

supporters in 1974 was 38.5 years, more than six years younger than the population average of 44.8 years; by 2003, the SNP average had grown to 46.9 years, whereas the population average had grown only to 47.7 years. The party's main rival, the Labour Party, has to some extent shifted in the opposite direction. In 1974, it had under 30 per cent support among people aged under 35, but 35–40 per cent among people in the groups aged over that. By 2003, its support was around one third in all age groups.

The second notable change is in relation to gender. It has long been noted that the SNP seemed more attractive to men than to women, and the surveys from 1974 to 1999 confirm that (see Table 4.1): in the first and last of these, the level of support among men was about one half greater than among women. The party leadership around John Swinney after 2000 – prompted by the quite high levels of female representation in the Scottish Parliament's SNP group – tried to appeal more directly to women, and the results may be seen in the surveys of 2001 and 2003, where the gap was closed and then in fact reversed. (The attribution of responsibility for this change to Swinney's leadership which began in the autumn of 2000 is made more plausible when we note that the proportions of men and women backing the SNP in the 2000 Scottish Social Attitudes Survey, conducted in the spring and summer of 2000, were similar to those in 1999 in Table 4.1, at 22 per cent among men and 17 per cent among women, whereas the figures for 2002 were similar to those for 2001 in Table 4.1, at 17 per cent among men and 16 per cent among women.)

The third change concerns social class and social mobility. The bottom segment of Table 4.1 shows that the party has never had much appeal to people in professional jobs. In the 1970s, however, it did have quite high support in intermediate groups, an advantage it had probably lost thirty years later, by which time its support was concentrated in working-class groups (the bottom three in the table). This shift from a somewhat mixed class base to a more clearly working-class one might seem consistent with the party's shift to the left in its rivalry with Labour, but the problem for the SNP is that the working class is shrinking and the middle class growing (Paterson et al. 2004).

Nevertheless, the story is actually more complex because it is partly about how people arrived at their current class position. The party of the 1970s appealed to upwardly mobile people – people whose own jobs were further up the social hierarchy than their parents' had been. An illustration of the situation in Scotland is in Table 4.2 (further detailed analysis is in Kendrick 1983, summarised by McCrone 1992: 166). The table shows the proportions supporting each of four parties according to the broad occupational class the respondent was in and to whether they had been socially mobile to get

Table 4.2 Party support by social mobility and broad current class, 1974

Current class	Mobility	Con	Lab	Lib Dem	SNP	Sample size
		%	%	%	%	
Non-manual	down or immobile	60	14	10	10	42
	up	37	23	13	22	167
Manual	down	24	47	6	20	175
	immobile	15	54	1	28	214
	up	25	43	10	16	216

Current class based on social grade. Mobility based on difference between current social grade of respondent and social grade of father: see text.

there; note that the social mobility was defined in terms of the full set of six classes shown in Table 4.1, not only in terms of the dichotomy shown in Table 4.2, so that, for example, being upwardly mobile in the lower segment would mainly mean moving up from an unskilled manual background to a skilled manual job. The SNP in 1974 seemed to rely on two main groups: those who had been upwardly mobile to the non-manual class (22 per cent support), and also people who were stable in the manual class or had been downwardly mobile to the manual class (28 per cent and 20 per cent); that combination represented the class coalition which the party had assembled then. By 1999, however – as illustrated in Table 4.3 – only one of these two concentrations of support remained: the party no longer had any advantage among the upwardly mobile, and even seems to have come to appeal particularly to the downwardly mobile. The contrast with Labour is rather stark: from a profile not dissimilar to the SNP's in 1974 (although with much higher levels of support in the manual class), it had become associated with upward mobility from lower-manual to upper-manual classes by 1999.

Table 4.3 Party support by social mobility and broad current class, 1999

Current class	Mobility	Con	Lab	Lib Dem	SNP	Sample size
		%	%	%	%	
Non-manual	down	9	34	15	23	145
	immobile	20	33	12	23	340
	up	17	37	11	23	577
Manual	down	9	38	6	33	300
	immobile	8	43	3	31	157
	up	9	59	4	19	55

Current class based on Goldthorpe class. Mobility based on difference between current Goldthorpe class of respondent and Goldthorpe class of parents: see text.
Source: Respondents in Scotland to British Household Panel Survey 1999. For further details, see the appendix to this chapter.

The fourth social change concerns religion. The SNP used to have a problem with Catholics: in 1974, only 12 per cent of them supported the party, in contrast to 27 per cent of people with no religion and to 19 per cent of adherents of the Church of Scotland and of other Presbyterian churches. In 2003, the differential was weaker, essentially because support was lower among the non-religious (19 per cent) and among the Presbyterians (17 per cent) but had barely changed among Catholics (13 per cent). Much fuller analysis of this slow secularisation of Scottish politics is provided by Rosie and McCrone (2000: 213–5), McCrone and Rosie (1998: 86–90) and Seawright and Curtice (1995).

The fifth and final point about social change concerns national identity. Most people in Scotland (over nine out of ten) choose 'Scottish' or 'British' as the label which best defines their national identity. Here, the story is in one respect of no change. The SNP has always had much stronger support among the 'Scottish' than among the 'British': 22 per cent to 5 per cent in 2003, and 15 per cent to 2 per cent in 1979. But there is underlying change here, because the size of the 'Scottish' group has been growing and that of the 'British' group has been declining (Paterson 2002c: 32): the 'Scottish' proportion was 56 per cent in 1979 and 72 per cent in 2003, while the 'British' proportion fell from 38 per cent to 20 per cent. So, the SNP is commanding a constant share of a growing group. Further analysis of this question of identity and the SNP is provided by Bond (2000) and Bond and Rosie (2002: 42–5).

In summary of this evidence on the social base of SNP support, the most striking contrast may be summed up through an oversimplified contrast. The SNP used to be the party of the aspirational – the young, upwardly mobile, male children of the welfare state, groups which gave Margaret Thatcher her victories in England. The SNP is now the party of the downwardly mobile and is no longer the party particularly of the young.

That rather crude contrast might make depressing reading for the party, although there are other ways of reading the data which point to a rather more optimistic potential. The SNP seems to have broadened its appeal in some ways even while losing the support of the upwardly mobile. It has apparently stopped alienating Catholics. It has swum with the tide of rising Scottishness. And, for the first time, it has appealed more to women than to men (although its strategy was presumably not to do so at the expense of its male support, which seems to have been what has happened). There is also a further way in which its loss of upwardly mobile support need not be disastrous: there is in fact less upward mobility among younger age groups than among people who grew up in the 1950s and 1960s, the main reason being that young people today are the children of these earlier generations, and opportunities for middle-class careers have not been expanding rapidly enough to absorb them at the rate that the parents could achieve. Thus some of the sons and daughters of people who were upwardly mobile in the 1950s and 1960s have had to settle for jobs at the lower end of the middle-class spectrum. (Further details are in Iannelli and Paterson, forthcoming.) As this tide advances as well, perhaps the SNP will find itself carried along with it just as it was by the rising upward mobility of the 1960s.

SNP SUPPORT AND CONSTITUTIONAL CHANGE

It has long been noted that support for the SNP and support for independence are quite distinct (see, for example, Bond 2000). Table 4.4 shows the data that have formed the basis of that conclusion, and extends the picture to 2003. The party has always been much stronger among people who favour independence than among others, but even there the party's support has dropped to barely two in five as the proportion of people supporting independence has grown (McCrone and Paterson 2002: 57). Thus the party has not benefited from the long-term growth in support for independence, and its capacity to attract such support has been waning even further recently: support for independence rose from 6 to 7 per cent in the 1974 and 1979 surveys to around a quarter from 1993 to 2003, and yet the party's share of independence supporters fell from about 60 per cent in the 1970s to just under 50 per cent in the 1990s and under 40 per cent in the two most recent surveys. The same has broadly been true since 1999 of the more general question of strengthening the Scottish Parliament's powers, as Table 4.5 shows: in 2003, among all those who 'agreed' or 'agreed strongly' that the parliament should be strengthened (59 per cent of the sample), only 26 per cent supported the SNP, in contrast to 35 per cent supporting Labour.

The SNP also has stronger support among those who are most enthusiastic in their evaluation of the parliament's performance, and so the perception that the parliament has been lacklustre may have limited the SNP's support: see the upper part of Table 4.6.[3] For example, among people who, in 2003, agreed that the parliament was increasing the say which ordinary people have in government, 20 per cent supported the SNP; the figure was 16 per cent among those who believed that the parliament was making no difference. The levels of SNP support on a question about the parliament's impact on the quality of the health service were 22 per cent among those who believed that it was improving, but only 14 per cent among those who believed it was not changing, and on the performance of the economy the proportions were 24 per cent and 13 per cent respectively.

Table 4.4 Support for the SNP by constitutional preference, 1979–2003

Constitutional preference	1979		1992		1997		1999		2001		2003	
	%	N	%	N	%	N	%	N	%	N	%	N
Independence outside EU	56*	50	54	54	44	69	47	148	35	152	44	145
Independence in EU			45	164	44	158	45	247	35	299	35	242
Strong domestic parliament **	14	189	16	474	11	368	13	753	9	851	13	730
Weak domestic parliament **	3	205			2	81	10	130	4	90	5	103
No directly elected body	2	189	2	232	2	156	1	129	3	146	3	193

* The two kinds of independence were not distinguished in the 1979 survey.

** Strong domestic parliament was referred to in 1979 as a 'Scottish Assembly which would handle most Scottish affairs', and from 1997 onwards as a 'Scottish Parliament within the UK with some taxation powers'. Weak domestic parliament was referred to in 1979 as a 'Scottish Assembly which would handle some Scottish affairs and would be responsible to Parliament at Westminster', and from 1997 onwards as a 'Scottish Parliament within the UK with no taxation powers'. No distinction was made in 1992.

All cell entries show percentage of those in that group supporting the SNP.

Table 4.5 Support for the SNP by desire for the Scottish Parliament to have more powers, 1999–2003

Strength of agreement with proposition that parliament should have more powers	1999		2001		2003	
	%	Sample size	%	Sample size	%	Sample size
Agree strongly	47	213	29	328	45	199
Agree	25	623	17	769	20	708
Neither	11	291	5	224	6	244
Disagree	2	263	4	199	4	237
Disagree strongly	0	50	2	62	1	89

All main cell entries show the percentage of those in that group supporting the SNP.

(On a question about education, however, there was little difference in analogous levels of SNP support, 19 per cent compared to 18 per cent.) Labour's share, by contrast, was only a few percentage points higher among those with a positive view of the parliament's performance than among those who believed that it had had little impact (details not shown in the table).

Table 4.6 Support for the SNP by evaluations of the Scottish Parliament, 2003

	Evaluation of the Scottish Parliament					
	improved		no difference		declined	
	%	Sample size	%	Sample size	%	Sample size
All respondents						
Say in government	20	562	16	839	9	58
Health service	22	567	14	701	15	144
Education	19	357	18	876	7	104
Economy	24	522	13	710	11	175
Respondents who 'agree' or 'strongly agree' that powers of parliament should increase						
Say in government	27	407	25	461	18	23
Health service	26	441	23	363	33	59
Education	24	271	27	510	14	41
Economy	29	419	21	390	31	49

The columns are defined as follows:
'say in government': 'improved' is those who believed that the parliament was giving people more say, and 'declined' is those who believed that it was giving people less say.
'health service' and 'economy': 'improved' is those who believed that the parliament would make the standard of the health service or the performance of the economy 'a lot better' or 'a little better', and 'declined' is those who believed that it would make these 'a lot worse' or 'a little worse'.
'education': 'improved' is those who believed that the parliament was increasing the standard of education, and 'declined' is those who believed that it was reducing the standard of education.
All main cell entries show percentage of those in that group supporting the SNP.

In some ways, this is surprising. One interpretation of the data on party support tabulated against constitutional option (Table 4.4) is that they show SNP popularity to be higher among people who rejected the old Scottish Office than among those who favoured that way of governing Scotland, and yet those who are unhappy with the new status quo are not, on the face of it, so inclined to support the party. The key to resolving the paradox is in how people react to their disappointment at the parliament's performance, as the lower part of Table 4.6 shows. Among those who want the parliament's powers to be increased, there is little or no difference in the levels of SNP support between those who have a positive evaluation of the parliament's performance and those who do not: on 'say in government', the proportions are 27 per cent and 25 per cent, on the health service they are 26 per cent and 23 per cent, and on education they are 24 per cent and 27 per cent. Only on the economy did the difference remain, but the gap had narrowed from 11 points to 8 (29 per cent against 21 per cent). Moreover, on the economy and on the question about the health service, the highest level of SNP support was found among the small minority who believed that the parliament had had a harmful effect. It would appear from this that the parliament's performance is not directly the explanation of levels of SNP support: what does explain these are the ways in which people are responding to that performance by thinking about alternative constitutional arrangements.

In that sense, the SNP's approach to the sense of disappointment with the parliament has been astute, arguing as it does that the way of improving matters is to increase the parliament's powers: the percentages in the lower panel of Table 4.6 suggest that only by expanding the group of people who agree with that (already a majority) can the party benefit from the disappointment. In reacting in this way, it has also implicitly modernised its very long-standing role as the motor of the constitutional debate. However, unless it can extend its support by this means sufficiently to form a government, it may well – as in the past – see the mantle of further constitutional reform being stolen from it by others, notably Labour.

STABILITY OF SNP SUPPORT

In some respects, cross-sectional surveys taken at one point in time underestimate the amount of change in allegiance and attitudes. This has been shown for attitudes to the Scottish constitution, where, in the five years following the 1997 election, around half of people favoured independence at some point, even though only about a quarter favoured it at any point in time (McCrone and Paterson 2002: 69). Similar findings have been reached concerning the British electorate (Clarke et al. 2004: 175–216). We can similarly use panel studies conducted in 1992–7 and 1997–2001 to examine the stability of party support in Scotland: as noted in the appendix to this chapter, these surveyed the same respondents every year or so, and thus allow us to track changes in individuals' views over time.

Table 4.7   Frequency of support for various parties, 1997–2001

Number of waves at which support party:	Con	Lab	Lib Dem	SNP
	%	%	%	%
0	78	40	79	71
1	4	7	5	7
2	2	4	3	5
3	1	7	1	3
4	2	7	5	3
5	12	35	6	10
Sample size	496	496	496	496

Source: Respondents in 1997–2001 British Election Panel Study who were resident in Scotland in 1997.

Table 4.7 summarises the results from the panel which ran every spring from 1997 to 2001.[4] There were five waves, and so a wholly consistent person would choose the same party five times. It may be seen that only 10 per cent of the electorate were consistent SNP supporters in that sense, similar to the Conservatives and much less than Labour's 35 per cent. Moreover, 60 per cent of people chose Labour on at least one of the five occasions; thus, as well as the 35 per cent who always supported Labour, there were another 25 per cent who were not averse to supporting it, not much less than the SNP's 29 per cent. That size of Labour's core, and of its appeal beyond that core, is a measure of the SNP's problem. It (and the other parties) are in effect competing for the two-thirds of people who sometimes do not support Labour; but Labour itself is almost as often able to attract these as is the SNP.

Table 4.8 then compares the two panels. Because the 1992 panel asked the relevant questions only in 1994 and 1996, the 1997 panel has here been restricted to the analogous years of 1997, 1999 and 2001. Since its British victory in 1997, Labour has probably consolidated its core vote, the proportion supporting that party on all three occasions rising from 28 per cent to 38 per cent. The SNP, by contrast, has at best made no progress in this respect: it is no closer to having a core base than it was before a Scottish Parliament was in prospect.

Table 4.8 Frequency of support for various parties, 1992–6 and 1997–2001*

Number of waves at which support party:	Con		Lab		Lib Dem		SNP	
	92–96	97–01	92–96	97–01	92–96	97–01	92–96	97–01
	%	%	%	%	%	%	%	%
0	68	80	51	43	81	80	70	75
1	11	6	11	10	8	7	10	9
2	6	3	11	9	7	6	8	5
3	16	12	28	38	5	7	13	11
Sample size	391	542	391	542	391	542	391	542

* Based on three waves from each panel: 1992–1994–1996, and 1997–1999–2001.
Source: respondents in 1992–7 British Election Panel Study who were resident in Scotland in 1992, and respondents in 1997–2001 British Election Panel Study who were resident in Scotland in 1997.

A simpler but more limited way of doing this analysis is to calculate the proportion of supporters of a party in the first wave of the panels who remained loyal to the party in all subsequent relevant waves (1992, 1994 and 1996, or 1997, 1999 and 2001). In this sense, Labour still had by far the strongest loyalty, 89 per cent in the 1992 panel and 82 per cent in the 1997 one. The SNP had much weaker loyalty: respectively 62 per cent and 66 per cent. Labour loyalty did not rise according to this measure between the panels, partly because it was already, at 89 per cent, almost as high as it could go; but, as we saw in Table 4.8, its core support did rise (from 28 per cent to 38 per cent). The SNP failed to achieve this, as we have seen from Table 4.8; but that is not the SNP's only failure in these respects. The loyalty of initial Conservatives rose from 53 per cent in the 1992 panel to 72 per cent in the 1997 panel; the proportions for the Liberal Democrats were 42 per cent and 58 per cent. Thus, between the panels, the SNP also failed to improve significantly the proportion of its initial supporters who stuck with it.

Where do these disloyal SNP supporters go? Now, returning to the five-wave version of the 1997 panel, we find that 47 per cent of people who supported the SNP at least once moved to Labour at least once, by contrast to 13 per cent to the Liberal Democrats and 6 per cent to the Conservatives. The problem for the SNP is, again, that the favour is not reciprocated: among people who supported Labour at least once, only 23 per cent ever supported the SNP. Indeed, among people who supported Labour at least once, 59 per cent always supported Labour, much more than the 36 per cent sticking with the SNP among people who supported that party at least once. Because Labour support in any given year is more than twice the SNP's, these figures mean similar absolute numbers of people flow from Labour to the SNP as in the other direction, but that merely then has the effect of consolidating Labour's dominance.

This impression of a rather small core support for the SNP may be confirmed by more subtle statistical analysis of the panel studies. The details are not given here, but the main point is that in the 1997 panel around one-fifth of the electorate was very willing to experiment with supporting the party, but a quarter of them deserted between waves. The other four-fifths of the electorate rarely supported the party, and around 90 per cent of those who did so deserted between waves. In this latter group, the desertion rate rose to over 95 per cent among people who never supported independence.[5]

SNP VOTES

Thus far, we have been looking only at general support for the SNP. This approach has the advantage of allowing party support to be tracked between elections, and also probably revealing underlying attitudes as distinct from the possibly tactical motives that influence people at elections. However, ultimately parties have to gather votes, and so this section looks at the relationship between votes and support over the same period of time we have been studying so far. We deal first with votes at UK general elections in Scotland, and then turn to the rather different and more complex issues which arise in the proportional electoral system for the Scottish Parliament.

Table 4.9 Vote for the SNP at UK general elections, by party support, 1974–2001

Party support	1974		1979		1992		1997		2001	
	%	N	%	N	%	N	%	N	%	N
Conservative	13	332	5	222	4	250	7	144	4	164
Labour	5	437	3	274	7	332	4	415	1	735
Liberal/Liberal Democrat	10	93	10	67	5	67	5	96	1	154
SNP	85	226	81	75	73	186	64	147	57	253
No party	16	37	9	65	12	90	10	58	4	181

All main cell entries show the percentage of those in that group voting for the SNP.

Table 4.9 shows, first, that, except in 1974, the SNP has not been good at attracting votes from people who identify with other parties. Second, it used to attract some votes from people who identify with no party at all, but that capacity had almost vanished by 2001. Above all, however, the SNP used to be able to mobilise its own supporters to vote for it (85 per cent doing so in 1974), but spectacularly lost that capacity by 2001 (the proportion being down to 57 per cent).

Table 4.10 Proportion of party supporters who voted for that party at UK general elections, 1974–2001

Party support	1974		1979		1992		1997		2001	
	%	N	%	N	%	N	%	N	%	N
Conservative	70	332	81	222	76	250	63	144	61	164
Labour	83	437	81	274	78	332	79	415	69	735
Liberal/Liberal Democrat	60	93	46	67	81	67	71	96	75	154
SNP	85	226	81	75	73	186	64	147	57	253

Main cell entries show the proportion voting for the party they support.

It is true that all parties are becoming less effective at mobilising their supporters, as Table 4.10 shows; but the drop for the SNP has been greater. In particular, comparing the party again with its main rival, Labour, whereas both parties mobilised similar proportions of their supporters from 1974 to perhaps as late as 1992, the SNP fell behind thereafter. This deficiency is partly explained by different tendencies of each party's supporters to abstain altogether, as Table 4.11 shows: SNP abstention rose from 10 per cent in 1974 to 30 per cent in 2001, a somewhat larger rise than Labour's from 10 per cent to 25 per cent. For the SNP, it is also explained by a greater amount of desertion of supporters to other parties: in 1974, only 4 per cent of SNP supporters voted for other parties, whereas in 2001 the proportion was 12 per cent; the analogous proportions for Labour were 7 per cent in 1974 and 6 per cent in 2001. The SNP's vote has also suffered from the fact that people who identify with no party were, by 2001, nearly all abstaining.

Table 4.11 Proportion of party supporters who did not vote at UK general elections, 1974–2001

Party support	1974		1979		1992		1997		2001	
	%	N	%	N	%	N	%	N	%	N
Conservative	10	332	10	222	13	250	14	144	24	164
Labour	10	437	10	274	11	332	17	415	25	735
Liberal/Liberal Democrat	13	93	16	67	10	67	10	96	17	154
SNP	10	226	11	75	14	186	22	147	30	253
No party	35	37	22	65	32	90	54	58	87	181

Main cell entries show proportion of identifiers with that party not voting.

Table 4.12   Vote for the SNP at Scottish general elections, by party support, 1999 and 2003

Party support	1999			2003		
	constituency vote	list vote	Sample size	constituency vote	list vote	Sample size
	%	%		%	%	
Conservative	4	6	231	6	7	230
Labour	7	8	625	5	5	483
Liberal Democrat	6	3	166	6	1	163
SNP	75	70	290	62	55	254
Green	–	–	–	5	5	23
Scottish Socialist Party	–	–	–	5	2	43
No party	12	13	115	1	3	181

The number of Green Party supporters was too small to give reliable results in 1999, while identification with the SSP was not asked in 1999.

A similar conclusion can be drawn from the shorter history of voting at Scottish Parliament elections. Table 4.12 shows the SNP attracting few of the supporters of other parties. In 1999, it was moderately successful at gaining the votes of some people who did not identify with any party, almost indeed back at the 1974 levels in this respect (see Table 4.9). But even that collapsed in the election of 2003. Meanwhile, as can be seen from Table 4.13, the decline between 1999 and 2003 in the SNP's capacity to mobilise its own supporters was greater than for the three other large parties. Whereas in 1999 it was much better at mobilising its own supporters, that advantage was mostly lost in 2003. Indeed, we can calculate that, if the SNP had attracted in 2003 the same share (70 per cent) of its supporters as in 1999, its overall vote share would probably have been about four to five percentage points higher, cancelling out most of its loss in the total share of the vote between these two elections.

The same picture emerges if we compare the votes on the two ballots in the Scottish Parliament elections. For example, whereas in 1999 the SNP retained on the list ballot 83 per cent of those who voted for it in the constituency ballot, by 2003 this had fallen to 71 per cent. The change for Labour was less severe, from 78 per cent to 73 per cent.

One notable feature of vote retention was the success of the Conservatives at mobilising their supporters. We can see from Table 4.13 again that in 2003 they attracted 60 per cent of their supporters in the list ballot, even more than the SNP. These list voters included 85 per cent of those who had supported the party on the constituency ballot (compared with the 73 per cent for Labour and the 71 per cent for the SNP). This feature of the Tory vote might be interpreted with cautious optimism by the SNP, because some media commentators have suggested that the Tories might be about to overtake the SNP as the second party in Scotland. These figures suggest that that is unlikely: the Conservatives did moderately well in 2003 mainly because they were excellent at mobilising and retaining their quite small body of support. The SNP failed in these respects, but it continues to operate from a somewhat larger if more diffuse base, as Table 4.7, for example, shows. If the Tories had only been able to mobilise their supporters on the list vote at the level achieved by Labour or the Liberal Democrats (45–50 per cent instead of 60 per cent, from Table 4.13), their share of the total vote would have been about four percentage points lower, leaving them with a total of around fourteen instead of eighteen seats, and hence in fourth place behind the Liberal Democrats.

Table 4.13 Proportion of party supporters who voted for that party at Scottish general elections, 1999 and 2003

Party support	1999			2003		
	constituency vote	list vote	Sample size	constituency vote	list vote	Sample size
Conservative	57	57	231	61	60	230
Labour	60	53	625	53	45	483
Liberal Democrat	61	58	166	54	48	163
SNP	75	70	290	62	55	254
Green	–	–	–	–	35	23
Scottish Socialist Party	–	–	–	37	37	43

Main cell entries show the proportion voting for the party they support.
The number of Green Party identifiers was too small to give reliable results in 1999, while the party did not field candidates in the constituency ballot in either election; identification with the SSP was not asked in 1999.

The SNP might also be somewhat encouraged by a further contrast with Labour and the Liberal Democrats. Both of these latter two parties were less successful in 2003 at persuading their supporters to vote for them than they had been in the 2001 UK general election (see Table 4.10): in the constituency ballot, the proportions were respectively 53 per cent and 69 per cent for Labour, and 54 per cent and 75 per cent for the Liberal Democrats. The SNP, by contrast, mobilised 62 per cent of its supporters in 2003, slightly higher in fact than the 57 per cent in 2001.

CONCLUSIONS

Analysing the social basis of a party's support, and the flows of votes between it and other parties, is only one aspect of understanding why it is or is not successful, and the data offered here therefore provide only one way of understanding the SNP's dilemmas. But, however much party strategists might want to supplement such an analysis, the lessons from it do seem to offer both problems and opportunities for the party.

On the negative side first, we have concluded that the SNP is no longer the party of the young and the upwardly mobile. The party's shift to the left may have been understandable as an attempt to take votes from Labour in the 1980s and 1990s, but it seems now to have lodged the party in a shrinking working class and in an ageing segment of the population. If the SNP was once the vehicle by which the aspirational sought to modernise Scottish society, it may now be the resort of the disgruntled, the down-wardly mobile. It also has a declining capacity to mobilise its own supporters, to attract votes from supporters of other parties and to secure the votes of those who do not support any party. The support it does attract is more transient than that of its main rival, Labour. It has not benefited much from the growth in support for home rule since the 1970s, nor even very much from the recent growth in support for strengthening the powers of the Scottish Parliament or for independence. It is clear from this, further, that Scotland could easily over the next decade or so reach a position of majority support for something like independence with the SNP still in a minority.

But these are not the only conclusions warranted by the data, and there are countervailing tendencies that promise rather better prospects for the party. It has broadened its social base, appealing more successfully to women and to people of a variety of religious persuasions than at any time in the past thirty years. If it has come to attract the support of the downwardly mobile more than those moving in the opposite direction, that is in fact in keeping with an important social trend. There are more downwardly mobile people among young people today because the oppor-tunities to move up have not been expanding rapidly enough (a trend common across Britain and probably other developed societies). If the SNP is a party of the disgruntled, then that might in due course resonate with a disgruntled society.

The SNP is not the only party that is coming to be less effective at mobilising its supporters, and it seems likely that, in due course, Labour will suffer from similar problems. If the only way of avoiding that is to concentrate on a small but beleaguered core support, as the Tories seem to have done, then perhaps both these parties would prefer the alternative of more pluralistic competition. Differential turnout of supporters is, after all, as important in elections as absolute levels of support. The SNP's difficulties in mobilising its supporters, moreover, are probably not related to the setting-up of the Scottish Parliament: almost the same rather low proportion of supporters voted for the party in the 2001 UK general election as in the 2003 Scottish Parliament election. In this sense, compared to Labour and the Liberal Democrats, it is less successful in UK elections and more successful in Scottish elections.

The main reason why party activists ought to be cautiously optimistic, however, is a rather perverse conclusion from the statistics. The SNP's base of support since the Scottish Parliament was set up is clearly higher than it has been at any time since the mid-1970s. Indeed, the level and social profile of its support in 1999 resembles that in 1974 fairly closely, as may be seen from Table 4.1, the main exceptions probably stemming from the points about downward mobility that have ambiguous implications. The results of the 2001, 2003 and 2005 elections were not anywhere nearly as poor as those of 1979. When we consider that 1999 was regarded as somewhat disappointing for the party, following its very high ratings in opinion polls after the 1997 referendum, and that 1974 was its best ever performance, we have a measure of how far it has come. The very fact that it can be doing so well, in historical terms, despite all the problems sketched in this chapter, should be a warning to those who would dismiss its prospects out of hand. The problem remains, however, that after 1974 the party had to wait until the mid- or late 1980s before it started to recover again. Dating its most recent high point as 1997–8, and its current problems from 1999, that would place the serious revival of its electoral fortunes at around the time of the Scottish Parliament elections of 2011.

APPENDIX: SURVEYS

Some of the analysis in this chapter is based on data generated by the Scottish respondents to two surveys not used elsewhere in this book. These are the 1992–7 and 1997–2001 British Election Panel Studies and the 1999–2001 waves of the British Household Panel Study.

The 1992–7 election panel study reinterviewed respondents to the 1992 Scottish Election Study on a number of occasions up to and including the 1997 UK general election. The 1997–2001 study conducted a similar exercise amongst respondents to the 1997 Scottish Election Study. Among the 957 respondents to the election survey in 1992, the subsequent panel study achieved response rates of 61 per cent in 1994 (588 respondents) and

44 per cent in 1996 (418 respondents). Likewise, among the 882 respondents to the 1997 election survey, the panel study achieved response rates of 76 per cent in 1998 (672 respondents), 71 per cent in 1999 (626 respondents), 66 per cent in 2000 (586 respondents) and 68 per cent in 2001 (596 respondents). Although the panel studies thus had quite high levels of attrition, they do have the unique virtue of letting us study the ways in which individuals do or do not change their minds in their political attitudes. Moreover, the attrition did not vary strongly by relevant attitudes (as measured in 1992 or 1997): it was much the same among supporters of various constitutional options for Scotland, of various political parties, and in various demographic groupings defined by social class, gender and age. The only statistically significant variation in response rates were that, in both the 1992 and the 1997 panels, older people (aged over 54) were less likely to respond than younger, and that, in the 1992 panel only, people who had supported the Conservatives and Liberal Democrats in 1992 were more likely to respond than others. The main effect of this variable attrition would be to exaggerate somewhat the Conservative and Liberal Democrat support in the 1992–6 columns of Table 4.8. This would not affect the main comparison we have looked at, that between the SNP and Labour. The British Election Panel Studies were funded by the Economic and Social Research Council (ESRC), and the fieldwork was undertaken by the National Centre for Social Research.

The British Household Panel Survey is an annual panel survey of households and adults that has been running across Britain as a whole since 1991; it is funded by the ESRC and is carried out by the Research Centre on Micro-Social Change at Essex University. Since 1999, the Scottish sample has been enhanced to about 1,500 households and about 3,000 adults, including respondents from the original sample living in Scotland. The new sample included full representation of the area north and west of the Great Glen, although the original (1991) sample did not. Further information is available from the survey's website, at www.iser.-essex.ac.uk/bhps/index.php

NOTES

1. In the survey series which is used here, this is recorded in a variable labelled 'party identification', the main contribution to which are survey responses to two questions, one on whether the respondent is a supporter of a party, and the other (for those who decline to call themselves party supporters) on whether they feel closer to one party than to the others. In the surveys other than those of 2001 and 2003,

respondents were prompted on these questions with the names of the four main parties. In these two surveys, instead of that prompting, a further supplementary question was added: for those who declined to say whether they felt close to any party, identification was recorded as how they would probably vote 'if there were a general election tomorrow'. The rationale for this alternative way of asking about identification is that providing a list of parties artificially increases the level of identification with these parties, but the identification variables defined in these two ways do tend to yield levels of identification with each party that are similar. Nevertheless, to test whether our conclusions have been distorted by the difference of definitions, we can rerun the 2003 analysis with identification defined as in the election study series (ignoring the absence of prompts). This gave similar patterns to those commented on in the first two substantive sections of this chapter (and Tables 4.1 to 4.6), although at an overall lower level: the overall level of not identifying with any party rose from 12 per cent to 38 per cent, and the level of identification with the SNP fell from 17 per cent to 12 per cent; the falls for the other large parties were from 15 per cent to 12 per cent for Conservative, from 33 per cent to 27 per cent for Labour, and from 10 per cent to 7 per cent for Liberal Democrat. Because this definition of identification omits those with the weakest attachment to the parties, it also raised by a few percentage points the proportions of party supporters who voted for each party (for example, in Table 4.13), but none of the trends commented on in the text were affected by this: for example, in 2003 the proportion of SNP supporters defined in this way who voted for the party was 70 per cent in the constituency ballot and 63 per cent on the list ballot, both down from 1999. It is important to emphasise, however, that this rerun analysis undoubtedly underestimates the levels of identification with the parties, because of the absence of prompts in the questions, and so should not be preferred to the definitions used in the text.

2. A test of the validity of any inferences drawn from the survey series can be had by comparing the percentage SNP vote (among all who reported voting) with the actual results of the parliamentary elections that took place in the corresponding years, measuring the constituency and list elements of the Scottish parliamentary ballots separately. For all but two of the years, these survey percentages were within two percentage points of the actual result (and, except in 1974, were within one percentage point). In 1997 and 2001, the survey under-reported the actual vote (respectively, 18 per cent compared to 22 per cent and 15 per cent compared to 20 per cent). If there was a similar small under-reporting of

party support, then the stability of the series shown in the first row of Table 4.1 would be even more striking.

3. These questions on the parliament's performance are analysed in greater depth in chapter 2.

4. Although the sample size is quite small here, analysis of the much larger sample in Scotland in the 1999–2001 British Household Panel Study showed similar results to the election panel for these years.

5. The analysis used Mixed Markov Latent Class models, as explained by Langeheine and van de Pol (1994) and as used extensively in the analysis of surveys conducted in connection with the 2001 British election by Clarke et al. (2004: ch. 6). The software used was LEM (Vermunt 1997).

References

Bond, R. (2000), 'Squaring the circles: demonstrating and explaining the political "non-alignment" of Scottish national identity', *Scottish Affairs*, 32: 15–35.

Bond, R. and Rosie, M. (2002), 'National identities in post-devolution Scotland', *Scottish Affairs*, 40: 34–53.

Clarke, H. D., Sanders, D., Stewart, M. C. and Whiteley, P. F. (2004), *Political Choice in Britain*, Oxford: Oxford University Press.

Curtice, J., McCrone, D., Park, A. and Paterson, L. (eds) (2002), *New Scotland, New Society?*, Edinburgh: Edinburgh University Press.

Dewar, D. (1988), Williamson Lecture, Stirling University, 21 October, extracts reprinted in Paterson (ed.) (1998), pp. 169–73.

Finlay, R. J. (1994), *Independent and Free*, Edinburgh: John Donald.

Finlay, R. J. (1997), *A Partnership for Good?*, Edinburgh: John Donald.

Iannelli, C. and Paterson, L. (forthcoming), 'Social mobility in Scotland since the middle of the twentieth century', *Sociological Review*.

Kellas, J. (1984), *The Scottish Political System*, Cambridge: 3rd edn, Cambridge University Press.

Kendrick, S. (1983), *Social Change and Nationalism in Modern Scotland*, Ph.D. thesis, University of Edinburgh.

Langeheine, R. and van de Pol, F. (1994), 'Discrete-time Markov latent class models', in A. Dale and R. Davies (eds), *Analysing Social and Political Change*, London: Sage.

Lynch, P. (2002), *The History of the Scottish National Party*, Cardiff: Welsh Academic Press.

McCrone, D. (1992), *Understanding Scotland*, 1st edn, London: Routledge.

McCrone, D. and Paterson, L. (2002), 'The conundrum of Scottish independence', *Scottish Affairs*, 40: 54–75.

McCrone, D. and Rosie, M. (1998), 'Left and liberal: Catholics in modern Scotland', in R. Boyle and P. Lynch (eds), *Out of the Ghetto?*, Edinburgh: John Donald.

Paterson, L. (ed.) (1998), *A Diverse Assembly: The Debate on a Scottish Parliament*, Edinburgh: Edinburgh University Press.

Paterson, L. (2002a), 'Governing from the centre: ideology and public policy', in J. Curtice, D. McCrone, A. Park and L. Paterson (eds), *New Scotland, New Society?*, Edinburgh: Edinburgh University Press.

Paterson, L. (2002b), 'Scottish social democracy and Blairism: difference, diversity and community', in G. Hassan and C. Warhurst (eds), *Tomorrow's Scotland*, London: Lawrence and Wishart.

Paterson, L. (2002c), 'Is Britain disintegrating? Changing views of "Britain" after devolution', *Regional and Federal Studies*, 12: 21–42.

Paterson, L., Brown, A., Curtice, J., Hinds, K., McCrone, D., Park, A., Sproston, K. and Surridge, P. (2001), *New Scotland, New Politics?*, Edinburgh: Edinburgh University Press.

Paterson, L., Iannelli, C., Bechhofer, F. and McCrone, D. (2004), 'Social class and social opportunity', in L. Paterson, F. Bechhofer and D. McCrone (eds), *Living in Scotland: Social and Economic Change since 1980*, Edinburgh: Edinburgh University Press.

Rosie M. and McCrone, D. (2000), 'The past is history: Catholics in modern Scotland', in T. M. Devine (ed.), *Scotland's Shame?*, Edinburgh: Mainstream.

Seawright, D. and Curtice, J. (1995), 'The decline of the Scottish Conservative and Unionist Party 1950–92: religion, ideology or economics?', *Contemporary Record*, 9: 319–42.

Surridge, P. and McCrone, D. (1999), 'The 1997 Scottish referendum vote', in B. Taylor and K. Thomson (eds), *Scotland and Wales: Nations Again?*, Cardiff: University of Wales Press.

Vermunt, J. K. (1997), *LEM: A General Program for the Analysis of Categorical Data*, available from the website of the University of Tilburg at http://www.tilburguniversity.nl/

Part 2

Devolved Elections

CHAPTER 5

Holyrood 2003 – Where were the Voters?

Catherine Bromley

INTRODUCTION

Voting in elections held in Scotland, as well as those across the UK, has fallen markedly in recent years. Although, at the time, the 1997 UK general election turnout of 72 per cent was the lowest in the post-war era, such a turnout would now be regarded as a high point. In the 2001 general election, turnout fell to just 59 per cent, the lowest level since 1918, and only recovered slightly to 61 per cent in 2005. Scottish elections have suffered a similar fate. That 67 per cent voted in the 1997 devolution referendum could arguably be called respectable. But, when invited to participate in the Scottish Parliament's first ever democratic election in 1999, just 58 per cent took up the opportunity. Although these turnout levels were historically low, they all shared one redeeming feature: more people voted in them than did not. But, in the second Scottish Parliament election in 2003, this was not the case. With a turnout of just 49 per cent, abstention (even if only by a very small margin) was the act of the majority. Given the high hopes and aspirations which accompanied devolution during the course of its planning and inception – and in particular an alleged ability to re-engage voters in the political process (Dewar 1998) – it must be a disappointment to its advocates that after the second Holyrood election the parliament was being dogged by the question of why half the electorate did not even consider it worth voting for.

This chapter has two broad aims. The first is to explain why people did not vote in the 2003 election. The second is to answer the perhaps slightly trickier question of why turnout was even lower in 2003 than in 1999. In particular, we attempt to establish whether the decline in turnout between 1999 and 2003 was a reflection of the electorate's rather lukewarm evaluations of four years of devolution (as discussed in detail in Chapter 2) or whether it was simply the result of wider trends that are helping to depress turnout at all elections. Understanding which of these processes was the more significant will help us to draw conclusions about the future prospects for turnout in Holyrood elections. Is it the case that so low a turnout early on in Holyrood's history means that it now faces a future of low turnouts, or is it the case that what has gone down could come up again?

Turnout in 2003

First, however, it is worth reflecting for a moment on the fact that the reported level of turnout among the sample of respondents whom we interviewed in 2003 is, at 60 per cent, eleven points higher than the actual official turnout in the election. Equally, in our 1999 survey, 72 per cent said that they had voted, compared with an actual turnout of 59 per cent. There is a number of reasons why this gap happens (Swaddle and Heath 1989). First, it is perhaps inevitable that a survey being conducted in the aftermath of an election, much of whose content is focused on politics, will interview a disproportionate number of voters. Put simply, the kinds of people who do not vote are also reluctant to take part in surveys, whether about politics or about something else. Another reason is poor or defective recall on the part of survey respondents. Some people who did not vote will report that they did, through either forgetfulness or the perception that admitting to not having voted might be socially unacceptable – though, given that a majority did not vote in 2003, this latter reason might be thought to have had less force in 2003. Meanwhile, the official turnout itself is subject to error, as those who have died recently will still be on the register, while others will legitimately be registered to vote at more than one address. However, the analysis in this chapter is primarily concerned with differences *between* various groups in their level of turnout rather than the overall level. And there is no reason to believe that the discrepancy between our survey and the official result in respect of the latter means that our survey does not accurately capture the key differences in the level of turnout between different groups.

We start our substantive discussion by describing the characteristics of those who did vote in 2003. In common with much of what has been found in previous literature on voter turnout, both domestically and cross-nationally (Bromley and Curtice 2002; Wattenberg 2003; Wolfinger et al. 1990), the people least likely to have voted in 2003 were predominantly young, living in private rented accommodation and working-class (see Table 5.1). They also had little interest in politics and had only a very weak sense of identification with any political party. Indeed, not only were the kinds of people who abstained in 2003 similar to 1999 and 2001, but in many cases they were the same individuals. Over 90 per cent of those who voted in 1999 or 2001 did so again in 2003, whereas only around half of those who abstained in 1999 or 2001 turned out in 2003.

Indeed, one piece of analysis of the 2003 turnout carried out on behalf of

Table 5.1 Turnout by age, social class, housing tenure, interest in politics and party identification, 2003

	% voted	*Sample size*
Age		
18–34	37	*345*
35–44	55	*307*
45–54	71	*247*
55–64	70	*260*
65+	78	*346*
Social class		
Professional/managerial	69	*461*
Intermediate	60	*145*
Small employers	71	*123*
Lower supervisory	54	*209*
Semi-routine/routine	54	*437*
Tenure		
Owner occupier	65	*986*
Social renter	53	*386*
Private renter	39	*114*
Interest in politics		
None at all	33	*208*
Not very much	52	*432*
Some	65	*473*
Quite a lot	75	*281*
A great deal	82	*111*
Party identification		
None	10	*181*
Not very strong	64	*688*
Fairly strong	74	*409*
Very strong	83	*99*
All	60	*1,508*

Note: Social class is measured by National Statistics Socio-Economic Classification. For further details, see the Technical Appendix.

the Electoral Commission suggested that one in ten of the electorate could be defined as 'serial non-voters' (Boon and Curtice 2003). This same study also found that around one in five non-voters gave circumstantial reasons for their not having voted (for example, that they had been busy, ill or just away at the time). While such reasons are undoubtedly important in explaining who does and does not vote at any particular election, they do not necessarily help to explain why the overall level of turnout changes over time. True, the working population has been expanding, and working hours are increasing, so it is therefore possible that more people nowadays are hard pressed to vote because of other demands on their time.[1] But these trends are in no way large enough to account for the drop in voting between the 1999 and 2003 Scottish elections.

Having sketched a profile of voters in 2003, we now attempt to understand what might lie behind these patterns. We do this by drawing a distinction between the kinds of factors that help account for low turnout in most elections, that is, between what we might term 'the usual suspects' and the kinds of 'home-grown' factors that might in particular help to explain voting behaviour at a Holyrood election.

THE USUAL SUSPECTS

First, we look at a number of factors that are commonly associated with turnout at all elections, some of which we have already shown to have been significant in 2003. These are:

- age
- interest in politics
- how strongly people identify with a political party, if any; and
- political efficacy, that is, whether people feel that the political system responds to their wishes.

There are two ways in which an examination of these factors might help us account for the decline in turnout in 2003. The first possibility is that more people fell into the categories of people among whom turnout is always lower. For this to be the case, we would need to demonstrate that in 2003 as compared with previous years there were more young people, fewer people interested in politics, fewer people with a sense of identity with a political party, and fewer people who felt efficacious. The second possibility is that these various factors had even more influence on turnout in 2003 than they had before, that is, that turnout fell most heavily among younger voters, the uninterested, non-identifiers and the inefficacious.

The age structure of Scotland's population did not, of course, change over the four-year period between 1999 and 2003, and so cannot account for the decline in turnout. But what about our other factors? There is some evidence that their incidence did change but only slightly. As Table 5.2 shows, the well-charted long-term decline in party identification appears to have continued yet further, with just one in three (35 per cent) having a very or fairly strong level of identification with a party at all compared with half (51 per cent) in 1999. At the same time, however, the proportion who profess to have no party identification has only increased from 7 to 12 per cent; and, as we shall see below, this is the key group of interest when it comes to turnout.[2] Meanwhile, so far as political efficacy is concerned, in 2003

73 per cent agreed with the proposition that 'parties are only interested in people's votes, not in their opinions', that is, they gave an *inefficacious* response, seven points higher than in 1999. A slightly smaller upward trend can also be detected on the question about whether 'MPs lose touch with people quickly'. (For further discussion of these items, see Chapter 3.) However, the 26 per cent who said they had a 'great deal' or 'quite a lot' of interest in politics was exactly the same as in 2001 and actually three points higher than in 1999. All in all, these changes are not sufficient to account for the nine point decline in turnout between 1999 and 2003.

Table 5.2 Trends in political interest, party identification and efficacy, 1999–2003

	1999	2001	2003
	%	%	%
Political interest			
A great deal	6	7	7
Quite a lot	17	19	19
Some	36	33	32
Not very much	31	27	28
None at all	9	13	13
Parties only interested in votes			
Agree	65	73	73
Disagree	20	16	15
MPs soon lose touch			
Agree	66	72	71
Disagree	15	15	13
Party identification			
Very strong	10	8	7
Fairly strong	41	31	28
Not very strong	40	46	46
None	7	11	12
Sample size	1,482	1,605	1,508

On the other hand, what certainly appears to be true is that many of these 'usual suspects' were even more strongly associated with turnout in 2003 than they were in either 1999 or 2001. Consider, for example, differences in turnout by age, as shown in Table 5.3. At the first Scottish election in 1999, there was a twenty-nine-point difference between the level of turnout among those aged 65 and over and those aged under 35. In 2001, that figure grew to thirty-nine points and in 2003 it edged up yet further to forty-one points. Similarly, in 1999 there was a fifty-point difference between the level of turnout among those who identified with a party very strongly and those who did not identify with a party at all. In 2001, the gap had widened to seventy points, while in 2003 it was no fewer than seventy-three points. There has also been equivalent growth in the differences in turnout by political interest and by one of our measures of political efficacy.

Table 5.3 Turnout by age, political interest, party identification and efficacy, 1999, 2001 and 2003

% voted	1999	Sample size	2001	Sample size	2003	Sample size
Age						
18–34	57	400	47	411	37	345
35–44	69	259	67	320	55	307
45–54	76	247	78	254	71	247
55–64	84	209	79	219	70	260
65+	86	356	83	400	78	346
Turnout gap	29		36		41	
Interest in politics						
None at all	41	138	39	226	33	208
Not very much	67	467	63	439	52	432
Some	75	527	75	525	65	473
Quite a lot	88	256	83	312	75	281
A great deal	87	94	73	101	82	111
Turnout gap	46		34		49	
Party identification						
None	36	115	13	181	10	181
Not very strong	68	567	70	727	64	688
Fairly strong	80	614	82	490	74	409
Very strong	86	153	83	125	83	99
Turnout gap	50		70		73	
Parties only interested in votes						
Agree	71	959	67	1,179	58	1,115
Disagree	79	290	76	251	73	222
Turnout gap	8		9		15	
MPs soon lose touch						
Agree	71	959	67	1,179	59	1,078
Disagree	80	290	79	251	66	189
Turnout gap	9		12		7	

So, the lower level of turnout in 2003 compared with 1999 or 2001 cannot simply be blamed on the electorate being more disconnected from politics in general. The public were no more uninterested in politics than they had been two or four years previously, while they were only slightly more inefficacious. Rather, turnout appears to have fallen in 2003 because turnout dropped most heavily among those who were already relatively disconnected from politics. As this was a pattern that had already been evident in the 2001 UK general election,[3] it is at least quite possible that this too might have little to do with devolution. But, of course, it might also be an indication that devolution has been particularly unsuccessful in reaching out to the relatively politically uninterested. The next section considers the extent to which devolution itself might have been responsible for the fall in turnout in 2003.

HOME-GROWN FACTORS

If what we discussed in the previous section is correct, we would expect to find direct evidence that those who were disenchanted with or who felt themselves to be untouched by devolution were less likely to vote. That evidence is in fact less easy to find than might be supposed. The 'home-grown' factors that might arguably impact on people's willingness to vote include:

- evaluations of the performance of devolution
- the belief that Westminster is more powerful than Holyrood
- perceptions of the importance of Scottish Parliament elections
- perceptions of the inevitability of the election's outcome, that is, that it was a foregone conclusion[4]
- the perceived differences between the larger parties in Scotland
- knowledge of the Scottish party leaders
- concern about the cost of the new parliament building.

Following the logic of our analysis in the previous section, there are two possible ways in which these might account for the decline in turnout in 2003. One is that more people simply fell into the categories where turnout is always lower. The other is that their impact on turnout was even greater in 2003 than in 1999.

We start with evaluations. We saw in Chapter 2 that, on a number of measures, evaluations of devolution were less favourable in 2003 than they were four years previously. However, for the most part, these evaluations were at most only weakly associated with turnout. Thus, for example, in 2003 turnout among those who thought that having the Scottish Parliament was helping to improve the standard of education was, at 65 per cent, only six points higher than among those who thought that the parliament was making no difference. Similarly, those who thought that the parliament has given ordinary people more say in how they are governed were only five points more likely to vote than those who thought it had not made any difference.

We also saw in Chapter 2 that, by 2003, far fewer people thought that the Scottish Parliament had more influence on what happens in Scotland than thought in 1999 that this would be the case. This change could be thought to have depressed turnout somewhat, as those who think that the UK government has most influence were eight points less likely to vote in the

2003 election than were those who thought that the Scottish Parliament did. But, at the same time, we should bear in mind that those who think that the UK government has most influence were also six points less likely to have voted in the 2001 UK general election too. So, we should be wary of rushing to the conclusion that the advent of the widespread perception that the UK government still has most influence in Scotland was in any way principally responsible for the particularly low turnout in 2003.

One perception that does have a particularly strong impact on turnout in Scottish Parliament elections is whether the outcome of such elections is thought to matter. There was no less than a twenty-nine-point difference in 1999 between the level of turnout among those who think that it makes 'a great deal' or 'quite a lot' of difference who wins a Scottish Parliament election, and participation among those who think that it makes little difference or 'none at all'. Meanwhile, there was no less than a fifteen-point drop between 1999 and 2003 in the proportion who think that who wins a Scottish election makes 'a great deal' or 'quite a lot' of difference.[5] This fall clearly helped to depress the turnout in 2003 and was firmly a 'home-grown' rather than a UK-wide trend.

Of course, this finding begs the question as to why the perceived importance of Scottish Parliament elections has declined. While this could simply be because there is a perception that the parliament has insufficient powers for it to matter who has most power within it, it could also be because there is thought to be little difference between the parties' policies anyway. As Table 5.4 shows, this was certainly a fairly widespread perception among the public in 2003. Fewer than one in three thought that there was a 'great deal' of difference between the Labour Party and the SNP in 2003, while just one in four thought that there was a 'great deal' of difference between the Conservative and Labour Parties in Scotland. Moreover, the parties were rather less likely to be thought to be far apart than had been the case four years earlier.

This perceived lack of difference between the parties is indeed associated with the perception that the outcome of Scottish elections does not make much difference. Those who think that there is a great deal of difference between Labour and the SNP are more than twice as likely to think that who wins a Scottish election matters a great deal or quite a lot than are those who think that there is not much difference between them. Meanwhile, as Table 5.5 shows, not only was there a twenty-point gap between the turnout in 2003 among those who said that there is a great deal of difference between Labour and the Conservatives and the level of participation among those who felt that there was not much difference, but also the size of this gap was twice what it was in 1999. There was also an equivalent sixteen-point gap between those who felt that there is a great

Table 5.4   Perceptions of differences between the parties, 1999, 2001 and 2003

Perceived difference between . . .	1999	2001	2003
	%	%	%
Conservative and Labour			
A great deal	30	21	23
Some	35	39	36
Not much	32	38	37
Labour and the SNP			
A great deal	41	33	31
Some	40	42	43
Not much	15	19	20
Sample size	1,482	1,605	1,508

deal of difference between Labour and the SNP and those who reckoned that there was not much difference, though in this case the figure had been somewhat higher in 1999. Evidently, the growth in the perception that there was not much difference in the parties had the potential to reduce turnout, though it is far too small to account for any more than a minor portion of the decline in turnout in 2003.

Table 5.5   Turnout by perceived difference between the parties, 1999, 2001 and 2003

Perceived difference between . . .	% voted					
	1999	*Sample size*	2001	*Sample size*	2003	*Sample size*
Conservative and Labour						
A great deal	79	*452*	78	*356*	75	*343*
Some	73	*497*	71	*588*	61	*523*
Not much	68	*482*	62	*626*	54	*586*
Turnout gap	11		16		21	
Labour and SNP						
A great deal	82	*598*	76	*516*	71	*458*
Some	72	*578*	69	*666*	59	*636*
Not much	58	*235*	58	*326*	55	*341*
Turnout gap	24		18		16	

The other factor worth considering here is whether people felt that the result of the 2003 election was simply a foregone conclusion and therefore felt less inclined to bother voting. While there is a more proportional voting system in Scottish elections than in Westminster contests, Labour appears – barring disasters – almost guaranteed to win the largest number of seats of any of the parties. The party has, after all, managed to win the majority of

Westminster seats at every election in Scotland since 1959, a very different position from that across Britain as a whole. So, Scotland's electoral history might have been thought to have encouraged the perception that the outcome of elections is done and dusted even before the polls are open. To test the extent to which this was a popularly held view at the time of the 2003 election, we asked people whether they agreed or disagreed with the following statement:

It was obvious who was going to win the election long before election day.

Under half (44 per cent) felt that it was a foregone conclusion, a quarter (24 per cent) disagreed, and three in ten (30 per cent) said that they neither agreed nor disagreed or that they didn't know. So, although the most common answer given was that the outcome was a foregone conclusion, a sizeable minority couldn't judge the matter either way. Unfortunately, this question was not asked in our 1999 survey, so we cannot establish whether this perception was more common in 2003 than in 1999. But, in any event, it is evident that this measure is not closely associated with turnout. As many as two-thirds (66 per cent) of those who said that the election result was obvious voted, only a little less than the figure of almost three-quarters (73 per cent) who disagreed that this was the case.

But elections are not just about the performance of the parties. They are also about personalities. If voters have clear likes and dislikes among their potential rulers, they may be more motivated to vote than if they do not. Yet, as Table 5.6 demonstrates, it appears that, for many voters in 2003, Scotland's party leaders were something of an unknown quantity. When asked to give each of the party leaders a mark out of ten, one in three could not pass judgement on the Liberal Democrat leader (and Deputy First Minister), Jim Wallace, or the leader of the SNP, John Swinney. Meanwhile, this was true of more than two in five when they were asked about the Conservative leader, David McLetchie. In fact, the only leader who appeared to evoke a strong reaction among the public was Tommy Sheridan of the SSP; almost half (46 per cent) gave him a poor mark of three or less.

Indeed, only half of the respondents to our 2003 survey felt able to give a mark out of ten to all of Jack McConnell, John Swinney, David McLetchie, Jim Wallace and Tommy Sheridan, while nearly one in ten felt unable to give *any* of the party leaders a score. In contrast, just 2 per cent felt unable to pass judgement on Tony Blair when asked about his performance as Prime Minister. Meanwhile, as Table 5.7 shows, the fewer party leaders that someone felt able to rate, the less likely they were to vote. Indeed, this pattern was not only evident in 2003 but also in the 1999 Scottish election.

Table 5.6 Evaluations of party leaders, 2003

	Evaluation (mark out of ten)			
	Poor (0–3)	Middle (4–6)	Good (7–10)	Don't know
	%	%	%	%
Jack McConnell (Lab)	18	48	20	14
Jim Wallace (LD)	17	36	15	32
John Swinney (SNP)	28	31	7	33
David McLetchie (Con)	20	30	8	42
Tommy Sheridan (SSP)	46	23	13	18

Sample size: 1,508

Note: Respondents were asked to rate McConnell's actual performance as First Minister, while in the case of the other party leaders they were asked how a good job they thought the leader would do as First Minister.

While in contrast it was less strong in the 2001 election. It appears that the failure of the Scottish party leaders to make much impression upon the Scottish public, whether favourable or unfavourable, managed to discourage from voting those who had at least bothered to vote in the low-turnout contest in 2001.

Table 5.7 Turnout in 2003 and knowledge of party leaders

		Voted in 2003	Sample size	Voted in 2001	Sample size	Voted in 1999	Sample size
No. of Scottish party leaders respondent could evaluate							
None	%	18	141	43	125	23	123
One	%	40	115	52	100	41	108
Two	%	46	158	71	150	57	148
Three	%	60	140	78	128	67	130
Four	%	60	200	81	190	63	194
Five	%	74	754	87	735	79	742

Note: Figures for 1999 and 2001 are based on respondents' recall in 2003 of whether they voted in 1999 and 2001. Those too young to vote in those elections have been excluded from the calculation.

One negative evaluation of the parliament that might be thought to have had an adverse influence on the turnout does not, however, seem to have done so. The Holyrood building saga has undoubtedly been the single most criticised aspect of the devolution project to date. There were concerns at the time of the election that the escalating cost of building the new parliament might depress turnout. In fact, those who took the most critical view of the new Scottish Parliament building were *not* more likely to stay at home. As many as 64 per cent of those who said that the building should never have been built turned out to vote, slightly higher than the 57 per cent figure among those who thought that the building should have been built but not cost so much, and the 61 per cent among those who thought that the new building would be worth it in the end. So, the row about the cost of the building cannot be said to have contributed to the decline in turnout.

GUILTY AS CHARGED?

So far, we have presented two alternative accounts of the low turnout in 2003. The usual suspects certainly appear to have had a major role. Young people were particularly disinclined to vote in 2003. So too were those with little or no attachment to the political parties and those with little interest in politics generally. While these groups had not grown markedly in size since 1999, membership of them appears to have had an even greater impact than before. These results echo previous work on why turnout was so low in the 2001 general election (Bromley and Curtice 2002, 2003). However, there is also evidence that some Scottish-specific, home-grown factors also played their part. For example, perceptions of the importance of Holyrood elections have declined since 1999, while fewer people now think that there is much difference between Scotland's main parties. Furthermore, there was a fairly widespread (though not overwhelming) perception that the result itself was a foregone conclusion. But is it possible to establish which of these two accounts played the bigger role in depressing turnout in the 2003 election?

In order to answer this, we need to undertake an analysis of whether people voted in 2003 that takes into account what they did or would have done at other elections. To that end, we have undertaken three sets of regression analysis of our 2003 survey data. In these analyses, we identify what was significantly associated with higher rates of abstention after taking into account whether someone said that (1) they would have voted on 6 May 2003 if a Westminster election had been taking place then rather than a Holyrood one, (2) they voted in the 2001 UK general election, and (3) they voted in the 1999 Scottish Parliament election. All of the variables which we investigated in the two preceding sections were eligible for inclusion in each model so long as they were statistically significantly correlated with turnout after taking into account the impact of the other variables in the model – including whether or not the respondent voted (or would have voted) at the other election. This means that our models identify what was different about the pattern of turnout in 2003 as compared with other elections. If that difference is better explained by our 'usual suspects', then one or more of the variables that we introduced under that heading should appear in the model.

Alternatively, if the difference is better accounted for by one or more variables that comprise our 'home-grown' factors, then it is those that will appear.

The results of these analyses are presented in full in the appendix to this chapter, but Table 5.8 contains a summary of what we found. The results of the three analyses are on the whole very similar. In each one, age and strength of party identification were found to be the most significant influence on turnout in 2003 after taking into account turnout at the other election in the model. In other words, younger people and those with no party identification were even less likely to vote in 2003 than they were at other elections. The perception that the election result was a foregone conclusion also features in each model, as does one or other of our two measures of political efficacy. Those who felt that the outcome was a foregone conclusion and those who had a low level of efficacy stayed at home. In two of the models, knowledge of the party leaders was also significant; those who could not offer an opinion on the leadership qualities of Holyrood's key politicians were less likely to have voted in 2003 even if they would have voted in a Westminster election on the same day or they had voted in 2001. This factor was not, however, significant when we controlled for turnout in 1999; instead, here we find that interest in politics was critical.

So, the above analysis presents us with an interesting picture. Neither home-grown factors nor usual suspects alone were responsible for the decline in turnout. Rather, they each contribute something to the overall account. Among the former, we have included in our models age, party identification and political efficacy; among the latter, we have both knowledge of the party leaders and the perception that the election was a foregone conclusion. Indeed, we should bear in mind the possibility that there is an interaction between these two sets of factors. If the outcome of the election was deemed to be relatively unimportant, the parties perceived to be largely offering the same and the key political actors in the election largely unrecognisable to all but a handful of strongly motivated and politically interested people, then this may help to explain why those groups who always have a low propensity to vote were particularly likely to stay at home in 2003. In short, the usual suspects mattered more thanks to home-grown factors.

It is worth pointing out, however, two sets of items that do not appear in the multivariate analysis. Lukewarm, even critical they may have been, but neither people's evaluations of the impact of devolution on services such as health and education nor their views about the Holyrood building project contributed to the low turnout in 2003. It would therefore be wrong to conclude that devolution per se, that is to say, the policy consequences of having a devolved government, was to blame. Rather, it seems that the *politics* of post-devolution Scotland might be more culpable, though of course whether people's evaluations of Scottish politicians and their parties might have been more generous if people believed that they had some positive outcomes to point to in their name is perhaps a moot point.

Table 5.8 Factors associated with 2003 Holyrood turnout using multivariate analysis

	Model 1	Model 2	Model 3
Other election	Would have voted in a Westminster election on the same day	Voted in the 2001 UK general election	Voted in the 1999 Holyrood election
Usual suspects	Age	Age	Age
	Strength of party identification	Strength of party identification	Strength of party identification
	MPs lose touch	Parties are only interested in votes	MPs lose touch
			Interest in politics
Home-grown factors	Election a foregone conclusion	Election a foregone conclusion	Election a foregone conclusion
	Knowledge of party leaders	Knowledge of party leaders	

Note: In Models 2 and 3, respondents who would not have been old enough to vote in 2001 or 1999 are excluded.

Conclusions

The decline in turnout in 2003 as compared with 1999 and 2001 cannot simply be accounted for by an increasing lack of interest in politics on the part of voters. True, the motivations that voters brought to the polls changed somewhat over that period, but not to an extent that could beget such a large decline over a relatively short time period. Rather, what appears to have happened is that the election failed to an even greater extent than did the 1999 or 2001 elections to engage those who are always relatively difficult to get to the polls. While that pattern might itself in turn be partly accounted for by a lack of perceived difference between the parties and the failure of the Scottish party leaders to attract the attention of the electorate, it also appears to reflect a decline in the perceived status of the parliament itself. Still, the Scottish Parliament is far from being alone in finding it increasingly difficult to persuade the politically uninterested to go to the polls, and to that extent at least the disappointments of devolution should not shoulder all of the blame.

Whether or not voters will go to the polls in 2007 in greater numbers than in 2003 will depend on a number of factors. Given that the problem lies most acutely among the kind of people who tend not to vote anyway, it certainly suggests that it will be an uphill struggle. That turnout was once again relatively low in the 2005 UK general election cannot have helped, if only for the reason that some people are starting to get out of the habit (or have failed to get into the habit) of voting in elections. But the overriding issue for the prospects for 2007 must be the stature of Holyrood and the esteem with which people hold the politicians within it. If, eight years into devolution, people are no more able to pass judgement on Scotland's political leaders than they were after four, then politicians could find it even harder to persuade the electorate to vote at all, let alone vote for them.

APPENDIX: MODELLING TURNOUT

The following tables present the results of the three multivariate models discussed in the text. Forward stepwise logistic regression was used. The dependent variable was vote at the 2003 election versus not. Because of the small sample sizes of some of the key categories of interest, the deviation method was used rather than contrast with a reference category. This means that the odds for each category of having voted in 2003 were compared against the average for that variable.

The independent variables available for inclusion in each model were: age, sex, social class, education level, housing tenure, national identity, constitutional preference, whether ever lived anywhere other than Scotland, strength of party identification, MPs soon lose touch, parties are only interested in votes, trust in government (UK government and Scottish Parliament), perceived difference between Labour and the Conservatives, perceived difference between Labour and the SNP, which body has most influence in Scotland, evaluation of impact of devolution on education since 1999, evaluation of impact of devolution on NHS standards since 1999, attitudes towards the parliament building, perceived extent of co-operation between MSPs of different parties, perceived extent of cooperation between MPs of different parties, election result was a foregone conclusion, number of leaders people could evaluate, and relative importance of Scottish Parliament and UK government elections.

Each model also included a different control for people's past and hypothetical voting behaviour as follows:

- The first model controlled for Westminster voting on the same day as the Holyrood election.

- The second controlled for turnout at the 2001 election (and excluded those who would not have been old enough to vote in 2001).
- The third controlled for turnout at the 1999 Holyrood election (and excluded those who would not have been old enough to vote in 1999).

Table 5A.1   Model 1: Regression analysis of turnout in 2003, controlling for turnout in hypothetical Westminster election

Dependent variable = voted in 2003 v. did not vote	Coefficient	Standard error	Impact on odds	
Hypothetical Westminster vote				
Would not have voted if Westminster election instead	−1.363	0.161	0.256	**
Would have voted	1.363	0.161	3.908	**
Age				
18–34	−0.885	0.165	0.413	**
35–44	−0.393	0.161	0.675	*
45–54	0.195	0.182	1.216	
55–64	0.338	0.185	1.402	
65+	0.744	0.208	2.105	**
Strength of party identification				
Very strong	1.041	0.354	2.833	*
Fairly strong	0.122	0.185	1.130	
Not very strong	0.181	0.171	1.199	
No party identification	−1.446	0.323	0.235	**
Don't know	0.101	0.314	1.107	
It was obvious who was going to win the election				
Agree	0.338	0.157	1.403	*
Neither	0.268	0.180	1.308	
Disagree	0.721	0.180	2.056	**
Don't know	−1.327	0.319	0.265	**
Number of party leaders evaluated				
None	0.462	0.149	1.588	**
One	−0.040	0.199	0.961	
Two	0.148	0.241	1.160	
Three	−0.019	0.249	0.981	
Four or five	−0.551	0.266	0.576	*
MPs soon lose touch				
Agree	−0.339	0.134	0.712	*
Neither	0.390	0.184	1.476	*
Disagree	−0.050	0.190	0.951	
Constant	−0.669	0.223	0.512	

** $p < 0.001$, * $p < 0.05$
R^2 = 30 per cent; sample size = 915

Table 5A.2 Model 2: Regression analysis of turnout in 2003, controlling for turnout in 2001 UK general election

	Coefficient	Standard error	Impact on odds	
2001 vote				
Did not vote in 2001	−0.921	0.121	0.398	**
Voted in 2001	0.921	0.121	2.511	**
Strength of party identification				
Very strong	0.929	0.340	2.533	*
Fairly strong	0.387	0.182	1.473	*
Not very strong	0.340	0.166	1.404	*
No party identification	−1.514	0.348	0.220	**
Don't know	−0.142	0.269	0.867	
Age				
18–34	−0.564	0.172	0.569	**
35–44	−0.368	0.157	0.692	*
45–54	0.093	0.176	1.097	
55–64	0.332	0.178	1.394	
65+	0.508	0.193	1.661	**
Number of party leaders evaluated				
None	0.569	0.147	1.767	**
One	−0.104	0.198	0.901	
Two	0.108	0.239	1.115	
Three	−0.214	0.242	0.807	
Four or five	−0.359	0.276	0.698	
It was obvious who was going to win the election				
Agree	0.305	0.153	1.357	*
Neither	0.155	0.178	1.168	
Disagree	0.552	0.174	1.737	**
Don't know	−1.013	0.311	0.363	**
Parties only interested in votes				
Agree	−0.390	0.139	0.677	*
Neither	−0.034	0.195	0.967	
Disagree	0.424	0.188	1.528	**
Constant	−0.375	0.203	0.687	

** $p < 0.001$, * $p < 0.05$
R^2 = 28 per cent; sample size = 908

Table 5A.3 Model 3: Regression analysis of turnout in 2003, controlling for turnout in 1999 Scottish election

	Coefficient	Standard error	Impact on odds	
1999 vote				
Did not vote in 1999	−1.247	0.167	0.287	**
Did vote	0.779	0.130	2.180	**
Don't know if voted in 1999	0.468	0.179	1.597	**
Age				
18–34	−0.801	0.177	0.449	**
35–44	−0.322	0.156	0.724	*
45–54	0.200	0.173	1.221	
55–64	0.303	0.175	1.353	
65+	0.620	0.196	1.860	**
Strength of party identification				
Very strong	0.813	0.344	2.256	*
Fairly strong	0.263	0.186	1.301	
Not very strong	0.323	0.168	1.382	
No party identification	−1.440	0.319	0.237	**
Don't know	0.040	0.270	1.041	
It was obvious who was going to win the election				
Agree	0.268	0.153	1.308	
Neither	0.176	0.178	1.193	
Disagree	0.674	0.179	1.961	**
Don't know	−1.118	0.318	0.327	**
Interest in politics				
A great deal	0.599	0.300	1.821	*
Quite a lot	0.386	0.193	1.471	*
Some	−0.241	0.157	0.785	
Not very much	−0.296	0.168	0.744	
None at all	−0.448	0.246	0.639	
MPs lose touch				
Agree	−0.405	0.139	0.667	*
Neither	0.424	0.193	1.529	*
Disagree	−0.019	0.195	0.981	
Constant	0.262	0.198	1.299	

** $p < 0.001$, * $p < 0.05$
R^2 = 28 per cent; sample size = 917

NOTES

1. However, it should also be noted that the rules for voting by post have been relaxed significantly since 2001, thereby removing the need for perennially busy people to visit a polling station in order to vote.
2. We should also note that party identification was acquired in the 2001 and 2003 surveys using a sequence of questions that tends to produce a lower level of identification than the sequence used in the 1999 survey (Bromley and Curtice 2002: 162–3). The former used the sequence normally used in the British Social Attitudes series, whereas the latter used that used in the British Election Study series.
3. See Bromley and Curtice (2002, 2003).
4. This factor could, of course, be regarded as a problem facing all British elections. That one party was almost bound to win most seats in 2003 could be seen as part of a wider trend in British elections that began in 1997, before which election Labour had been outpolling the Conservatives for almost five years.
5. While there was also a decline in the perceived importance of Westminster elections between 1999 and 2003, at six points the drop was far smaller than in the case of Scottish Parliament elections. We should also note that, while those who think that it matters who wins a Scottish Parliament election were also more likely to vote in the 2001 UK general election too, at twenty-one points the gap was rather smaller than the twenty-nine-point gap that existed in 2003.

REFERENCES

Boon, M. and Curtice, J. (2003), *Scottish Elections Research May–June 2003*, London: The Electoral Commission. Available at http://www.electoralcommission.org.uk

Bromley, C. and Curtice, J. (2002), 'Where have all the voters gone?', in A. Park, J. Curtice, K. Thomson, L. Jarvis and C. Bromley (eds), *British Social Attitudes: the 19th Report*, London: Sage.

Bromley, C. and Curtice, J. (2003), 'The lost voters of Scotland: devolution disillusioned or Westminster weary?', *British Elections and Parties Review*, 13: 66–85.

Dewar, D. (1998), 'The Scottish Parliament', *Scottish Affairs: Special Issue on Understanding Political Change*, pp. 4–12.

Swaddle, K. and Heath, A. (1989), 'Official and reported turnout in the British general election of 1987', *British Journal of Political Science*, 19: 537–70.

Wattenberg, M. P. (2003), 'Electoral turnout: the new generation gap', *British Elections and Parties Review*, 13: 159–73.

Wolfinger, R., Glass, D. and Squire, P. (1990), 'Predictors of electoral turnout: an international comparison', *Policy Studies Review*, 9: 551–74.

CHAPTER 6

Is Holyrood Accountable and Representative?

John Curtice

INTRODUCTION

In creating the Scottish Parliament, advocates of devolution aimed to put Scots themselves in charge of deciding who ran their government. In contrast to what happened during the eighteen years of Conservative rule between 1979 and 1997, who ran Scotland would be determined by who could win elections in Scotland rather than who was most popular in England. Scottish governments that presided over failure in Scotland would have to endure the wrath of the voters of Scotland. Parties that wanted to introduce new policies in Scotland would need to secure the consent of the voters of Scotland. No longer could a policy like the poll tax be foisted on an unwilling nation as a result of votes cast further south.

Yet there was never any guarantee that creating a separately elected Scottish Parliament would ensure that its politicians were accountable to the public for their past actions or that the balance of opinion within the body would be representative of public opinion. For this to happen, Scottish Parliament elections have to be not only elections *to* the Scottish Parliament but also elections *about* the Scottish Parliament. If Scottish Parliament elections are to be occasions when the country's rulers are held to account, then voters need to vote on the basis of how well they think the Executive and the opposition parties have performed over the previous four years. Equally, if elections to the parliament are to register the balance of public opinion and ensure that it is represented on the floor of the chamber, then voters need to take into account the policy proposals of the parties when deciding how to cast their ballots.

But why might voters not to take such considerations into account? Of course one possibility is that they lack the necessary knowledge about what has happened over the last four years or of what the parties propose to do in future in order to make an informed judgement. Just how well informed voters are or need to be to vote effectively in any election is in fact the subject of some dispute (Bartels, 1996; Delli Carpini and Keeter, 1996; Page and Shapiro, 1992; Popkin, 1991). However what concerns us here is the possibility that irrespective of their levels of knowledge Scottish voters may not be motivated to hold their politicians to account when they vote in a Scottish election. After all, there is plenty of warning in the existing literature that this may be the case when voters are asked to vote in elections to bodies that are regarded as subsidiary or less important. For example, both European and local elections have been characterised as 'second-order' elections in which, thanks to the perceived unimportance of the body being elected, voters opt to use the occasion as an opportunity to express their views on the performance of the national statewide government of the day rather than what they think of the performance of their local authority or about the future of Europe (Heath et al., 1999; Reif 1984; Reif and Schmitt, 1980). So if the Scottish Parliament is regarded as a relatively unimportant body then we might find that voters prefer to use Scottish Parliament elections to express a judgement about what is happening at Westminster rather than about what they think has happened or should happen at Holyrood.

The first aim of this chapter is to ascertain whether voters in Scotland do indeed hold Scottish politicians to account when they vote at Scottish elections. Do they vote on the basis of how well they think the Scottish Executive has performed over the last four years? Or is it in fact how well the UK government is performing that is uppermost in their minds? Meanwhile, the second aim is to discern whether at Scottish elections voters can be said to give anyone a mandate to pursue particular policies. When they choose how to vote at Scottish elections, do voters reflect their policy preferences on those topics that lie within the Scottish Parliament's competence? Or are they as likely to be influenced by issues that are confronting the House of Commons as they are by anything that might be facing Holyrood?

In pursuing these aims, we focus in particular on the 2003 election. In 1999, voters were electing a wholly new body that had no track record to defend. In 2003, in contrast, they could judge an Executive that had a four-year-old record to defend. So, the 2003 election was the first occasion on which voters could actually hold their own government to account for what it had done, as well as express a view about the policy proposals for the future being put forward by the parties. It is thus our first chance to assess fully whether voters have the motivation to vote in Scottish Parliament elections in the way that the advocates of devolution assumed that they would.

We proceed as follows. First, we consider some preliminary evidence on the relative importance of Scottish Parliament elections in the eyes of Scottish voters and on the motivations they bring to the ballot box. Then we look at what voters made of the record of the Scottish Executive over the last four years and on the impact that their evaluation appears to have had on how they voted. In addition, we also look here at the impact of their evaluations of the performance of the First Minister. Thereafter, we turn to some of the policy proposals that were put before the electorate in the 2003 election and ask whether these appear to have influenced the way that people voted. Finally, the conclusion assesses whether the evidence which we have presented suggests that Scottish politicians are indeed held accountable by Scottish Parliament elections and whether they can be considered occasions when the public's policy preferences are registered.

Preliminaries

We have suggested that voters would be less likely to vote on the basis of the record of the parties in the Scottish Parliament over the last four years or take into account the promises they make for the next four years if they think that the Scottish Parliament is relatively unimportant. As we have already seen in Chapter 2, this does indeed appear to have been the perception which they formed over the course of the parliament's first term. At the time of the first Scottish Parliament election in 1999, slightly more people thought that the parliament would have most influence over the way that Scotland is run then thought that the UK government would (see Table 6.1). But, within twelve months, two-thirds were saying they thought that it was the UK government that actually had most influence, while only around one in eight thought that the Scottish Parliament did. Thereafter, those figures barely changed.

Table 6.1 Who runs Scotland, 1999–2003

Which has (1999: will have) most influence over the way Scotland is run?	1999	2000	2001	2003
	%	%	%	%
The Scottish Parliament	41	13	15	17
The UK government at Westminster	39	66	66	64
Local councils in Scotland	8	10	9	7
The European Union	5	4	7	5
Sample size	1,482	1,663	1,605	1,508

Still, the fact that people do not think that the Scottish Parliament has as much influence as the UK government does not necessarily mean that they consider it or its elections to be unimportant. Perhaps the parliament is simply regarded as the somewhat less important of two bodies that are both thought to matter. Certainly, a glance at Table 6.2 suggests that this might be the case. In 2003, slightly over two in five thought that it mattered a great deal or quite a lot who won a Scottish Parliament election, only 7 per cent fewer than said the same about Westminster. However, four years earlier, there had not been any difference in the perceived importance of the two elections. Meanwhile, we should bear in mind that some people think that the outcome of an election matters not because they think that the institution being elected matters but because they always want their preferred party to win irrespective of the body in question.

Table 6.2 Perceived importance of elections, 1999–2003

% say it matters 'a great deal' or 'quite a lot' who wins elections to . . .	1999	2001	2003	1999–2003 change
the Scottish Parliament	56	43	41	−15
the House of Commons	54	45	48	−6
Sample size	1,482	1,605	1,508	

However, despite the perceived unimportance of the parliament and its elections, there is one other piece of evidence that suggests that voters do not simply regard Scottish Parliament elections as an imitation of a Westminster contest. In Table 6.3, we show for both the 1999 and 2003 Scottish elections and the 2001 UK general election the percentage of people who said that they had decided to vote on the basis of what was going on in Scotland in particular rather than across Britain as a whole. In both 1999 and 2003, well over half said that they voted on the basis of what was going on in Scotland, and only between a quarter and a third on what was happening in Britain as a whole. In contrast, at the 2001 UK election, a plurality said they had voted about what was happening in Britain as a whole.

Table 6.3 What people vote on, 1999–2003

Decided to vote mostly on what is going on in . . .	1999	2001	2003
	%	%	%
Scotland	53	34	57
Britain as a whole	31	44	26
Sample size	1,482	1,605	1,508

So, although the Scottish Parliament might be regarded as a relatively unimportant body, it may not be considered so unimportant that people are simply inclined to regard its elections as a chance to express an opinion on the performance of the UK government. Voters claim at least that in a Scottish election they are voting about Scotland rather than Britain. But can we demonstrate that this is so when we look at how far their votes reflected their evaluations of the Scottish Executive over the previous four years?

THE RECORD

We have already seen in Chapter 2 what people felt had happened to the standard of the NHS, the quality of education and living standards in Scotland during the four years between 1999 and 2003 (see Table 2.5). To recap, while nearly a quarter felt that the general standard of living had fallen over the last four years, they were outnumbered by the third who felt that it had increased. The Scottish public was evidently reasonably happy with the economic record of the first four years. Meanwhile, despite the well-publicised problems experienced by the Scottish Qualification Authority in 2000 in processing examination results accurately (Paterson 2000), only slightly more people felt that the quality of education had declined than felt that it had increased. However, the Scottish public was a lot less happy about the state of its health service; nearly half felt that its standards had declined, while only one in five reckoned that it had improved. Moreover, if we compare these results with those obtained in England when the same question was asked as part of the 2003 British Social Attitudes survey, we find that while the balance of opinion on both living standards and the quality of education was much the same in Scotland as it was in England, the NHS Scotland was not regarded as highly as its counterpart south of the border. It looks as though people in Scotland noticed the greater difficulty that the health service in Scotland was having in reducing waiting times as compared with the service in England.

So, voters in Scotland felt that the country had advanced more in some respects than in others over the previous four years. Still, it appears that the Scottish Executive entered the election with a record that would not necessarily result in a heavy loss of votes should voters take these evaluations into account in deciding how to vote. There is also further reason why this might be the case. For, as we also discovered in Chapter 2, the Scottish Executive was not necessarily regarded as responsible for what had been happening in the country over the previous four years. In respect of each of the NHS, education and living standards, more people reckoned that the policies of the UK government had been principally responsible for what had happened than felt that the policies of the Scottish Executive had been responsible (see Table 6.4). This perception is of course consistent with the evidence presented earlier in Table 6.1 that most people feel that the UK government has most influence over what happens in Scotland.

Table 6.4 Perceived responsibility for policy outcomes in Scotland

	Perceived responsibility for trends in		
	NHS standards	Quality of education	Standard of living
	%	%	%
UK government's policies at Westminster	38	30	43
Scottish Executive's policies	21	25	18
Both UK government and Scottish Executive	7	7	9
Some other reason	17	12	16
Sample size	1,508	1,508	1,508

But this is not the only reason why the Scottish Executive need not necessarily have feared the wrath of the voters in 2003. For, as we also discovered in Chapter 2, Scots seemed inclined to award the plaudits to the Scottish Executive and the brickbats to the UK government at Westminster. As a result, the minority who did consider the Scottish Executive to be responsible for what had happened over the previous four years held relatively positive evaluations. Almost half of the respondents reckoned that standards in the health service and the quality of education had increased, while well over half said that the general standard of living had improved. All of these figures are at least twice the level obtained among those who felt that the UK government was responsible.

But, whatever their evaluations were of what had happened and who was responsible, did voters act on them in the polling station? In particular, were those who felt that responsibility lay with the Scottish Executive more likely to reflect their view of what had happened in how they voted than were those who gave the praise to or laid the blame on the UK government? If voters who believe that the UK government was responsible allow their vote in a Scottish Parliament election to be influenced by their perceptions of that government's record, they could be considered to be doing precisely what we would expect if Scottish Parliament elections are considered to be 'second-order' occasions which present an opportunity to protest at the record of the UK government. Only if those who think that the Scottish

Executive was responsible for trends in health, education and living standards act on their evaluations can we claim that Scottish Parliament elections help hold the country's devolved politicians to account.

Table 6.5 presents one way of answering our question. It looks at those voters who said that four years previously they voted for the Labour Party and examines how many of them reported backing Labour again in 2003. In so doing, it breaks these voters down according to their evaluations of what had been happening to the health service, education and living standards in Scotland, both irrespective of whom they regarded as responsible for those trends and then separately for those who regard the UK government as responsible and those the Scottish Executive. Included among the latter are those who felt that the UK government and the Scottish Executive were both responsible; they at least have some reason to hold the Executive accountable.

Table 6.5 How Labour voters responded to trends in the NHS, education and living standards

% 1999 Labour supporters voting Labour in 2003			Assign responsibility for trend to			
Perceived trend in	All 1999 Labour supporters	Sample size	UK govt	Sample size	Scottish Executive	Sample size
NHS standards						
Increased	60	98	83	30	50	57
Stayed same	63	109	70	51	52	29
Fallen	49	158	50	79	46	34
Quality of education						
Increased	57	131	63	39	57	71
Stayed same	59	94	57	46	62	29
Fallen	45	94	40	52	55	25
Standard of living						
Increased	58	143	57	73	69	67
Stayed same	62	133	67	70	59	38
Fallen	50	94	47	62	44	19

There are some features of this approach to our answering our question that we should consider before examining the substantive results. The first is that we have decided to take into account how people voted in 1999. There are two reasons for doing so. First, voters' evaluations are not necessarily independent of the party that they support. Some may feel that standards in the health service, the quality of education and living standards have improved because they are Labour supporters rather than vice versa. Taking into account some measure of their partisanship prior to the 2003 election enables us to control for this *ex post hoc* rationalisation to some degree. Second, it may be argued that central to the process of holding politicians accountable is that voters withdraw support from the government where it is no longer felt to be justified, and this is precisely the process that Table 6.5 highlights.[1]

But of course it could be objected that the Scottish Executive was not simply run by Labour between 1999 and 2003 but by Labour in coalition with the Liberal Democrats. We have in fact replicated the analysis in this section looking at Labour and Liberal Democrat voters combined rather than just Labour voters alone, and doing so makes no difference to our substantive conclusions. Meanwhile, our approach has the advantage that, as Labour were in sole control of the UK government, it unambiguously uncovers any evidence that voters might have used the Scottish election to express dissatisfaction with the performance of the UK government.

A third feature of the analysis undertaken in Table 6.5 that should be borne in mind is that those who abstained in 2003 are included in the analysis. As a result, the more who said they voted Labour in 1999 but abstained in 2003, the lower the figure in the table. Of course, some 1999 Labour supporters who abstained in 2003 are likely to have done so for the kinds of reasons discussed in Chapter 5 on turnout, reasons that have little to do with their views of the performance of the Executive. But one possible way in which those former Labour voters who were disenchanted with the performance of the UK government or the Scottish Executive could have expressed their feelings is by abstaining rather than by voting for a different party.

Finally, we have of course to bear in mind that voters could cast two votes. Our measure of their 1999 vote is their recall of how they voted in the constituency ballot in that election, this being the ballot in which Labour was the more successful. However, in 2003, irrespective of how they actually voted in the constituency or list ballot, we have for those who voted an indication of which party they regarded as their first preference party in that election. It is this first preference that we use as our measure of the 2003 vote, both in Table 6.5 and in subsequent tables in this chapter.

Bearing these considerations in mind, what do the results in the table suggest about the relationship between people's evaluations of what had been happening over the previous four years and how people voted in the Scottish election? First, there does appear to be some evidence that those 1999 Labour voters who felt that standards had fallen were less likely to back the party again than were those who felt that standards had at least stayed the same. For example, while 63 per cent of those 1999 Labour voters who felt that the standards of the health service had stayed the same supported the party again in 2003, only 49 per cent of those who felt that those standards had fallen did so, a gap of fourteen points. There are similar gaps of fourteen and twelve points in respect of education and living standards. Second, however, it would appear that, while voters were inclined to blame Labour when they felt that things were going wrong, they did not give them credit when they felt they were doing well. In each case, slightly fewer people voted for the party again if they felt that standards had increased than if they merely felt that they had stayed the same.

But is there any evidence that it is the Scottish Executive that is being held to account rather than the UK government? There is in fact relatively little. Among those who felt that the Scottish Executive was mainly (or least jointly) responsible, the proportion backing Labour a second time varies little according to people's evaluations. Only the small number who believed that living standards had fallen stand out as markedly less loyal to Labour. In contrast, among those who regarded the UK government as principally responsible, in all three cases the probability that someone voted Labour again varied systematically with their evaluation. It appears that, if anything, former Labour voters were more inclined to hold the UK government accountable in the 2003 Scottish election than they were the Scottish Executive.

There are, however, two obvious limitations to this analysis. The first is that it takes no account of the possibility that Labour might have gained votes among those who did not support it four years previously but who looked favourably on developments in Scotland in the intervening years. In other words, the party might have been rewarded by those with positive evaluations who did not previously vote for it. Secondly, our analysis does not provide guidance as to whether any of the differences we have observed are statistically significant or not. What we can see in some cases is that the number of observations on which our figures are based is rather small.

To overcome these limitations, we can undertake a logistic regression where the dependent variable is whether or not the respondent voted Labour in 2003. Our first independent variable is how they said they voted in 1999. Note that, in doing this, we allow for the possibility that those who abstained in 1999 or who voted for one party rather than another might vary in their propensity to switch to Labour in 2003 irrespective of their evaluations. We then allow each of our three evaluations of what had happened since 1999 to enter as independent variables. In so doing, we have used a forward stepwise procedure under which only those evaluations that are significantly related to voting Labour in 2003 at the 5 per cent level of probability are allowed to enter the equation.

Table 6.6 Logistic regression model of Labour voting and retrospective evaluations

	Model 1			Model 2		
	Coefficient	Standard error		Coefficient	Standard error	
Recall vote 1999						
Conservative	−0.81	0.50		−0.84	0.51	
Labour	2.87	0.22	**	2.89	0.22	
Liberal Democrat	−0.09	0.44		−0.08	0.44	
SNP	−0.80	0.44	*	−0.78	0.44	
Other	−0.04	1.24		−0.23	1.25	
(Abstained)						
Quality of education						
(Increased)						
Stayed same	−0.22	0.23		−0.15	0.30	
Fallen	−0.66	0.23	**	−0.80	0.31	**
Don't know	0.29	0.25		0.38	0.29	
Quality of education and Scot. Exec. responsible						
(Increased)						
Stayed same				−0.12	0.47	
Fallen				0.55	0.47	
Scot. Exec. not responsible/Don't know				−0.17	0.30	
Nagelkerke R^2	43 per cent			45 per cent		

Main cell entries are contrast coefficients. The reference category is indicated in brackets.
** significant at 5 per cent level. * significant at 10 per cent level.

The results are shown in the first model in Table 6.6. Just one of our three evaluations enters our model, that is perception of the quality of education. Even after taking into account how they had voted in 1999, those who felt that the quality of education had fallen were significantly less likely to vote Labour than were those who felt that it had increased. But, after taking this pattern into account, neither health nor living standards are significantly related to voting Labour. Meanwhile, in our second model in Table 6.6, we test whether there is any evidence that those who felt that the Scottish Executive was at least jointly responsible for what had happened to education were particularly likely to reflect their evaluations in their vote choice. This we do by entering an additional variable that measures the evaluations of educational standards of just those who think that the

Scottish Executive was responsible while putting into a separate category those who reckoned that responsibility lay elsewhere. Doing so does not offer any evidence that those who felt that responsibility lay with the Executive were particularly likely to act on that perception in the polling station. If that were the case, the coefficient for those who on the additional variable said that standards had fallen would have been negative and significant (while the equivalent coefficient for the variable, already included in model 1, that registers the perceptions of all respondents might even become small and insignificant). In practice, it is positive (suggesting that, if anything, voters who felt that the Executive was responsible were less likely to abandon Labour than were those who assigned responsibility elsewhere) and not significant. Meanwhile, the equivalent coefficient for all respondents has actually become larger in model 2 than it was in model 1, suggesting that it was among those who did *not* hold the Scottish Executive responsible that evaluations of the quality of education in Scotland's schools had most impact on their voting behaviour.

So, it appears on our evidence so far that Scottish elections are not particularly effective mechanisms for holding the Executive to account. Evaluations of what had happened in Scotland over the previous four years were only weakly related to how people voted. Moreover, those who felt that the Scottish Executive was responsible for what had happened were, if anything, less likely to reflect their evaluations in their voting behaviour than were those who felt that the UK government was. The 2003 election may not simply have been a judgement on what was going on at Westminster, but it was certainly not evidently much of a judgement on how well the devolved politicians had performed at Holyrood.

FIRST MINISTER AND PRIME MINISTER

However, acting on their evaluations of trends in health, education or living standards is not the only way in which voters might hold their politicians accountable for past performance. Perhaps they are more moved to act on their judgements as to how well their rulers have performed rather than more abstract perceptions of whether the state of the country has improved or not. To assess this possibility, our 2003 survey invited respondents to say how good a job they thought Tony Blair had done as Prime Minister and then how good a job Jack McConnell had done as First Minister. In both cases, they were invited to give the leader a mark out of ten (for details of the marks given to other party leaders in Scotland, see Chapter 5). In Table 6.7, we show what proportion gave these two leaders a 'good' mark (that is, one of at least seven), how many a 'middling' mark (between four and six) and how many a bad one (three or less).[2] It also shows how many said they did not know how well the Prime Minister or the First Minister had done.

Table 6.7 How Scots judged Tony Blair and Jack McConnell

Mark out of 10	Tony Blair	Jack McConnell
	%	%
Good (7–10)	41	20
Middle (4–6)	39	48
Bad (0–3)	18	18
Don't know	2	14

Sample size = 1,508

Scotland's voters evidently rated Tony Blair more highly than they did Jack McConnell. Twice as many gave the Prime Minister a good score as gave one to the First Minister. Not that Jack McConnell was necessarily thought to be doing a bad job; nearly half simply gave him a middling score. In addition, rather more voters were uncertain about how well the First Minister had done than was the case with Mr Blair.

Table 6.8 How Labour voters responded to their judgements of Tony Blair and Jack McConnell

Mark out of 10 given to	% 1999 Labour voters who in 2003			
	Voted Labour	Abstained	Voted for another party	Sample size
Tony Blair				
Good (7–10)	68	22	10	243
Middle (4–6)	48	33	20	105
Bad (0–3)	6	50	44	34
Jack McConnell				
Good (7–10)	67	22	11	127
Middle (4–6)	57	26	17	193
Bad (0–3)	30	40	30	39

But did these evaluations make any difference to how people voted? In Table 6.8, we look at how 1999 Labour voters behaved in 2003 according to how well they thought the two leaders had performed. Such evaluations do seem to have made a difference. Those 1999 Labour voters who gave Tony Blair a good mark were over ten times more likely to have voted Labour than were those who gave him a bad score. Equally, those who gave Jack McConnell a good mark were more than twice as likely to have voted Labour again than were those who gave him a bad rating. However, this of course means that evaluations of Tony Blair appear to have had more impact on how people voted than did evaluations of Jack McConnell. Voters in the 2003 Scottish election may have held the First Minister to account to some degree, but their vote was even more likely to reflect their judgement of the Prime Minister.[3]

POLICY PREFERENCES

We turn now from the degree to which voters reflected their judgements of the past in how they voted in the 2003 election to the extent to which the way they voted reflected their views about some of the key policy issues debated during the 2003 election campaign. Policy issues are of two kinds (Butler and Stokes 1974). Some are 'valence' issues, where the desirability of the outcome is rarely disputed and the parties simply differ in how best to achieve it. Arguably, such issues dominated the 2003 election campaign. All the main parties indicated that they would provide some mixture of more nurses, more teachers and more police (Allardyce 2004), developments that few would want to reject, thereby making it very difficult to distinguish between them. Other issues, in contrast, are 'position' issues, where the desirability of what is proposed is disputed and debated between the parties. It is on these that it might be thought particularly desirable that the balance of opinion in the parliament should reflect the balance of Scottish public opinion. Three such issues that did arise in the campaign and lay within the competence of the Scottish Parliament to deliver were proposals for free bus passes for the over-60s that would be valid across the whole of Scotland (backed by Labour and the Liberal Democrats together with the SSP), a reduction in taxes on business (proposed by both the Conservatives and the SNP), and the introduction of free school meals for all children (advocated by the SSP).

As Table 6.9 shows, the first two of these were relatively popular. Fewer than one in five opposed either, while between three in five and three in four backed them. Free school meals for all, in contrast, were more controversial. On these, the country appears to have been divided down the middle.

But the election campaign was not confined to a discussion of devolved matters. For the second time in a row, a Scottish election campaign was conducted against the backdrop of gunfire. In 1999, the Kosovo war broke out as the campaign began at the beginning of April. In 2003, the second

Table 6.9 Scotland's policy preferences

	% Agree	% Disagree
Devolved matters		
Free bus passes to all over-60s even though lots could afford to pay	74	18
Cut business taxes to strengthen Scotland's economy	60	16
Free school meals to all children even though lots of parents can afford to pay	45	45
Reserved matters		
Asylum-seekers should be kept in detention centres while cases are considered	62	26
Britain was wrong to go to war with Iraq	42	40

Sample size: 1,508

Gulf War in Iraq had already begun by the time the campaign had started, though it did at least conclude well before polling day. This latter war was highly controversial, and the legitimacy of Britain's involvement in it was hotly debated. The UK Labour government's decision to join the US-led invasion was backed by the Conservatives but was opposed by the Liberal Democrats and the SNP as well as the Greens and the SSP, all of whom invited voters to back them in the Scottish election in order to express their opposition to the war. In short, the war was a reserved issue that seemed capable of swamping whatever impact debates about devolved matters might otherwise have had.

The deep divisions between the parties over the invasion of Iraq were reflected in public opinion. Scotland appears to have been divided down the middle on the subject, with almost equal numbers agreeing and disagreeing that 'Britain was wrong to go to war with Iraq' (see Table 6.9). In contrast, there was rather more of a consensus on another reserved issue that was the subject of some debate at the time of the 2003 election campaign, the processing of applications made by asylum-seekers. In criticising the UK government's handling of this issue, the Conservative Party proposed that all applicants (as opposed to some, as was currently the case) should be held in detention centres until their applications were accepted or rejected. This, they argued, would help to ensure that those applicants whose applications were rejected could then be easily and effectively expelled from the country. Critics argued that such a policy would infringe the human rights of people who had not committed any criminal offence. Little more than one in four Scots backed this latter view, while over three in five supported the position upheld by the Conservatives.

Table 6.10 Policy preferences and vote choice on devolved matters

Vote	Free bus passes		Free school meals		Cut business taxes	
	Agree	Disagree	Agree	Disagree	Agree	Disagree
	%	%	%	%	%	%
Con	19	28	18	21	21*	20
Lab	37*	30	38	33	38	36
Lib Dem	13*	17	12	18	12	10
SNP	24	21	24	21	24*	24
Other	8	4	8*	6	6	11
Sample size	610	145	367	366	485	131

* shows which party or parties supported that proposition. In the case of free school meals, the 'other' party in favour was the Scottish Socialist Party. It won 5 per cent of the vote among those who agreed with the policy and 3 per cent among those who disagreed.

But how far were these attitudes reflected in the ballot box? In particular, were the views of the public on devolved matters in line with how they voted? Or did the election become a referendum on hotly disputed policy questions that lay within the remit of the Westminster Parliament? In Table 6.10, we show how those who voted divided their votes, broken down by their views on our three devolved issues. This suggests that there is very little evidence that voters' attitudes were reflected in how they voted. True, those who supported free bus passes for over-60s were seven points more likely to vote Labour, while opponents were inclined to support the Conservatives. But, at the same time, supporters were actually four points less likely than opponents to back the Liberal Democrats, even though that party was in favour of the bus passes. As a result, the total level of support given to the two main parties in favour of free bus passes by those who agreed with the policy was just three points higher than it was among those who were opposed.[4] Meanwhile, attitudes towards cutting business taxes hardly seem to have made any difference at all to how people voted. Equally, support for the SSP was only two points higher among those in favour of free school meals than it was among those who were opposed. Indeed, Labour performed relatively well among supporters of this policy despite having voted it down in the Scottish Parliament.

In contrast, we appear to be able to identify some rather clearer differences in voting behaviour between those on the two sides of our reserved policy issues (see Table 6.11). Those who opposed the war were fifteen points more likely to vote for an anti-war party (with the SSP doing particularly well among this group), while Labour in particular received a much lower level of support among opponents of the war. Meanwhile, support for the Conservatives was more than twice as high among those who favoured the detention of asylum-seekers than it was among its opponents, though we

Table 6.11 Policy preferences and vote choice on reserved matters

Vote	Britain wrong on Iraq		Detain asylum-seekers	
	Agree	Disagree	Agree	Disagree
	%	%	%	%
Con	18	23	23*	11
Lab	30	41	34	41
Lib Dem	17*	12	12	17
SNP	24*	21	25	20
Other	11*	4	6	11
Sample size	365	326	508	210

* see note to Table 6.10

should note that the SNP also did rather better among the supporters of detention despite the party leadership's opposition to the policy.

A multivariate analysis (not shown) in the form of a nominal regression of party support against all of these five issues largely confirms these findings. Opposition to the Iraq war was significantly associated with a lower level of support for both Labour and the Conservatives, while support for detention of asylum-seekers was associated with a higher level of Conservative and (perversely) SNP support. In contrast, this analysis confirms that there is no significant relationship between support for free school meals and support for the SSP or indeed any other party. However, it does confirm that opponents of free bus passes were particularly likely to vote Conservative, while it also suggests that, once we take into account these other relationships, those who favoured cutting business taxes were in fact significantly more likely to vote Conservative or SNP. Even so, of all of these relationships, it is clear that by far the strongest is that between opposition to the war and lower support for Labour.

Voters' choices in the 2003 election reflected, then, their attitudes towards some key reserved matters of particular controversy at the time of that election. Moreover, their choices seem to have been moved by these issues to a greater extent than they were by some of the proposals for devolved matters put forward at the election. Even so, it would be a mistake simply to label the election as a referendum on the war. Among those who voted Labour in 2001, the proportion of those who turned out and backed the party again was, at 47 per cent, just five points lower among the opponents of the war than it was among its supporters. If that gap had not existed, Labour's share of the overall popular vote would have been just one point higher. The war may have cost Labour some support, but it far from determined the outcome of the election.

Indeed, there is an illuminating comparison we can make that helps put the importance of attitudes towards the Iraqi war, and indeed of the other issues we have been examining here, into perspective. In each case, the relationship between how people voted and their attitudes is far weaker than is the relationship between how they voted and their constitutional preference. This can be seen by comparing the results in Tables 6.10 and 6.11 with those in Table 6.12, which shows how those with differing constitutional preferences voted in 2003. This shows that there was no less than a fifty-four-point difference between the level of support secured by the SNP among supporters of independence and the amount of backing it won among those who did not want any kind of separate parliament in Scotland. Equally, in the case of the Conservative Party, there was a forty-nine-point gap in the opposite direction. The largest equivalent gap anywhere in the two previous tables is the eleven-point difference in the level of support given to Labour by supporters and opponents of the Iraqi war. While it may be true that voting in Scotland far from simply reflects people's constitutional preferences (Bond and Rosie 2002), it is in fact relatively speaking a highly divisive issue at the ballot box and has remained so in the wake of devolution's introduction. After four years of devolution, whether or not the Scottish Parliament should exist and, if so, what status it should have appears much more likely to be reflected in how people vote than are any of the issues that the Scottish Parliament itself can currently determine.

Table 6.12   Constitutional preference and vote choice

	Constitutional preference		
Vote	Independence %	Devolution %	No parliament %
Con	4	19	53
Lab	23	43	24
Lib Dem	7	18	13
SNP	58	12	4
Other	9	7	6
Sample size	472	111	208

Conclusion

Our evidence suggests that Scottish Parliament elections may well not be very effective at achieving some of the objectives that it was hoped they would deliver. On the evidence of the 2003 election at least, such elections look like neither an effective mechanism for holding the Executive accountable for its actions nor an effective means of registering the policy preferences of Scottish voters on devolved matters. Indeed, in 2003, the election seems to have been most successful at registering voters' views of the performance of the UK government at Westminster and their stance on at least one key reserved matter of the day, namely Iraq. As a result, the degree to which Holyrood's politicians are being delivered of a mandate that is clearly independent of that of the House of Commons is open to doubt.

At the same time, however, our evidence does not suggest that Scottish Parliament elections are so overshadowed by events at Westminster that they can simply be described as 'second-order' affairs in the manner that local and European elections often are. Attitudes towards events at Westminster, even one so momentous as the decision to go to war, did not appear to matter that much. Rather, what the election outcome reflected most clearly was where people stood on Scotland's long-standing constitutional debate.

That this constitutional debate still matters may perhaps be a clue as to the true function of Scottish Parliament elections. As we have seen in Chapter 2, despite the trials and tribulations of the parliament building, most Scots still want to have a parliament and indeed to have one that is more powerful than it appears to have been so far. The legitimacy of government in Scotland requires, it seems, the existence of an institution that is elected separately from anything that exists England. Rather than to provide accountability or representation, the function of Scottish Parliament elections may simply be to act as a ritual that provides that legitimacy. But whether in the long run ritual alone will be sufficient to maintain the interest and participation of voters in Scottish Parliament elections is perhaps a more debatable question.

NOTES

1. We should of course bear in mind that some respondents will misremember how they voted in 1999 and that, in particular, voters may be inclined to align their past behaviour with their current preference (Himmelweit et al. 1978). This, of course, would have the effect of reducing the proportion of people identified by our survey as having switched away from Labour in 2003. However, this will only affect the validity of our analysis if those who misremember how they voted were different from those who did not in their evaluations of health, education and living standards – and there is no particular reason to believe that this is the case.

2. We opted to treat the scale as a rank order rather than an interval level measure, as in subsequent analysis this procedure resulted in a stronger relationship with vote. It may well be that the degree of discrimination required of respondents to use a ten-point scale effectively was greater than they were able to deploy.

3. Multivariate analysis similar to that in Table 6.6 confirms this conclusion. Evaluations of both Tony Blair and Jack McConnell are significantly related to voting Labour in 2003 after controlling for 1999 constituency vote, but evaluations of the former are clearly the stronger of the two. In particular, even those who give Mr Blair a middling score were significantly less likely to vote Labour than were those who gave the Prime Minister a good score, whereas this was not true of evaluations of Mr McConnell. It should of course be borne in mind that evaluations of party leaders may be influenced by current vote choice rather than vice versa (and to a greater degree than evaluations of health, education or the economy) and that, as a result, the effects of evaluations of both leaders may be overestimated in our analysis.

4. Even if we take account of those supporting the SSP, this figure only increases to five points.

REFERENCES

Allardyce, J. (2004), 'Scotland 2003: the election campaign and the political outcome', in M. Spicer (ed.), *The Scotsman Guide to Scottish Politics*, 2nd edn, Edinburgh: Scotsman Publications.

Bartels, L. (1996), 'Uniformed votes: information effects in presidential elections', *American Journal of Political Science*, 40: 194–230.

Bond, R. and Rosie, M. (2002), 'National identities in post-devolution Scotland', *Scottish Affairs*, 32: 15–35.

Butler, D. and Stokes, D. (1974), *Political Change in Britain*, 2nd edn, London: Macmillan.

Delli Carpini, M. and Keeter, S. (1996), *What Americans Know about Politics and Why it Matters*, New Haven, CT: Yale University Press.

Heath, A., McLean, I., Taylor, B. and Curtice, J. (1999), 'Between first and second order: a comparison of voting behaviour in European and local elections in Britain', *European Journal of Political Research*, 35: 389–414.

Himmelweit, H., Jaegar, M. and Stockdale, T. (1978), 'Memory for past vote: implications of a bias in recall', *British Journal of Political Science*, 8: 365–84.

Page, B. and Shapiro, R. (1992), *The Rational Public*, Chicago: Chicago University Press.

Paterson, L. (2000), *Crisis in the Classroom: The Exam Debacle and the Way Ahead for Scottish Education*, Edinburgh: Mainstream.

Popkin, S. (1991), *The Reasoning Voter: Communication and Persuasion in Presidential Campaigns*, Chicago: Chicago University Press.

Reif, K. (1984), 'National electoral cycles and European elections 1979 and 1984', *Electoral Studies*, 3: 244–55.

Reif, K. and Schmitt, H. (1980), 'Nine second-order national elections: a conceptual framework for the analysis of European Election results', *European Journal of Political Research*, 8: 3–44.

CHAPTER 7

A Chance to Experiment?

John Curtice

Probably the most remarkable feature of the outcome of the 2003 election was the success of parties and candidates other than those representing one of Scotland's four largest parties. Such 'other' candidates accounted for no fewer than seventeen of the 129 MSPs sent to fill the Holyrood chamber. As many as seven of them came from the Scottish Green Party, another six represented the Scottish Socialist Party (SSP), while the remainder comprised three independents and a candidate from the Scottish Senior Citizens' Unity Party, a party representing pensioners that had been formed only weeks before the 2003 election. This major breakthrough by parties and candidates from outside Scotland's political establishment led to the newly elected body being dubbed by the media a 'rainbow parliament'.

One reason why parties like the SSP and the Greens were able to secure such levels of representation despite never having come close to winning a seat in the House of Commons is that the Scottish Parliament election was held using a system of proportional representation. While two of the independents who secured election did so in a constituency contest, all of the remaining 'other' MSPs were elected via the proportionately allocated regional party list seats. Nevertheless, the use of a more proportional system would not have resulted in such a diverse legislative assembly if voters had not also voted for 'others' in far greater numbers than they had ever done in a Westminster election. In the constituency contests in the 2003 election, nearly one in ten (9.6 per cent) voted for an 'other' party, while on the party list ballot more than one in five (22.0 per cent) did so. In contrast, in the 2001 UK general election, just 4.0 per cent of voters in Scotland voted for an 'other' candidate, while in 1997 just 1.9 per cent did so. Given that a party needs to secure between 5 and 6 per cent of the vote in a region to be sure of winning a party list seat, it is evident that few if any 'other' MSPs would have been elected in 2003 if voters had behaved in the way they usually do in UK general elections.

The success of 'other' candidates in 2003 was not, though, simply a flash in the pan. Such candidates also performed relatively well in the first Scottish Parliament election in 1999. True, at 2.7 per cent, the proportion voting for 'other' candidates on the constituency ballot in that election was not particularly remarkable. But, on the party list vote, no less than 11.3 per cent did so. So, it appears from the evidence of both Scottish Parliament elections to date that voters are in fact more inclined to vote for a smaller 'other' party or candidate in a Scottish Parliament election than they are in an election to the House of Commons.

Two possible explanations as to why this should be so immediately suggest themselves. First, given that voters are more likely to vote for an 'other' party or candidate on the party list vote than they are in the constituency contests, perhaps they are more inclined to vote for them because they think they have more chance of winning a seat. That voters are more likely to vote for a smaller party if proportional representation is in place has long been one of the claims made about the effect of using a proportional system (Duverger 1976). At the same time, however, given that it seems that voters are also more likely to vote for an 'other' party on the constituency ballot of a Scottish Parliament election than they are in a constituency contest for the House of Commons, it may be that the relative success of 'other' parties in Scottish Parliament elections is the result of the fact that voters approach Scottish Parliament elections rather differently. It is often argued that voters are more willing to vote for smaller parties if they regard an election as a relatively unimportant, 'second-order' affair (Reif and Schmitt 1980; Reif 1984). If an election is not thought to be important to them, it is argued, voters are less concerned about 'wasting' their vote on a party or candidate that apparently has little chance of winning, and are more inclined to give a 'chance' to a party that has not had power before. In short, they are inclined to use their vote to have a harmless flutter or perhaps, more pejoratively, to engage in an ill-informed experiment.

However, whatever the encouragement to vote for a smaller party provided by the electoral system or the perceived character of an election, we would still not expect a voter to support, say, the Greens if they did not have some affinity with that party. This suggests that we should also consider the kinds of people who voted for one of the 'other' parties. The character of the appeal made by the two principal 'other' parties at the 2003 election, the Greens and the SSP, certainly suggests ways in which those who voted for them might well have been distinctive. In the case of the Greens, previous research would suggest that the party would draw its support most heavily from well-educated people who have a liberal, 'post-materialist' outlook on life (Inglehart 1977, 1990, 1997; Dalton 1994; Fuchs and Rohrschneider 1998; Dalton 2006). Someone with a 'post-materialist' outlook is simply someone who is less concerned about their physical security and material well-being (perhaps because these are already assured) than they are about acquiring a better 'quality of life', including opportunities for 'self-expression' and 'self-actualisation'. Meanwhile, in the case of the SSP, we might anticipate that its relatively left-wing appeal would attract voters with a left-wing outlook. If so, this could mean that it performs relatively well among working-class voters, among whom support for left-wing values tends to be higher (Heath et al. 1985, 1991; Surridge 2003; but see Evans 2000). In any event, if we can demonstrate that the Greens and the SSP appeal to clear and distinctive strands of support, it will be more difficult to argue that the success of the other parties in Scottish Parliament elections is simply the result of an ill-thought-through flutter or experiment; rather it reflects an expression of support for a distinctive point of view.

This chapter examines who supported 'other' parties in Scottish Parliament elections and why. We concentrate in particular on the 2003 election and especially the ballot on which such parties were most successful, the list vote. We begin by reviewing the evidence that people vote for 'other' parties because they do not consider the outcome of a Scottish Parliament election to be very important. We then consider the possible impact of the electoral system before considering the degree to which the pattern of support for the Greens and the SSP in particular is in line with what one might expect given the character of their appeal.

AN UNIMPORTANT ELECTION?

As we have already discovered in Chapter 6, only just over two in five (41 per cent) of those interviewed as part of our 2003 survey reckoned that who won a Scottish Parliament election mattered 'a great deal' or 'quite a lot'. Even among those who voted, only just over half (52 per cent) were of this view. So, there certainly were plenty of voters who voted in the 2003 election even though they felt that the event in which they were participating was not particularly important.

Yet, those who felt that the election was unimportant were not significantly more likely than those who did think it was important to support one of the other parties on the list vote in 2003. In our survey, among those who said that it makes either 'not very much' difference who wins a Scottish Parliament election or no difference at all, 17 per cent said that they voted for one of the 'other' parties on the list vote. This is just two points higher than the figure among those who think that it matters 'a great deal' or 'quite a lot', and is actually three points *lower* than among those who were of the intermediate view that it makes 'some' difference. It seems hard to argue that those who backed an 'other' party did so because they thought that the election did not matter very much.

We might wonder, too, whether those who supported an 'other' party consist disproportionately of those for whom politics holds little interest or attention. In fact, the very opposite is true. No less than 29 per cent of those who said they had a 'great deal' or 'quite a lot' of interest in politics voted for an 'other' party on the list vote in 2003. In contrast, just 10 per cent of those with 'some', 'not much' or no interest in politics did so. Equally, those who were better informed about how devolution works were also more likely to vote for a smaller party.[1] Rather than being an ill-considered flutter or experiment, backing an 'other' party appears in fact to have been the particular preserve of the politically interested and informed.

THE IMPACT OF THE ELECTORAL SYSTEM

There are two ways in which we might attempt to ascertain whether people are more willing to vote for a smaller party in a Scottish Parliament election because of the use of proportional representation. The first is one we have in fact already made some use of in our introductory remarks; that is, to compare how voters behaved on the list vote with the way that they voted in the non-proportional constituency contests. The second approach, meanwhile, is to examine whether voters actually feel that there was more point in voting for a smaller party in a Scottish Parliament election because proportional representation is in use, and whether those who share that perception are more likely to vote for a smaller party. Neither approach, however, is without its difficulties.

As we have already noted, more than twice as many people voted for an 'other' party on the list vote in 2003 than did so in a constituency ballot. But there is one simple reason why this may not be considered definitive evidence of the impact of proportional representation. Voters had far more opportunity to vote for an 'other' party or candidate on the list vote than they did in the constituency ballots. Most notably, the Scottish Green Party did not fight any constituency contests at all. So, the 6.9 per cent of voters who backed them on the list vote were unable to vote for a Green candidate in their local constituency contest even if they wanted to. Moreover, such voters were far from alone. Overall, no less than 12.2 per cent of the list vote was cast for a party that did not fight any of the constituency contests, almost enough wholly to account for the 12.4 point difference between the vote for 'others' on the constituency and list vote.[2] Meanwhile, we should note that the SSP, which did contest all but three of the seventy-three individual constituency seats, won almost as high a share of the constituency vote (6.2 per cent) as it did of the list vote (6.7 per cent). It no longer looks so obvious that voters were more inclined to vote for an 'other' party on the list vote, rather than their simply having more opportunity to do so.

However, this approach presumes that voters draw a clear distinction between the proportionality of the list vote and the non-proportionality of the constituency contests. Perhaps voters are more inclined to vote for an 'other' party on both ballots of a Scottish Parliament election simply because they have more chance of winning a seat somewhere along the way even though in practice there is relatively little prospect of that happening via a constituency contest. So, we need to establish whether voters do in fact think that there is more point in voting for a smaller party on the list vote and whether this perception affects their apparent propensity to vote for such a party.

In both our 1999 and 2003 surveys, we asked respondents whether they agreed or disagreed with the following statement:

There is more point voting for a small party on the second vote than there is on the first vote.

In fact, only 28 per cent agreed with this statement, though equally only 20 per cent actually disagreed. No fewer than half either said they neither agreed nor disagreed, or said they did not know. While those who actually voted were rather more likely to have a view one way or the other, still only 34 per cent agreed with the proposition while 22 per cent disagreed. Evidently, it would be wrong to suggest that the perception that it makes more sense to vote for a small party on the list vote is a widespread one.

Nevertheless, this perception does appear to have made a difference to the behaviour of the minority who did share it. In Table 7.1, we compare the voting behaviour of those who agreed with our proposition with that of those who disagreed. In particular, we show what proportion backed a smaller party on, first, the list vote and, second, the constituency vote. We can see that, while those who did feel that there was more point in voting for a small party on the second vote were in fact most likely to vote for an 'other' party on the constituency ballot, they were only marginally ahead of those who actively disagreed with the proposition. In contrast, on the list vote, they gave far more support to 'others' than did any other group. Meanwhile, those who disagreed with the proposition were no more likely to have voted for an 'other' party on the list vote than they were on the constituency ballot. Equally, there was only a modestly higher level of voting for an 'other' party on the list vote among those with no firm views on the efficacy of voting for a smaller party on the list vote.

Table 7.1 Voting for an 'other' party, 2003, by perceptions of the electoral system

% vote for other party for	More point in voting for a small party on second vote			
	Agree	Neither agree nor disagree	Disagree	Can't choose
List	34	8	7	8
Constituency	10	2	8	5
Difference	+24	+6	−1	+3
Sample size	259	222	165	89

Indeed, if we take these perceptual data at face value, we might conclude that the perception that there was more point in voting for a smaller party on the list vote resulted in a six-point higher vote for 'others' on the list vote than on the constituency vote.[3] But how far we should take the data at face value is in some doubt. There is a danger that some of those who decided to vote for an 'other' party on the list vote, while supporting one of the established parties in their constituency contest, may then have subsequently rationalised their behaviour when they answered our question about the merits of voting for a smaller party on the list vote. If so, then our estimate would overstate the impact of the proportional treatment of the list vote on people's willingness to vote for an 'other' party.

We are left, then, with some uncertainty about the degree to which the ability of 'other' parties to win votes in the 2003 election can be put down to the use of a more proportional electoral system. One approach suggests that, once we take into account the difference between the opportunity to vote for an 'other' party on the more proportional list vote and that in the constituency contests, voters may not have been any more *inclined* to vote for a smaller party on the list vote at all. Meanwhile, no more than a third of those who participated in the election felt that there was more point in backing a smaller party on the list vote. These two facts certainly caution against simply ascribing the success of the 'others' to the use of a proportional system. On the other hand, the distinctive behaviour of the minority who did think that there was more point in voting for a smaller party on the list vote suggests that it may well have had some impact. We should bear in mind, too, that some voters may have been more willing to vote for 'others' on both ballots because of the greater proportionality of the system as a whole,[4] while fewer smaller parties may have been willing and able to give voters the chance of voting for them on the list vote but for its more proportional character. So, perhaps the system did provide some encouragement to vote for an 'other' party after all. But, if it did, it seems unlikely to have had much impact unless some of those parties had also been successful in capturing the interest and attention of a section of those to whom their substantive message might have had some appeal. So, we now examine just who it was who voted for 'others', looking in particular at the Scottish Green Party and the SSP.

Who votes for the Greens and the SSP?

As we indicated earlier, the nature of the appeals made by the Greens and the SSP lead to some quite clear expectations about the kind of voter that the two parties should have attracted. In the case of the Greens, we anticipate that they should be supported by those of a liberal post-materialist disposition, and as a result by those with a university education. So far as the SSP are concerned, we would expect them to be supported by those with strongly left-wing views, and thus by those in working-class occupations.

Table 7.2 Support for the Greens and the SSP, 2003, by educational qualification

% vote for list of	Highest educational qualification					
	Degree	Professional	Higher	Standard Grade 1–3	Standard Grade 4–7	None
Greens	17	10	7	4	1	3
SSP	13	3	5	4	5	3
Sample size	131	137	120	81	129	227

Our main expectation about the social character of those who voted for the Greens is clearly upheld. Table 7.2 shows the proportion of those with various levels of educational attainment who voted for the Greens and for the SSP on the list vote in 2003. No fewer than one in six of those with a university degree voted for the Greens, compared with just 4 per cent of those whose highest educational qualification is a Standard Grade or its equivalent. As one might anticipate, given that far more younger people have had access to a university education, support for the Greens is also much higher among those in younger age groups. No fewer than 13 per cent of those aged 34 or under supported the Greens on the list vote in 2003 compared with just 5 per cent of those aged 65 and over.[5]

More surprisingly, however, we can see from Table 7.2 that support for the SSP was highest among university graduates too. Meanwhile, the socialists were no more successful than the Greens in securing support among those with no educational qualifications. Although education appears to have had less impact on the probability of someone voting SSP than it did in the case of the Greens – the gap between the level of support among graduates and those with none is ten points, as opposed to fourteen points in the case of the Greens – this is hardly the profile that we would expect if the party were winning working-class votes. And, indeed, as Table 7.3 shows, the SSP was not particularly successful in winning support among those in semi-routine and routine occupations. Those in this group were no more likely to vote for the SSP than were those who were employers, managers or in professional occupations. Still, the pattern of the party's support does here at least appear rather different from that of the Greens, whose support was markedly lower among both those in routine occupations and those in lower supervisory ones than it was among those in more 'middle-class' occupations.

Table 7.3 Support for the Greens and the SSP, 2003, by social class

| % vote for list of | NS-SEC class group | | | | |
	Employers and professional	Intermediate	Self-employed	Lower supervisory	Semi-routine and routine
Greens	11	9	12	2	3
SSP	7	3	3	7	5
Sample size	287	81	77	104	220

But what of the values of those who supported the Greens and the SSP? We look first of all in Table 7.4 at whether adherence to a post-materialist outlook made a difference to the chances of someone backing the Greens or the SSP. In order to ascertain whether respondents had a post-materialist or a materialist outlook, we asked them which of a set of four items they thought it was most important for Britain to do, and then which was the next most important. The items they were asked to choose among were:

Maintain order in the nation
Give people more say in government decisions
Fight rising prices
Protect freedom of speech.

Those who picked the second and the fourth items as their top two priorities (in either order) are classified as post-materialist, while those who choose the first and the third are regarded as materialist. Those who selected any other combination are categorised as 'mixed'. This procedure is the one that has most commonly been used in previous research in order to identify post-materialists (Inglehart 1977).

In fact, only one in three people in our survey fell neatly into either the post-materialist or the materialist category. Just 14 per cent were post-materialists, while 19 per cent were materialist. The remaining two-thirds were 'mixed' in their orientations. Nevertheless, the minority that did occupy one or other end of the spectrum were very distinctive in their level of support for the Greens and the SSP. As we had anticipated, and as can be seen in Table 7.4, post-materialists were far more likely to support the Greens than were materialists – indeed, no less than six times more likely. Yet, strikingly, the SSP also performed well among post-materialists. Indeed, at 15 per cent their level of support among this group more than matched that given to the Greens. Perhaps the anti-capitalist message of the SSP appealed as much to this group as did the anti-growth message of the Greens.

Table 7.4 Support for the Greens and the SSP, 2003, by post-materialist/materialist orientation

% vote for list of	Post-materialist	Mixed	Materialist
Greens	13	7	2
SSP	15	5	1
Sample size	*115*	*551*	*163*

We have also suggested that the Greens should have had a particular appeal to those with more liberal views on social issues. In our survey, we carried a number of items designed to measure how libertarian or author- itarian an outlook someone adopts to such issues. Full details of these items are given in the Technical Appendix to this book. For our purposes here, we have collapsed our respondents' combined score on these items into four approximately equal-sized groups. So, at one end of the spectrum, we have a group that contains the quarter or so of the population that is most libertarian, and at the other end a group that comprises the quarter or so that is most authoritarian. In between are two groups with less polarised views that we can think of as 'moderately libertarian' and 'moderately authoritarian'.

As Table 7.5 shows, this procedure confirms our expectation that those who supported the Greens tended to have a liberal outlook. Indeed, the relationship is striking. Over one in five of those whose views we have classified as libertarian voted for the Greens on the list vote in 2003. Among the remaining three groups, in contrast, support for the Greens did not exceed 5 per cent. Meanwhile, those of a libertarian persuasion were also more likely to back the SSP than those who were not. But the gap in this case is somewhat smaller. Just 12 per cent of libertarians supported the SSP, while at the other end of the spectrum 4 per cent of authoritarians did so.

Table 7.5 Support for the Greens and the SSP, 2003, by libertarian/authoritarian value position

% vote for list of	Libertarian	Moderately libertarian	Moderately authoritarian	Authoritarian
Greens	21	5	3	2
SSP	12	3	4	4
Sample size	182	159	260	140

Indeed, and in line with our expectations, whether or not someone has predominantly left-wing or right-wing views makes more difference to whether someone voted for the SSP than does where they stand on the libertarian–authoritarian dimension. (Whether someone has predominantly left-wing or right-wing views was ascertained in similar fashion to how we identified whether they adopted a libertarian or an authoritarian standpoint, and the details can be found in the Technical Appendix to this book.) As Table 7.6 shows, while 13 per cent of those on the left of the political spectrum backed the SSP, none of the respondents that we classified as right-wing did so. Meanwhile, although the Greens did also perform somewhat better among those on the left, the differences are relatively small.

So, both the Greens and the SSP appealed to distinct bodies of voters in 2003.[6] In the case of the Greens, they did so in a manner that fully upheld our expectations. The Greens performed best among those of a liberal, post-materialist orientation, many of whom were university graduates. True, in the case of the SSP the picture was not entirely as we had anticipated. The party did not particularly succeed in winning over working-class voters; indeed, if anything, it shared with the Greens a particular strength among university graduates.[7] But its supporters were undoubtedly of a left-wing viewpoint; and, while they were also inclined to be both liberal and post-materialist, it was where they stood on the left–right spectrum that distinguished SSP voters above all.[8]

Table 7.6 Support for the Greens and the SSP, 2003, by left/right value position

% vote for list of	Left	Centre left	Centre right	Right
Greens	10	9	7	4
SSP	13	4	4	0
Sample size	171	242	150	184

CONCLUSION

Our analysis contradicts any assertion that the success of the smaller parties in the 2003 Scottish election was an ill-informed decision undertaken by voters because they thought that the election was of so little consequence that they could afford to experiment. The decision to vote for one of the smaller parties was one most commonly taken by those who were well educated, politically interested and politically well informed. In so doing, they for the most part gave support to a party whose ideological stance reflected their own views. And in any event, voting for a smaller party was not the particular preserve of those who felt that the election was not particularly important.

More debatable is the extent to which the level of support for smaller parties was enhanced by the use of a system of proportional representation. In so far as proportional representation did make a difference, it may have been not simply because voters understood that smaller parties had a better chance of winning a seat under such a system but rather because parties did – and as a result stood in the election and then secured the attention of the electorate (or perhaps more accurately the politically more aware section of the electorate) in a manner that they would not otherwise have done. In so far as that was the case, it meant that the outcome of the 2003 election reflected the diversity of public opinion in Scotland to a greater extent than any election to the House of Commons. That, at least, would be regarded by the advocates of proportional representation as a success.

Notes

1. Respondents were asked to identify which of the following statements were true or false:

   The Scottish Parliament cannot change the basic rate of income tax in Scotland (FALSE)

   The UK government, not the Scottish Parliament, makes all decisions about defence (TRUE)

   The Scottish Parliament can decide how much of its budget is spent on schools in Scotland (TRUE).

   Among those who identified the status of all three items correctly, 22 per cent voted for an 'other' party on the list vote; in contrast, just 10 per cent of those who could not identify any of the items correctly did so.

2. True, we should bear in mind that 0.7 per cent of the constituency vote was cast for parties that did not contest any of the regional list seats, while 0.5 per cent more votes were cast for independent candidates on the constituency ballot than on the party list vote. But equally, 1.9 per cent of the list vote was cast for two parties, the Scottish Senior Citizens' Unity Party and the Scottish People's Alliance, that contested only one and sixteen constituency seats respectively (securing just 0.4 per cent of the overall constituency vote).

3. We take the difference between the level of voting for 'others' on the constituency vote and the list vote among those who agreed with our proposition about the list vote and compare it with the equivalent difference among those who 'neither agree nor disagree'. The difference between these two figures is eighteen points (24 per cent less 6 per cent). This is regarded as the 'impact' of agreeing with the proposition. We then multiply this proportion by the proportion of those who voted who agreed with the proposition (34 per cent). This calculation results in an estimate of 6 per cent.

4. If this were the case, however, then it might be thought that those who agreed with a further statement in our survey, 'There is more point voting under the Scottish Parliament voting system because every vote counts', a statement that might be regarded as an indicator of the degree to which the proportionality of the system as a whole provides more incentive, should have been more likely to have voted for an 'other' party on the constituency ballot than those who disagreed. The evidence for this, however, is weak. While 8 per cent of those who agreed with the

statement voted for an 'other' party on the constituency vote, so also did 5 per cent of those who disagreed.

5. Further analysis indicates, however, that once we control for educational attainment, this difference is not statistically significant. In other words, the age profile of the Green vote is largely a function of its educational profile.

6. We might also note that their success seems in each case to have been at the particular expense of one of the larger parties. The Greens appear to have done most damage to the Liberal Democrats. No less than 13 per cent of those who voted for the Liberal Democrats on the constituency ballot voted for the Greens on the list vote. In contrast, only 5 per cent of those who backed Labour on the constituency ballot switched to the Greens, and just 3 per cent of Conservative and SNP constituency voters. Meanwhile, the SSP seem to have disproportionately secured the support of those who would otherwise have voted for the SNP. No less than 8 per cent of those who said they would have voted for the SNP if a Westminster election were being held in May 2003 voted for the SSP on the list vote. In contrast, only 5 per cent of Labour's hypothetical Westminster voters backed the SSP, 3 per cent of the Liberal Democrats' and none of the Conservatives' supporters. These findings are also in line with the evidence of the election results themselves (Curtice 2004).

7. At the same time, we should note that the SSP did score best in those constituencies with relatively high levels of socio-economic deprivation (Curtice 2004). It may well be the case that the middle-class, graduate support that the party secured came mainly from those in these categories who lived among less affluent neighbours.

8. We might note, however, that despite the fact that both parties were in favour of independence, neither party was particularly successful at winning support among those in favour of independence. While 8 per cent of those in favour of independence voted for the Greens, so also did 9 per cent of those who preferred devolution. And while, at 8 per cent, support for the SSP among those in favour of independence was three points higher than it was among the advocates of devolution, the gap is much smaller than those for the SSP in any of Tables 7.4, 7.5 or 7.6.

REFERENCES

Curtice, J. (2004), 'Adding up the figures: conclusions from 2003', in M. Spicer (ed.), *The Scotsman Guide to Scottish Politics*, Edinburgh: Scotsman Publications.

Dalton, R. (1994), *The Green Rainbow: Environmental Groups in Western Europe*, New Haven, CT: Yale University Press.

Dalton, R. (2006), *Citizen Politics: Public Opinion and Political Participation in Advanced Industrial Democracies*, 4th. edn, Washington, DC: CQ Press.

Duverger, M. (1976), *Political Parties: Their Organization and Activity in the Modern State*, 3rd edn, London: Methuen.

Evans. G. (2000), 'The working class and New Labour: a parting of the ways?', in R. Jowell, J. Curtice, A. Park, K. Thomson, L. Jarvis, C. Bromley and N. Stratford (eds), *British Social Attitudes: The 17th Report*, London: Sage.

Fuchs, D. and Rohrschneider, R. (1998), 'Postmaterialism and electoral choice before and after German unification', *West European Politics*, 21: 95–116.

Heath, A., Jowell, R. and Curtice, J. (1985), *How Britain Votes*, Oxford: Pergamon.

Heath, A., Jowell, R., Curtice, J., Evans, G., Field, J. and Witherspoon, S. (1991), *Understanding Political Change: The British Voter 1974–1987*, Oxford: Pergamon.

Inglehart, R. (1977), *The Silent Revolution*, Princeton, NJ: Princeton University Press.

Inglehart, R. (1990), *Culture Shift in Advanced Industrial Society*, Princeton, NJ: Princeton University Press.

Inglehart, R. (1997), *Modernization and Postmodernization: Cultural, Economic and Political Change in 43 Democracies*, Princeton, NJ: Princeton University Press.

Reif, K. (1984), 'National electoral cycles and European elections 1979 and 1984', *Electoral Studies*, 3: 244–55.

Reif, K. and Schmitt, H. (1980), 'Nine second-order national elections: a conceptual framework for the analysis of European Election results', *European Journal of Political Research*, 8: 3–44.

Surridge, P. (2003), 'A classless society? Social attitudes and social class', in C. Bromley, J. Curtice, K. Hinds and A. Park (eds), *Devolution – Scottish Answers to Scottish Questions?*, Edinburgh: Edinburgh University Press.

CHAPTER 8

Proportional Power

John Curtice

INTRODUCTION

The advent of devolution in 1999 brought with it not only a new institution, the Scottish Parliament, but also a new electoral system. Ever since the reorganisation of local government in the 1970s, all elections in Scotland, both local and parliamentary, had been held using the single-member plurality electoral system, a system under which voters place a single 'X' against the name of their most preferred candidate, and the candidate with the most votes is elected. Indeed, not since 1945, the last occasion on which university MPs, including those from the Combined Scottish Universities constituency, were elected using the Single Transferable Vote, had anyone from north of the border had the chance to vote in anything other than a plurality election, either single-member or multi-member. But when, in the early 1990s, Labour and the Liberal Democrats negotiated the details of devolution inside the forum of the Scottish Constitutional Convention, they agreed that Scottish Parliament elections should be conducted using an Additional Member System (AMS). While the two parties envisaged seventy-three MSPs being elected in single member constituencies using the familiar plurality rule, a further fifty-six MSPs would be elected from party lists, seven in each of eight regions, such that the total number of MSPs won by each party in each region would be as proportional as possible. Moreover, voters were no longer to have one vote but two, one a vote for their local constituency MSP, the second for the party list that they most preferred.

One key aim of the new system, which was similar to that used in post-war Germany, was to reduce the very substantial advantage that Labour currently derived from single-member plurality. In the 1992 UK general election, for example, Labour won just 39 per cent of the vote in Scotland, yet it secured no less than two-thirds of the country's seventy-two Commons seats. So, if single-member plurality were to be used in elections to the

Scottish Parliament, there was evidently a danger that the parliament would be continuously dominated by one party, even though the party in question could never win as much as half the vote in Scotland. Such a possibility was certainly not acceptable to the Liberal Democrats, who in any event had long been in favour of electoral reform for all elections in the UK.

But AMS also potentially had other advantages. It has long been recognised that single-member plurality can discourage people from voting for smaller parties because they fear that to do so would be a waste of a vote (Duverger 1976). They might be particularly disinclined to vote for a smaller party if they are concerned that a candidate whom they particularly dislike might win in their constituency, and reckon that someone other than the candidate whom they most prefer has a good chance of defeating that candidate. For advocates of proportional representation, at least, this psychological disincentive not to support smaller parties and instead to vote tactically for a less preferred candidate is one of the key disadvantages of single-member plurality. Better, they argue, that voters should be able to vote 'sincerely' for the party they most prefer so that the outcome of an election provides an accurate reflection of voters' real preferences. This is supposedly what AMS enables voters to do with their 'second' or party list vote, as on that ballot seats are allocated in direct proportion to votes cast.

In addition to this argument, which could be held to apply to virtually any form of proportional representation, other arguments are sometimes deployed in support of AMS in particular. Here, however, the emphasis is not on making it easier for voters to cast a sincere vote. Rather, it is on the opportunity that is provided to voters by the fact that they have two votes to express a more sophisticated choice (Bawn 1999). Voters do not have to cast their two votes for the same party, but rather can 'split' them between two different parties. This means, for example, that voters can vote for the candidate whom they like best in their constituency, irrespective of the party which that candidate is representing, while still backing the party that they like best in the list ballot. Moreover, they can do so secure in the knowledge that it is the list vote that is meant to determine the overall outcome in seats. Indeed, similar considerations might mean that voters are even less willing to vote in their local constituency contest for parties which have no apparent chance of winning because they now have the opportunity to vote for their first-preference party on the list ballot. Meanwhile, it is also argued that voters can use the fact that they have two votes to express their support for a particular coalition (Bogdanor 1981). Thus, for example, voters who would like Labour and the Liberal Democrats to form a coalition government could give one of their votes, say their constituency vote, to

Labour and the other, say their list vote, to the Liberal Democrats. The existence of such an opportunity, it can be argued, helps meet the objection that is sometimes raised by critics of proportional representation that voters lose influence over who forms the government if governments are the product of coalition negotiations.

But doubts have also been expressed about the degree to which split-ticket voting under AMS is the product of such sophisticated reasoning (Jesse 1988). Rather, it is argued that ticket-splitting may simply be the result of confusion among voters about how AMS actually works. Perhaps one potentially obvious source of confusion is the use, as in Germany, of the term 'first vote' to refer to the constituency ballot and 'second vote' to the list one. Such nomenclature might be thought to convey the mistaken impression that the list vote is a second-preference vote when in fact it is the more important vote of the two. Meanwhile, more generally, some critics have expressed a concern that the complexity of AMS might mean that voters are discouraged from voting at all, a tendency that might be reinforced if in fact voters dislike the system too.

In this chapter, we evaluate these two perspectives. First of all, we consider the degree to which voters appear in both the 1999 and 2003 elections to have been confused about the new electoral system or even to have disliked it. We also examine whether any confusion or dislike helps account for the failure of voters to vote at all or, if they did vote, to split their votes in a mistaken manner. Thereafter, we consider whether there is any evidence that voters used the system to vote sincerely to a greater degree than they did under single-member plurality, or to vote in a more sophisticated manner.

KNOWLEDGE

In both our 1999 and our 2003 surveys, we adopted two approaches to measuring voters' understanding of AMS. We presented our survey respondents with a series of statements about the system, some of which were true and some false, and asked them in each case whether they thought that the statement was true or false. This approach provides us with an 'objective' measure of the level of voters' understanding of the system. We also asked respondents in both years how easy or difficult they found it to understand the system. This gives us a more 'subjective' self-report of how well voters feel they understand AMS.

Table 8.1 indicates how well respondents were able to answer our knowledge quiz about the electoral system by showing for each statement the proportion that correctly identified it as either true or false. There were

Table 8.1 Proportion of respondents giving correct answers to knowledge quiz about the electoral system

	% correct	
	1999	2003
You are allowed to vote for the same party on the first and second vote (TRUE)	78	64
Regional party list seats are allocated to try to make sure that each party has as fair a share of votes as is possible (TRUE)	63	48
Unless a party wins at least 5 per cent of the second vote, it is unlikely to win any regional party list seats (TRUE)	43	33
No candidate who stands in a constituency contest can be elected as a regional party list member (FALSE)	31	24
The number of seats won by each party is decided by the number of first votes they get (FALSE)	30	26
People are given two votes so that they can show their first and second preferences (FALSE)	26	25
Average	45	37
Sample size	1,165	1,324

evidently some considerable gaps in voters' knowledge, and those gaps were even bigger at the time of the second election in 2003 than they were in 1999. Even in 1999, only in two instances did a majority of respondents correctly identify the statement as true or false; in 2003, this was true of just one statement. On all six items, the proportion able to say correctly whether it was true or false was lower in 2003 than in 1999. Of course, not all those who were unable to identify correctly whether a statement was true or false actually gave an incorrect answer – in each case many simply said they did not know whether a statement was true or false – but nevertheless it would appear that there was plenty of room for confusion among the electorate in both 1999 and 2003.

Still, we should note that voters were evidently better acquainted with some parts of the system than with others. For the most part, they seem to have been less knowledgeable about the details of the constituency and list contests than they were about the broad principles of the system. While knowledge about the former might be necessary to undertake effectively some of the forms of sophisticated voting that it is argued AMS makes possible, its absence may not generate actual confusion so long as voters do at least have a basic understanding of the aims and uses of the two votes. In any event, the picture painted by the objective knowledge quiz is reinforced by respondents' self-reporting of their understanding of the electoral system. As Table 8.2 shows, in both 1999 and 2003, relatively few (around one in ten) reported much difficulty in understanding what to do with the ballot paper. On the other hand, rather more (two in five) reported difficulty when it came to understanding how votes were translated into seats.

Table 8.2 Perceived difficulty of the electoral system

Some people say that filling in the ballot papers is very difficult. Others say that it is not at all difficult. How difficult do *you* think it is filling in the ballot papers for the Scottish Parliament election?

	1999 %	2003 %
Very difficult	1	1
Fairly difficult	8	11
Not very difficult	36	33
Not at all difficult	42	39
Can't choose	12	13

Some people say that it is difficult to understand how the number of seats a party wins in worked out under the new system. Others say that it is not at all difficult. How difficult do *you* think it is understanding how the seats are worked out?

	1999 %	2003 %
Very difficult	7	6
Fairly difficult	33	34
Not very difficult	33	35
Not at all difficult	12	9
Can't choose	14	14
Sample size	*1,165*	*1,324*

SUPPORT

Whatever the limitations of voters' understanding of AMS, at first glance the new electoral system appears to have been relatively popular. In 1999, no fewer than 66 per cent agreed with the proposition that 'the Scottish Parliament should be elected using proportional representation'. While at 59 per cent the equivalent figure in 2003 was a little lower, the use of an alternative system still appears to have been relatively popular. Indeed, a not dissimilar proportion, 55 per cent, agreed in 2003 that proportional representation should be used to elect the House of Commons as well.

However, two notes of caution are in order. First, the answers given by the public to questions about electoral systems are highly sensitive to question-wording (Curtice and Jowell 1998). This is illustrated by the fact that, among the very same respondents who gave majority support to the use of proportional representation in elections to the House of Commons, no fewer than 52 per cent also said in response to a different question that 'we should keep the voting system [for the House of Commons] as it is to produce effective government'. Only 39 per cent wanted to 'change the voting system for general elections to the House of Commons to allow smaller parties to get a fairer share of MPs'. Evidently, support for proportional representation depends on the terms in which it is presented. Even so, this does not suggest that there is widespread public opposition to the use of proportional representation. Instead, rather than being either firmly in support of or opposed to the use of proportional representation, it would seem that many people simply do not have firm and fixed views on the subject either way.

Our second note of caution is about how much support there might be for the use of AMS in particular as opposed to the principle of proportional representation in general. Support for AMS in particular seems to have declined between 1999 and 2003 to a considerably greater degree than did support for proportional representation in general (Curtice 2004). For example, by 2003, only 33 per cent agreed that 'the voting system used in Scottish Parliament elections should be used in future to elect MPs to the House of Commons', well down on the 50 per cent who took that view in 1999. Equally, only 36 per cent felt that the Scottish Parliament electoral system was 'fairer than the one usually used at elections', down from 54 per cent in 1999. Meanwhile, whereas in 1999 as many as 62 per cent thought that there was more point in voting under the Scottish Parliament system because every vote counts, in 2003 only 47 per cent took that view. These rather large falls in response to questions that refer to the voting system used in Scottish Parliament elections in particular – falls that are not replicated to the same degree when voters are asked about proportional representation in general – suggest that, by 2003 at least, there may have been a growth in dissatisfaction with AMS in particular among the general public.[1]

DID CONFUSION OR DISCONTENT MATTER?

We have, then, ascertained that the public does not appear to have been well informed in either 1999 or 2003 about how certain aspects of the Scottish Parliament electoral system worked – though the lack of understanding seems to have centred on the translation of votes into seats rather than the process of voting itself. We have found, too, that while there may be considerable if shallow support for the principle of proportional representation in general, by 2003 at least there may have been increased doubt among the public in Scotland about the merits of AMS in particular. But did any of this discontent or lack of understanding result in either abstention or confusion?

Table 8.3 suggests that those who dislike either proportional representation in general or the voting system used in Scottish Parliament elections in particular were not consistently or significantly more likely to abstain in either 1999 or 2003. Thus, for example, while those who supported the principle of electing the Scottish Parliament by proportional representation were four points more likely to claim to have voted in 1999, they were actually eleven points *less* likely to do so in 2003. Equally, while those who disagreed that there was more point in voting under the electoral system used in Scottish Parliament elections were three points less likely to have voted in 2003, they were twelve points more likely to have done so in 1999. Moreover, most of the differences in the table are small. In fact, rather than being particularly low among the opponents of the electoral system, turnout was by far and away lowest among those who neither agreed nor disagreed with the various propositions in our table. This is probably a reflection of the fact that members of this group express a much lower level of interest in politics than do either the supporters or the opponents of proportional representation.

Table 8.3   Turnout by attitude towards the electoral system

| | % who voted | | | |
| | 1999 | | 2003 | |
	Agree	Disagree	Agree	Disagree
SP should be elected using PR	81	77	66	77
Sample size	765	112	782	144
Use SP electoral system to elect MPs	83	79	73	69
Sample size	587	176	426	216
More point in voting under SP system, as every vote counts	78	90	71	68
Sample size	617	155	622	103
SP voting system is fairer	82	72	74	74
Sample size	624	113	446	108
Prefer SP voting system to elect SP *	77	73	66	58
Sample size	862	469	926	386

* Respondents were asked to choose between the Scottish Parliament (SP) system and that used in elections to the House of Commons.

But, if those who are indifferent to the use of proportional representation are both less interested in politics and less likely to have voted, perhaps they know less about it too. So, perhaps we will find that a lack of understanding of the electoral system was associated with a low level of turnout. We might particularly anticipate that those who subjectively felt that the system was difficult to understand would feel uncomfortable about going to the polls. However, the evidence for this is weak. It is the case, as Table 8.4 shows, that in both 1999 and 2003 those who said that the ballot paper was 'very' or 'fairly' difficult to complete were somewhat less likely to report having voted than were those who said that it was 'not very' or 'not at all' difficult. However, we should bear in mind that this is a small group, comprising just 10 per cent of respondents in 1999 and 12 per cent in 2003, so this perception cannot have discouraged many voters from going to the polls. Far more numerous (see Table 8.2) were those who said that it was very or fairly difficult to understand how the seats were worked out; yet the difference between their reported level of turnout and that among those who did not feel that matters were that complicated was only between one and four points.[2]

Table 8.4 Turnout by subjective knowledge of the electoral system

	% who voted			
	1999		2003	
	Difficult to fill in/understand	Not difficult to fill in/understand	Difficult to fill in/understand	Not difficult to fill in/understand
Ballot paper	74	86	66	72
Sample size	118	889	181	948
Seats	81	82	66	70
Sample size	470	521	547	571

However, there does appear to be rather stronger evidence that a low level of objective knowledge about the electoral system was associated with a lower propensity to vote. In 1999, no fewer than 83 per cent of those who were able to identify at least three of the quiz items correctly as true or false claimed to have voted, whereas only 63 per cent of those only able to identify two or fewer correctly did so. In 2003, the equivalent figures were 73 per cent and 52 per cent respectively. True, in part these gaps of twenty points or so are somewhat narrower (fifteen points in 1999, eleven in 2003) if we confine ourselves to those who said that they had voted at the previous general election, suggesting that in part those who know relatively little about the Scottish Parliament voting system consist disproportionately of those who are disinclined to vote in any kind of election. Nevertheless, even if we undertake a more elaborate multivariate analysis that, inter alia, takes into account people's interest in politics and their turnout at the last election, we still find that there was a significantly lower level of turnout among those who scored less well on our quiz.[3] While we might still wonder whether our quiz has simply proved to be a better indicator of interest in Scottish Parliament elections than were any of the other questions included in our surveys, it would seem that at minimum the relatively low level of knowledge of the workings of the Scottish Parliament electoral system among the general public was certainly not conducive to a high level of turnout in either 1999 or 2003.

But did a lack of knowledge among those who did turn out and vote result in confusion in how to use their two votes? Certainly, there were plenty of voters who did opt to vote for a different party in the list vote from how they voted on the constituency ballot. In 1999, 20 per cent voted differently on the two ballots, while in 2003 no fewer than 28 per cent did so. There certainly seems to be plenty of potential room here for confusion and misunderstanding.

If such confusion were widespread, one feature that we might expect to find, as we indicated earlier, is that voters failed to cast their list vote for their first-preference party in the mistaken belief that the 'second' or list vote was intended to be a mechanism for registering a second preference. In fact, in 1999 the proportion who voted for their first-preference party on the list vote was, at 84 per cent, only slightly below the proportion, 88 per cent, who did so on the constituency ballot. Moreover, those who on our quiz mistakenly cited as true the statement that 'People are given two votes so that they can show their first and second preferences' were no more likely to fail to vote for their first-preference party on the list vote than were those who correctly identified the statement as false. It would seem difficult to argue from this evidence that, at that election at least, misunderstanding of the meaning of the two votes led many voters to vote mistakenly for their second preference on the list vote. However, in 2003, the proportion voting for their first-preference party on the list vote was, at 75 per cent, both lower than it was in 1999 and more distant from the proportion who voted for their first-preference party on the constituency ballot (83 per cent). Moreover, those who mistakenly identified the purpose of the two ballots to be to show a second preference were rather less likely (72 per cent) to vote for their first-preference party than were those who correctly recognised the statement in our quiz to be false (81 per cent). It appears possible that, in

2003 at least, a few voters may have failed to vote for their first-preference party on the list vote because they mistakenly thought that it was intended to be a mechanism for registering a second preference.

However, we should also note that those who failed to vote for their first-preference party on the list vote were highly distinctive in how they voted on that ballot. Indeed, it is the behaviour of this group that accounts for much of the support won on the list ballot by parties other than Scotland's four largest. In 1999, a quarter of those who failed to vote for their first-preference party on the list vote backed someone other than one of Scotland's four largest parties, compared with just 2 per cent of those who did vote for their first preference on the list vote. In 2003, the equivalent figures were no less than 47 per cent and 5 per cent. The Greens in particular benefited from this phenomenon; just 17 per cent of those who in 1999 voted for the Greens on the list vote said that the Greens were their first-preference party, while equally in 2003 just 22 per cent were backing their first preference. It could be argued that, if those who failed to support their first-preference party on the list vote were doing so simply out of confusion, we would not expect their 'errors' to have benefited particular parties. True, the Greens, who did not stand in any constituencies at either election, may have helped to sow confusion among those who had some sympathy for them through their campaign slogan, '2nd Vote Green'. But equally it is also possible that those who decided to back the Greens or another party on the list vote then rationalised their behaviour when they answered our knowledge quiz (see also Chapter 7).

In any event, there is no consistent evidence that those who voted differently on the two ballots did so out of confusion. In both 1999 and 2003, the proportion of those who said that it was very or fairly difficult to understand how seats were allocated under the electoral system differed little in their propensity to split their votes than did those who reckoned that it was not particularly difficult to understand at all. In 1999, 25 per cent of the former group and 22 per cent of the latter voted differently on the two votes. In 2003, the equivalent figures were 29 per cent and 28 per cent respectively. Meanwhile, those who could correctly identify no more than two of our quiz statements as true or false were actually less likely to split their votes. This was especially so in 1999 when just 14 per cent of this group voted differently on the two ballots, compared with 25 per cent of those who identified three or more quiz statements correctly. In 2003, meanwhile, there was little difference between the two groups, with split-ticket rates of 26 per cent and 30 per cent respectively.

SINCERE AND SOPHISTICATED VOTING

If we can uncover little evidence to support the contention that voters split their ballots because they were confused, can we find any support for the argument that AMS makes it easier for people to vote sincerely for the party they most prefer rather than being influenced by the tactical situation in their constituency? As we noted earlier, we might expect this to be particularly true of the list vote, that is, the vote to which seats are allocated proportionately.[4] Indeed, we might even find that voters are more likely to be influenced by the tactical situation on the constituency vote than they are under single-member plurality, since under AMS they have the ability both to vote for the candidate best placed to defeat a candidate they particularly dislike and to vote for the party they like best on the list vote.

In order to ascertain whether or not voters were influenced by the tactical situation when they cast their constituency vote, we asked our respondents:

And thinking of this 'first' or 'constituency' vote, which one of the reasons on this card comes **closest** *to the main reason you voted for the party you chose?*

I always vote that way
I thought it was the best party
I really preferred another party, but it had no chance of winning in this constituency.

The last of these three responses is taken to indicate that a respondent voted tactically rather than sincerely. This exact same question was also asked after the 1992 and 1997 UK general elections in Scotland, which means that we can compare the incidence of tactical voting in the first two Scottish Parliament elections with that at recent UK general elections. Meanwhile, in 1999 and 2003 we also asked our respondents an equivalent question about their list vote:

And still thinking of this 'second' or 'party list' vote, which one of the reasons on this card comes **closest** *to the main reason you voted for the party you chose?*

I always vote that way
I thought it was the best party
I really preferred another party, but it had no chance of winning any party list seats in this region.

Our expectation that fewer people voted tactically on the list vote in 1999 and 2003 than had done at previous UK general elections held under single-member plurality is confirmed. On both occasions, just 4 per cent said that they had really preferred another party but that it did not have any chance of winning a seat in their region. In contrast, no fewer than 9 per cent of people in Scotland said that they had voted tactically in the 1992 UK general election, while 10 per cent did so in 1997. At the same time, however, and contrary to what we might have expected, reported tactical voting was also lower, just 5 per cent, in the constituency contests in 1999 and 2003 too. The introduction of AMS may well have facilitated an increase in sincere voting, but the fact that the increase occurred on the constituency ballot as well as on the list vote could mean that it occurred because by 1999 fewer voters had the impetus to vote tactically rather than because they were voting under a different electoral system.[5]

We identified earlier two possible ways in which people might use the fact that they had two votes to express a more sophisticated choice. One possible use is to express a preference for a particular coalition formation. In 1999, no fewer than 51 per cent said that they thought that it was better 'to have a government in Edinburgh formed by two political parties together in coalition' rather than a government 'formed by one political party', while an almost identical proportion, 50 per cent, said the same in 2003. So, there was no shortage of voters who preferred the principle of a coalition. Meanwhile, given that in most regions Labour were not expected to win any list seats (because of the anticipated strength of their performance in the constituency contests), their supporters in particular could opt to back a preferred coalition partner on the list vote without much fear that it would cost their party any seats.

There is, however, little consistent evidence of voters using the system in this way. One key group who might be expected to do so are those who voted Labour or Liberal Democrat on the constituency vote and who not only said that they preferred a coalition government in Edinburgh but also, in response to a further question, indicated a preference for a Labour–Liberal Democrat coalition rather than a Labour–SNP one. In 1999, members of this group were in fact far more likely to vote on the list ballot for the other partner in their preferred coalition than were those who voted Labour or Liberal Democrat on the constituency ballot but preferred single-party government. No fewer than 10 per cent of those who backed a Labour–Liberal Democrat coalition split their ballots between Labour and the Liberal Democrats, compared with just 3 per cent of those who opposed a coalition. However, even then, we should bear in mind that another 14 per cent of those Labour and Liberal Democrat constituency voters who backed a coalition between those two parties split their ballots by voting for someone other than Labour or the Liberal Democrats on the list vote. Meanwhile, if we look at the same key group of supporters of a Labour–Liberal Democrat coalition in 2003, we find that they were hardly more likely to split their ballots between Labour and the Liberal Democrats (6 per cent did so) than were those who opposed a coalition (5 per cent), while no fewer than 23 per cent of them split their ballot in some other way.

Meanwhile, there is not any evidence at either election that those Labour and SNP constituency voters who supported the idea of a Labour–SNP coalition (most were in fact SNP rather than Labour voters) used their two votes to express their coalition preference. In 1999, at 7 per cent, the proportion who voted on the list ballot for the other party in their preferred coalition, was barely any higher than it was among those who opposed a coalition (6 per cent). Meanwhile, in 2003 they were actually less likely to do so (2 per cent as compared with 8 per cent).

On the other hand, there is rather more evidence to support the view that some voters felt able to vote for the candidate whom they most preferred in their constituency irrespective of the party to which that candidate belonged. Indeed, this seems to have been the case particularly in 2003. In our surveys, we attempted to ascertain who voted for their preferred candidate rather than their preferred party by asking:

Still thinking of this 'first' or 'constituency' vote, which of the statements on this card comes **closest** *to the way you voted on the 'first' or 'constituency' vote?*

I voted for a party, regardless of the candidate
I voted for a party only if I approved of the candidate
I voted for a candidate, regardless of his or her party.

In 1999, 9 per cent said that they voted for a candidate regardless of his or her party, while in 2003 this figure increased to 13 per cent. Moreover, in consistency with this answer, in 1999 42 per cent of this group voted for a different party on the list vote, while in 2003 47 per cent did so. Both figures are higher than the levels of 20 and 28 per cent respectively which we have already seen pertained among voters as a whole. Equally, in 1999 only 61 per cent said that they were voting for their first-preference party, while in 2003 only 57 per cent did so. So, even if we only regard as a vote for a candidate one not only cast for a candidate regardless of party, but also one not cast for either a voter's first-preference party or for the party supported on the list vote, by 2003 around 4 per cent of all constituency votes appear to have been cast for a candidate rather than their party. While it would clearly be wrong to suggest that most MSPs win their seats on the basis of their personal popularity, a popular candidate can evidently make something of a difference.

CONCLUSION

The use of AMS in Scottish Parliament elections has not been as harmful as some critics anticipated. Voters have certainly not stayed away from the polls because they disliked the system. There is little evidence that confusion about the system meant that voters split their two votes in a mistaken fashion. While there might be thought to be some evidence that, in 2003 at least, misunderstanding of the system meant that some voters used their list vote to express a second-preference vote, the fact that such second preferences went so disproportionately to smaller parties, most notably the Greens, suggests that such behaviour was far from random error. Rather, it seems more likely that voters used the opportunity of the list vote to give a smaller party a 'chance'. Certainly, it is the willingness of voters to use their second vote in this way that appears to have been the biggest single impact on how voters have behaved.

Yet, equally, AMS has not been as successful as its advocates might have hoped. Knowledge of some of the workings of the system, at least, is low, and this certainly does not seem to have encouraged participation. Support for the system seems to have declined between 1999 and 2003. While more voters do appear to have voted sincerely than have done at recent UK general elections, it is not clear how far this is the result of the use of AMS. There is little sign that voters have used their two votes to express a coalition preference; and, while some have used their constituency vote to express a preference for a candidate rather than a party, it would be a mistake to presume that the outcome of the constituency contests is anything other than predominantly determined by the popularity of the parties.

As a result, it is perhaps little wonder that the future of AMS in Scottish Parliament elections remains in some doubt. In 2004, the UK government appointed a commission under the chairmanship of Sir John Arbuthnott charged with the task, among other things, of examining whether the system should continue to be used. Meanwhile, the Scottish Parliament itself has decided that a different proportional system, the Single Transferable Vote, should be used in local elections in Scotland. The evidence presented in this chapter is hardly an indictment of AMS. But it is also far from being sufficient of an endorsement to suggest that its use has been an unalloyed success.

NOTES

1. However, we should note that there was one item in our survey on which there was not a decline between 1999 and 2003 in support for the Scottish Parliament system. In 1999, 60 per cent said that they preferred 'the new way of voting for the Scottish Parliament' because 'it means all parties are represented', while 31 per cent said that they preferred 'the way of voting used in elections to the UK House of Commons . . . as it produces effective government'. In 2003, 61 per cent said that they preferred 'the current way of voting', while only 27 per cent wanted to use that in elections to the House of Commons. Unlike the other questions referred to in this paragraph, this question was included among questions that asked people about their constitutional preferences, and it may be that respondents who had just expressed their preference for a Scottish Parliament were then rather reluctant to express a preference for a voting system used in the House of Commons.
2. We might also note that most of the differences in Table 8.4 are somewhat smaller if we confine our attention to those who claimed to have voted (under single-member plurality) at the previous UK general election.
3. For both 1999 and 2003, we undertook a logistic regression of turnout against age, educational attainment, interest in politics, turnout at the last UK general election, strength of party identification, how much it matters who wins a Scottish Parliament election, and score on a separate knowledge quiz about devolution, together with score on our knowledge quiz on the electoral system. In both cases, score on our electoral-system quiz was still significantly associated with a higher level of turnout at the 1 per cent level.
4. There are, however, two possible reasons why this might not be true of AMS as implemented in Scottish Parliament elections. First, a party needs to secure nearly 6 per cent of the list vote in a region before it can be more or less sure of winning a seat, a threshold that might still be sufficiently high to discourage some people from voting for a smaller party. Second, Labour's success in winning constituency seats is such that the party is not eligible for any additional list seats; this proved to be the case in seven regions in 1999 and six in 2003. This could be thought to provide an incentive for Labour voters to choose a different party on the list vote, as a vote for Labour would effectively be 'wasted'.
5. However, we should note that no such decline is evident from the answers given to a somewhat differently worded question included on the 2001 and 2005 British Election Study (Fisher and Curtice 2006).

References

Bawn, K. (1999), 'Voter responses to electoral complexity: ticket splitting, rational voters and representation in the Federal Republic of Germany', *British Journal of Political Science*, 29: 487–505.

Bogdanor, V. (1981), *The People and the Party System: The Referendum and Electoral Reform in British Politics*, Cambridge: Cambridge University Press.

Curtice, J. (2004), 'Proportional representation in Scotland: public reaction and voter behaviour', *Representation*, 40: 329–41.

Curtice, J. and Jowell, R. (1998), 'Is there really a demand for constitutional change?', *Scottish Affairs – Special Issue on Constitutional Change*, pp. 61–93.

Duverger, M. (1976), *Political Parties: Their Organization and Activity in the Modern State*, 3rd edn, London: Methuen.

Fisher, S. and Curtice, J. (2006), 'Tactical unwind? Changes in party preference structure and tactical voting in Britain between 2001 and 2005', *Journal of Elections, Public Opinion and Parties*, 16: 55–76.

Jesse, E. (1988), 'Split-voting in the Federal Republic of Germany: an analysis of federal elections from 1953 to 1987', *Electoral Studies*, 7: 109–24.

Part 3

National Identity

CHAPTER 9

Routes into Scottishness?
Michael Rosie and Ross Bond

INTRODUCTION

For a number of years, there has been considerable interest in the illumination that large scale social surveys can bring to the investigation of national identities in Scotland (see, for example, Brown et al. 1999; McCrone 2001; Paterson et al. 2001; Rosie and Bond, 2003). To some extent, this interest has been driven by constitutional change. Devolution has encouraged an environment in which greater resources have been devoted to researching specifically Scottish questions, including those concerned with national identities. Equally importantly, constitutional change has increased the salience of national identity as an area of academic research and wider popular concern, both sharpening the focus on well-established questions and generating more novel lines of enquiry.

While the re-establishment of the Scottish Parliament is an obvious political manifestation of Scottish national identity, a key question remains as to whether devolution will further accentuate the depth and importance of this identity, or alternatively whether its political expression will in fact mean that people feel less need to emphasise their Scottishness (Paterson et al. 2001). In this chapter, we review, and place in historical context, the most recent evidence concerning the salience of national identities in Scotland. The plural 'identities' is important here because, as we shall see, in Scotland national identity often has a multiple nature, not least because most people can conceive of themselves as Scottish and/or British. But, as well as examining the importance of Scottishness as compared with other national identities, we also examine the extent to which national identities in Scotland are regarded by respondents themselves (and not just social scientists) as important aspects of their everyday lives and sense of self.

However, not only has devolution raised more questions about the salience of Scottishness, it also brings into sharper focus the *nature* of this identity. Regardless of their position on the best means of governing Scotland, all the parties in the Scottish Parliament stress their belief in an inclusive Scottishness determined by factors such as birthplace and residency rather than more exclusive determinants like ethnicity and parentage. Scotland's principal nationalist and opposition party, the SNP, very much stresses its 'civic' credentials, welcoming in-migration and encouraging newcomers to Scotland to join the campaign for Scottish independence. To this end, the party has even established groups such as 'Scots Asians for Independence' and 'New Scots for Independence'. Scotland lacks a nationalist party such as the Vlaams Blok, which, despite its high levels of popular support in Flanders, was in November 2004 ruled to be racist by Belgium's highest court.[1] Moreover, unlike similar 'neo-nationalist' (McCrone 1998) movements in places like Catalonia and Quebec, the SNP does not need to negotiate the issue of language as a significant barrier to an inclusive national identity.

Recent initiatives by the Labour/Liberal Democrat coalition Executive have also highlighted the extent to which an open and inclusive perspective of national identity prevails among Scotland's political elites. Most notable here are the *One Scotland, Many Cultures* campaign,[2] which seeks to highlight the positive features of Scotland's diversity, and the *New Scots* or *Fresh Talent* initiative, which aims to create conditions whereby more people from outwith Scotland can be attracted to work and live there.[3]

But such developments beg the question of whether this view of an open, civic Scottishness is shared by the population at large, the vast majority of whom were born in Scotland of Scottish parents. A central aim of this chapter is therefore to utilise new questions from the 2003 survey to investigate the extent to which Scottishness is popularly viewed as an inclusive national identity, and so offer some insights into the extent to which those most likely to be seen as 'outsiders' can indeed *become* Scottish. We do this from two perspectives. First, we examine the expressed national identities of those for whom Scottishness may be problematised by their birthplace, parentage or length of residence. We then go on to examine the beliefs of the majority population for whom we would expect Scottishness to be relatively unproblematic: what factors do they think are most central to Scottish national identity, and do their views suggest that this identity is indeed relatively inclusive? In doing this, we devote particular attention to those who see their Scottishness as particularly important to their sense of self, and we examine whether this group is particularly likely to hold an exclusive viewpoint.

National identities in contemporary Scotland

We begin by examining data arising from two measures of national identity in Scotland. The first is the most permissive, inviting respondents to indicate which of eight national/territorial identities, if any, describes the way they think of themselves. The benefit of such an 'unforced' question is that respondents are encouraged to go beyond any 'primary' or overarching identity and are invited to indicate any further identities they may possess. Several of these identities and other options – 'Irish'; 'Northern Irish', 'Ulster', 'Welsh', 'Other' and 'none of these' – are chosen only by small proportions of respondents (between 1 and 3 per cent), and we exclude them here from our analysis. Table 9.1 thus shows only the most common responses to these questions in recent Scottish surveys.

Table 9.1 National/territorial identities in Scotland, 1997–2003

% regarding themselves as	1997	2000	2001	2002	2003
Scottish	82	87	86	83	84
British	52	52	50	56	58
English	4	5	3	4	4
European	9	10	12	11	17
Sample size	882	1,663	1,605	1,665	1,508

Two particular identities stand out in Table 9.1 as being the most frequently chosen. Scottishness accounts for a very large majority of respondents, and its incidence has remained relatively stable over the period 1997–2003. Britishness accounts for a half or more in each survey, and it might appear that there has been a recent, if minor, increase in this sentiment, from 50 per cent in 2001 to 58 per cent in the most recent survey. In fact, as we shall discuss below, other measures of identity appear to indicate that any increase has been more modest than even these figures would suggest. Nevertheless, it is clear that these two identities together account for the identities of most respondents in Scotland; only a very small proportion (4 per cent in 2003) regard themselves as neither.

What is also notable in Table 9.1 is that, to a considerable degree, these identities cannot be understood as discrete and mutually exclusive categories. As simple arithmetic reveals, many respondents in Scotland have, at least, a dual sense of national identity (in that there is some overlap between those who regard themselves as Scottish and those who regard themselves as British). In fact, in 2003, almost half of all respondents (48 per cent) regarded themselves as *both* British and Scottish.

Given that most respondents in Scotland feel Scottish and/or British, it is valuable to examine the relative weight given by individuals to these two identities. One of the most useful, and well-known, ways of doing so is the so-called 'Moreno' question. This survey measure was designed in Spain to tease out how respondents balanced state-level and 'sub-state' identities (for example, being Spanish and/or being Catalan). It was first applied in Scotland in the mid-1980s by Luis Moreno, and thus provides a long-standing benchmark of the relationship between Britishness and Scottishness. The question, and the proffered responses, runs as follows:

Which, if any, of the following best describes how you see yourself?
Scottish, not British
More Scottish than British
Equally Scottish and British
More British than Scottish
British, not Scottish

Table 9.2 shows the pattern of responses to this question over the last decade or so. The surveys suggest that, during the 1990s, there was a marked reduction in the number of people who regard themselves as 'equally Scottish and British' and an increase in the proportion who described themselves as either 'more Scottish than British' or 'Scottish, not British'. Since the late 1990s, these two latter identities have between them accounted for around two-thirds of respondents, with most of the remainder regarding themselves as 'equally Scottish and British'. Very few indeed regard themselves as exclusively or primarily British. It might also be noted that almost all respondents feel able to assign themselves to one or other of the categories, with only about one in twenty unable to do so.

There are, we think, four main points to be taken from Table 9.2. Central to these is that a very large majority of respondents (91 per cent in 2003) assign themselves *some* degree of Scottishness, indicating a very high degree of salience for that identity. There are two qualifications to that point, however. Two-thirds assign themselves *some* degree of Britishness, and, leading on from that, a majority (60 per cent in 2003) regard themselves as *both* Scottish and British. The final point, then, is that Scottishness and Britishness are by no means incompatible and should not be regarded as such. Respondents can, and do, hold dual Scottish/British identities.

Table 9.2 The 'Moreno' question in Scotland, 1992–2003

	1992	1997	1999	2000	2001	2003
	%	%	%	%	%	%
Scottish, not British	19	23	32	37	36	31
More Scottish than British	40	38	35	31	30	34
Equally Scottish and British	33	27	22	21	24	22
More British than Scottish	3	4	3	3	3	4
British, not Scottish	3	4	4	4	3	4
Sample size	*957*	*882*	*1,482*	*1,663*	*1,605*	*1,508*

There is a subsidiary point we wish to make here: different measures of identity may produce slightly different results. For example, more respondents assigned themselves some form of Scottish identity on 'Moreno' (91 per cent) than regarded themselves as Scottish in Table 9.1 (84 per cent). Likewise, we found a slightly higher proportion of 'British' respondents on the 'Moreno' scale (64 per cent as compared to 58 per cent in Table 9.1).

Longer-term trends thus suggest that, while the salience of Scottishness has remained very high indeed over recent decades, attachment to British identity may have faded somewhat (see, for example, Bond and Rosie 2002). The data from Table 9.2, however, suggest that there was some stabilising in this respect around the time of devolution. We certainly cannot say that the re-establishment of the Scottish Parliament has increased the saliency of Scottish national sentiment and eroded Scotland's sense of Britishness. Rather, it would seem that the *level* of Britishness has become fairly stable since devolution, and this identity is still acknowledged by a majority of people in Scotland.

NATIONAL IDENTITIES AND ALTERNATIVE SOURCES OF IDENTIFICATION

A potential objection to the measures we have employed thus far is that they illuminate only those categories of identity to which respondents assign themselves when prompted, and tell us nothing about the importance that respondents assign to such identities. In order to explore whether national identities are more or less important than other facets of people's identity, the 2001 and 2003 surveys included a question specifically designed to tease out the kinds of identities which respondents regarded as crucial to their own sense of themselves. This question asks:

If you had to pick just one thing from this list to describe yourself – something that is very important to you when you think of yourself – what would it be?

Respondents were asked to pick an option, followed by a second and third option, from the following list (noted here in the order presented to the respondent):

Working class	A city person	A working person
British	A Protestant	Young
Elderly	A mother/father	White
A woman/man	Middle class	Asian
Not religious	Black	Unemployed
A wife/husband	Retired	Other
A Catholic	Religious	
A counrry person	Scottish	

In 2001, this question had a short preamble that highlighted the potential importance of national identity, but this was removed in the 2003 survey. The striking similarity of the results for the two years suggests that this change had little impact. This can be seen in Table 9.3, which shows the ten identities that proved most popular in 2003 alongside the total proportion of respondents who chose these same identities in the 2001 survey.

Table 9.3   **Most important identities, 2001 and 2003**

% choosing identity as one of their three options	2001	2003
Scottish	45	49
A mother/father	49	49
A working person	29	30
A wife/husband	28	29
A woman/man	25	27
Working-class	24	21
British	11	13
A country person	10	11
Young	9	9
Retired	11	9
Sample size	*1,605*	*1,508*

These data suggest that Scottishness is not simply a popular identity in Scotland but a very important aspect of the self-identity of around half of respondents. Indeed, the only identity which rivals Scottishness in its importance is parenthood. In both surveys, we find that (perhaps surprisingly) Scottish identity is even chosen more frequently than the more 'universal' identity of gender. In the 2003 survey, for example, more women chose being Scottish as one of their three most important identities than chose being a woman (47 per cent as compared to 35 per cent).

SCOTTISH IDENTITIES AND 'IDENTITY RESOURCES'

We are now in a position to disaggregate three types of respondent in Scotland according to their relationship with Scottishness. We will do this by combining the answers to the 'important identities' question with those to the earlier 'permissive' question on which national identities people acknowledge (see Table 9.1). Firstly, we have the large proportion (49 per cent) who in response to the first of these two questions choose being Scottish as key to their identity. The remaining respondents can then be divided according to their response to the second question. Most of the respondents who did not cite being Scottish as a key identity did nonetheless choose Scottish as a national identity they would use to describe themselves. But some 14 per cent of all respondents did not. We can thus summarise the pattern of attitudes towards Scottishness as follows:

'*Prioritised Scots*' (49 per cent): Regard themselves as Scottish and see that identity as very important to their sense of themselves;
'*Background Scots*' (36 per cent): Regard themselves as Scottish but do not view that identity as of central importance;
'*Non-Scots*' (14 per cent): Do not regard themselves as Scottish.

This last group, although numerically small, are of great sociological significance. Scottishness is both very salient and, for half of all respondents, 'very important' – yet here we find a minority who simply do not regard themselves as Scottish at all. Who are this minority, and in what respects do they differ from the two other groups?

Of central importance here are the identity resources that individuals possess. By 'identity resources' we mean the attributes which people hold which are most likely to be germane to their sense of national identity. Others have described these resources as 'markers' which people use to support a 'claim' to a particular national identity (Kiely et al. 2001). For example, we would expect that where people were born, where their family comes from, and the length of time they have lived in a particular country would all be important to their *own* feelings of national identity. And, just as importantly, these identity resources will also be important in determining the views of *other people* about one's national identity. We now use these three key identity resources – birth, ancestry and residence – to look at respondents' self-conceptions of national identity, and also to examine the relative importance which people in Scotland accord to these attributes in accepting others as Scottish. In doing so, we can assess the extent to which Scottishness is indeed an open and civic as opposed to exclusive and ethnic identity.

Table 9.4 illustrates how those born, and not born, in Scotland are distributed across our three identity groups. It suggests that birthplace is a crucial identity resource. The vast majority of respondents who were born in Scotland hold some kind of Scottish identity (95 per cent), while a majority of those respondents born outwith Scotland (61 per cent) describe themselves as 'non-Scots'.

Table 9.4 **Identity category and place of birth**

Identity category	Born in Scotland	Born elsewhere
	%	%
'Prioritised Scots'	56	18
'Background Scots'	39	21
'Non-Scots'	5	61
Sample size	*1,231*	*271*

Yet Table 9.4 also demonstrates that birth in itself does not wholly determine Scottish national identity. This is most evident in the group born outside Scotland, of whom a large minority regard themselves as Scottish; indeed, a notable minority actually *prioritise* this identity. Clearly, then, being born in Scotland is by no means a necessary condition for feeling Scottish. This suggests that, potentially at least, people are able to 'become' Scottish, and that there may be some process that 'opens up' Scottishness to migrants to Scotland and makes it possible for them to adopt a Scottish identity.

But the (limited) non-coincidence of birth and identity demonstrated in Table 9.4 need not necessarily be indicative of an open, civic national identity. It may be that those not born in Scotland have other resources upon which they can base a Scottish identity. Moreover, one such possible resource – ancestry – would connote a more 'ethnic' and therefore 'closed' interpretation of Scottishness. Table 9.5 examines the relationship between ancestry (as measured by where the respondent's parents were born) and identity.

Table 9.5 Identity category and parental place of birth

Identity category	Both parents born in Scotland	One parent born in Scotland	Neither parent born in Scotland
	%	%	%
'Prioritised Scots'	58	47	10
'Background Scots'	38	39	25
'Non-Scot'	5	14	65
Sample size	1,081	202	215

Here again, we find a fairly robust relationship. A very large majority of those with two Scots-born parents (96 per cent) and a slightly smaller majority of those with one Scots-born parent (86 per cent) adopt a Scottish identity. In contrast, among those with no Scots-born parents, nearly two-thirds (65 per cent) regard themselves as 'non-Scots'. But we should note that having Scottish-born parents is by no means a prerequisite for feeling Scottish. That more than one-third (35 per cent) of those with no Scottish parentage feel able to adopt some degree of Scottish identity again hints towards some kind of process by which individuals can 'become' Scottish.

A further instructive means of examining the extent to which such a process of 'becoming' may indeed take place is to look at people's length of residence. Table 9.6 shows a strong relationship between length of residence in Scotland and Scottish identity. A majority of those 'always' resident in Scotland have a prioritised Scottish identity, as do almost half of those resident for twenty-five years or more. While majorities of the two remaining groups are 'non-Scots', nearly half of those resident for between eleven and twenty-four years regard themselves as being at least in some way Scottish (with a notable minority prioritising it). Even among the most recent residents, about one in five assign themselves a Scottish identity. Thus Table 9.6 implies that, for some people at least, one can 'become Scottish' on the basis of residence, even if this may be a somewhat long-drawn-out process.

Table 9.6 Identity category and length of residence in Scotland

Identity category	Always	25 years or more	11–24 years	0–10 years
	%	%	%	%
'Prioritised Scots'	57	46	21	7
'Background Scots'	38	40	26	13
'Non-Scot'	5	15	53	80
Sample size	989	326	100	87

Tables 9.4 to 9.6 suggest that birth, ancestry and residence all act as 'resources' upon which individuals may draw to construct a sense of themselves as Scottish. We have shown, in turn, that respondents who are born in Scotland, have Scottish-born parents or have lived in Scotland for some considerable time are likely to adopt a Scottish identity and indeed to 'prioritise' it. Conversely, a majority of respondents born outwith Scotland, who are without Scottish-born parents or who have lived in Scotland for a relatively short period of time regard themselves as 'non-Scots'. These three kinds of 'resources' would seem to be of very great importance in mediating individuals' national identities, but we have also shown that no single one of them entirely determines these identities. As well as the evidence that suggests that a process of 'becoming' Scottish is possible even in the absence of one of these key resources, we have also consistently found that a very small minority who *do* possess such resources *do not* regard themselves as Scottish. Five per cent of those born in Scotland, and a similar proportion of those with two Scottish-born parents and those who have always lived in Scotland, regard themselves as 'non-Scots'. Although these people would seem to have little need to 'become' Scottish, in fact it appears that they have no desire to 'be' Scottish.

We will examine this group in more detail later, but for the moment let us return to the apparent process of becoming Scottish. While looking at each of our three key identity resources in isolation shows that their absence need not preclude the holding of a Scottish identity, it does not enlighten us as to whether people who lack the resource in question are in fact basing their Scottishness on one or more of the other key resources. It may well be that some of those respondents in Table 9.6 who appear to have 'become' Scottish through residence may in fact be deriving their Scottish identity from having a Scottish birthplace, or from the more 'ethnic' basis of parenthood. For example, we find that a clear majority (74 per cent) of the respondents in Table 9.6 who said that they had lived in Scotland for twenty-five years or more were in fact *born* in Scotland. Most of this sub-group, therefore, are Scots-born respondents who have, at some point in their lives, temporarily lived elsewhere.

In order to establish more firmly the extent to which one can become Scottish through residence alone, we therefore turn our attention to the relatively small number of respondents (12 per cent) who were *not* born in Scotland and who have two parents born *outside* Scotland. Most of these respondents do not think of themselves as Scottish, but a notable minority (27 per cent) do, with a small proportion (6 per cent) prioritising their Scottishness. But the prevalence of Scottishness among this group clearly varies according to *length* of residence, as Table 9.7 shows.

Table 9.7 Identity category by length of residence among those not born in Scotland and without Scottish-born parents

Identity category	25 years or more	11–24 years	0–10 years	All
	%	%	%	%
'Prioritised Scots'	20	–	–	6
'Background Scots'	42	20	12	27
'Non-Scot'	38	80	88	67
Sample size	51	48	81	186

Note: Six respondents who said they were not born in Scotland and whose parents were not born in Scotland, but who nevertheless claimed to have lived in Scotland all their lives, have been excluded from the table.

Table 9.7 appears to demonstrate the salience of birth and parental birth in mediating claims to a Scottish identity. Relatively few respondents who have neither of these 'routes' into Scottishness express Scottishness unless they have lived in Scotland for some considerable time. Rather strikingly, none of the respondents who had lived in Scotland for less than twenty-five years expressed a prioritised Scottish identity, while few expressed even a 'background' sense of Scottishness. Only among those resident for twenty-five years or more do we find a marked sense of Scottish identity: almost two-thirds of this group (62 per cent) express some degree of Scottishness. Nevertheless, even among those resident in Scotland for a relatively short period, small minorities express at least some sense of Scottishness. So, although the data suggest that a process of 'becoming' Scottish solely on the basis of residence is possible, they also suggest that such a process, if it occurs at all, is usually a fairly lengthy one.

'RESOURCED' AND 'UNRESOURCED' SCOTS

As we have seen above, a Scottish identity need not simply follow on from possessing the right kinds of resources. A small proportion (4 per cent) of those born in Scotland to at least one Scottish parent are 'non-Scots'. Who are these people, and why do they not adopt a Scottish identity? Our prime concern here lies with who these people think they are. We explore this by splitting the 'non-Scots' identity into two groups. These are:

'*Resourced non-Scots*' (4 per cent of all respondents): Were born in Scotland and/or have Scottish-born parent(s) and do not regard themselves as Scottish.

'*Unresourced non-Scots*' (11 per cent): Were not born in Scotland and have no Scottish-born parents and do not regard themselves as Scottish.

We already know that none of the respondents in these two groups regard themselves as Scottish, while all those in our other two groups do. But which other territorial/national identities, if any, do those in our four groups lay claim to? Table 9.8 reveals the proportions in each group who regard themselves as belonging to one of the other identities set out earlier in Table 9.1.

Table 9.8 Identity category and non-Scottish national/territorial identities

| | Identity category | | | |
| | Scots | | Non-Scots | |
% regarding themselves as	'Prioritised'	'Background'	'Resourced'	'Unresourced'
British	49	64	88	64
English	1	4	4	27
European	14	18	13	28
Sample size	749	540	84	133

We find a fairly high level of Britishness in all groups. Even among the 'prioritised Scots', nearly half say they are British. Meanwhile, among the 'resourced non-Scots', nearly nine out of ten regard themselves as British – and indeed Britishness is the only identity of note among this group. But, if Britishness is clearly present across all groups, the same cannot be said for an English identity. Only in the 'unresourced non-Scots' group do we find any notable degree of affiliation with Englishness, and even here it accounts for only just over a quarter of respondents. This may seem somewhat surprising, given that 'the English' (more accurately, the English-born) are Scotland's largest minority (Watson 2003; McIntosh et al. 2004). These data suggest that the English-born in Scotland may not, in fact, choose to describe themselves as English. The 'unresourced' group also contains relatively large proportions who choose 'European' (and, although not shown in Table 9.8, 20 per cent of this group also choose 'other'). Taken together, these data indicate that, while most 'resourced non-Scots' defined themselves as British, those in the unresourced group adhere to a mixture of identities.

BEING AND BECOMING SCOTTISH: MAJORITY PERSPECTIVES

The above data illustrate the key role of certain identity resources in mediating whether or not individuals see *themselves* as Scottish. In this final section, we turn to the question of how *other people* (the majority of whom possess all the key identity resources of Scottishness) view the national identities of those who lack (or appear to lack) these resources. We again base our investigation on birth, ancestry and residence, albeit that this time ancestry is measured by 'visible' ethnicity rather than parentage. At the same time, the additional identity resource of accent is also introduced. Assessing which of these factors are believed to be most central to Scottish national identity again helps us to ascertain whether this identity is indeed an open and inclusive one.

Respondents were offered two scenarios that depicted claims to Scottishness. In the first scenario, they were asked to think of someone who had been born in England but now lived permanently in Scotland and who claimed that they were Scottish. In the second scenario, they were asked to think of a 'non-white' person living in Scotland who spoke with a Scottish accent and who claimed they were Scottish. In each instance, the respondent was first asked whether they thought that *most people* would consider this notional person to be Scottish, and then whether they *themselves* would consider them to be Scottish.

Table 9.9 Responses to two scenarios of Scottishness

	An English-born person living in Scotland would be considered Scottish by		A non-white person with a Scottish accent and living in Scotland would be considered Scottish by	
	Most people	Respondent	Most people	Respondent
	%	%	%	%
Definitely would	5	11	5	23
Probably would	25	33	37	47
Probably would not	50	34	43	19
Definitely would not	18	20	12	9
Sample size	1,508	1,508	1,508	1,508

In both scenarios, we find a marked tendency for respondents to claim a more inclusive perspective than they assume is held by most other people (see Table 9.9). This tendency is more marked in respect of the non-white scenario than the English-born scenario. Thus, 30 per cent believe that most people would either definitely or probably consider the English-born person to be Scottish, but 44 per cent claim to hold this view themselves. In the non-white scenario, the respective figures are 42 per cent and 70 per cent.

Being born in England would seem to be a significant barrier to receiving a sympathetic response to any claim to be Scottish. Even accounting for the tendency of respondents to paint themselves in a more inclusive light than 'most people', we still find that more would definitely or probably *not* regard an English-born Scottish resident as Scottish (54 per cent) than definitely or probably *would* (44 per cent). It is also noticeable that rather fewer people would *definitely* view an English-born person as Scottish than would definitely view a 'non-white' person as such (11 per cent as compared to 23 per cent). Equally, rather more would *definitely not* view an English-born person as Scottish than they would a 'non-white' person (20 per cent as compared to 9 per cent). This is perhaps not so surprising, given England's long-standing status as Scotland's (often negative) 'Other', and of the existence of anti-English sentiments in at least some quarters of Scottish society (McIntosh et al. 2004).

It should be noted here that the 'non-white' scenario does not simply refer to a 'non-white' person living in Scotland, but accords to this notional person a recognisably Scottish accent. To some extent, accent may be regarded as a proxy marker for two of the identity resources discussed earlier, since possession of a 'Scottish' accent implies a substantial period of residence in Scotland, perhaps even to the point of being born there. We must thus recognise that the higher degree of inclusiveness seen towards the 'non-white' scenario may be to some extent due to people's tendency to regard accent as an identity resource. Likewise, given that accent (or, indeed, skin colour) may be discerned immediately in everyday interaction in the way that birth or ancestry cannot, one might speculate that accent is actually relatively salient when people are assessing who they consider to be Scottish. If so, it is probable that introducing a Scottish accent into our 'English-born' scenario would have led to more inclusive attitudes among respondents.

Moreover, while attitudes to members of Scotland's 'visible minority' groups who claim Scottish nationality appear considerably more inclusive than do attitudes to English-born people, this does not mean that people are unproblematically inclusive in their willingness to regard non-white people as Scottish, even when such people have a Scottish accent. While it is true that 70 per cent fall into one of the relatively inclusive response categories (that is, those who would definitely or probably consider such a person as Scottish) so far as their own views are concerned, less than a quarter (23 per cent) say that they would *definitely* consider a non-white person with a Scottish accent to be Scottish. Almost as many (19 per cent) say that they probably would *not*, and a small but significant minority (9 per cent) say that they *definitely* would not consider such a person to be Scottish. This suggests that, while most people in Scotland claim to see ethnicity as relatively unimportant to Scottish identity – or at least not as a barrier to claiming to be Scottish – a sizeable minority believe the opposite.

But might these perspectives on the identities of others be associated to some extent with people's own feelings of national identity? For example, if Scottishness is not in fact a relatively 'open' identity but instead is rather exclusive by nature, perhaps those who feel most strongly Scottish would be the least likely to accept as fellow Scots those who lack key identity resources? To explore this issue, we bring together self-identification and people's own opinions about the identity claims of others. Table 9.10 shows what proportion of those in each of the four categories of national identity we developed earlier said that they would regard an English-born person resident in Scotland as Scottish.

Table 9.10   Attitudes towards claims of those born in England to be considered Scottish, by identity category

	Identity category			
	Scots		Non-Scots	
Would consider Scottish	'Prioritised'	'Background'	'Resourced'	'Unresourced'
	%	%	%	%
Definitely would	10	12	12	8
Probably would	35	33	29	25
Probably would not	30	39	36	35
Definitely would not	23	15	16	29
Sample size	749	540	84	133

The differences between three of these groups – that is, both 'Scottish' groups and the 'resourced non-Scots' – are, in fact, fairly small. About two-fifths in each of these groups (ranging between 41 and 45 per cent) say that they would definitely or probably see this notional English-born person as Scottish, with just over half (52 to 54 per cent) saying that they would definitely or probably not. It is the 'unresourced' group (one that almost certainly contains a number of English-born respondents) which proves most distinctive. Nearly two-thirds of this group (64 per cent) adopt a relatively exclusive position on this identity-claim, with more than a quarter (29 per cent) saying that they *definitely* would not accept it.

To some degree, the same pattern is found if we look at perceptions of how 'most people' would see this matter. In the first three groups, around two-thirds (66 to 67 per cent) believe that most people would not see this person as Scottish, while this proportion rises to 79 per cent of the 'unresourced' group. Given the similarity between this group's own views and their perceptions of the views of 'most people', it seems likely that some part of their definition of themselves as 'non-Scots' is the result of a belief that they themselves would not (and perhaps should not) have any claim to Scottishness accepted by 'most people'.

By contrast, when it comes to the 'non-white' scenario, the views of those in the various identity groups are largely similar to each other. Large majorities of those in all four identity groups (ranging between 68 and 76 per cent) report that they definitely or probably would accept this 'non-white' person's claim to be Scottish – and such differences as do exist prove not to be statistically significant. Similarly, we found no statistically significant differences among these four groups on the question of how 'most people' would feel on this matter. Overall, it appears that those with the strongest sense of Scottishness are *not* more likely to uphold an exclusive attitude towards who can be considered Scottish.

CONCLUSIONS

The latest evidence from the Scottish Social Attitudes survey confirms the extent to which people in Scotland continue to emphasise their Scottish national identity in the wake of devolution. It also shows that this is an identity which, for around half of all respondents, is very important to their sense of self. But, while Britishness for most remains a secondary identity, there is no evidence that devolution is leading to its further eclipse by Scottish national identity: dual identities continue to be widely prevalent. At the same time, there is still a small minority for whom Scottishness is not only relatively unimportant but is entirely absent. To some extent, this is because they believe that they lack the necessary resources upon which to base a Scottish identity. In this respect, we found that birth, ancestry and length of residence were all important. Even so, there is still a yet smaller minority who possess these resources but do not feel Scottish.

Just as people's own feelings of national identity are influenced by the identity resources of birth, ancestry and residence, the relative importance accorded to these factors by the population as a whole when weighing up the identities of others is also illustrative of the nature of Scottishness. In this regard, we found that people thought themselves to possess more inclusive attitudes than those they believed were held by the wider population. The fact that place of birth was thought to be central to Scottishness to a greater extent than ethnicity provides at least some evidence to indicate that the kind of open, inclusive Scottish national identity favoured by Scotland's political classes is shared by a wider population. Evidence about the identities of those not born in Scotland and lacking Scottish parentage, but who had lived there for a considerable period, also suggests a degree of openness about the possibility of 'becoming' Scottish. While many do not 'become' Scottish, preferring instead to maintain or adopt other national identities, our evidence shows that this need not be a case of 'majority' attitudes obstructing the wishes of the 'minority'. For example, non-Scots who lacked any of the resources to claim a Scottish identity were least likely to regard a person born in England as Scottish. Nor did we find that having a strong sense of Scottishness was itself associated with relatively exclusive attitudes towards others adopting such an identity.

But this evidence should not be taken to mean that Scottishness is indeed the kind of open, inclusive identity that many would like to see. As well as widespread scepticism towards the notion of an English-born person becoming Scottish, perhaps of more concern is the relative reluctance wholeheartedly to accept the Scottishness of those from 'visible' minority ethnic groups, even when they may have other identity resources (such as residence and accent) that are important to being Scottish. This suggests that it may not be only 'New Scots' who find a Scottish identity less than completely open to them – some of those who one might expect should have no need to undergo a process of 'becoming' Scottish may face similar obstacles.

Notes

1. On this ruling and its context, see http://news.bbc.co.uk/1/hi/world/europe/3994867.stm.
2. See www.onescotland.com
3. See www.scotland.gov.uk/library5/government/afttm-00.asp

References

Bond, R. and Rosie, M. (2002), 'National identities in post-devolution Scotland', *Scottish Affairs*, 40: 34–53.

Brown, A., McCrone, D., Paterson L. and Surridge, P. (1999), *The Scottish Electorate*, Basingstoke: Macmillan.

Kiely, R., Bechhofer, F., Stewart, R. and McCrone, D. (2001), 'The markers and rules of Scottish national identity', *The Sociological Review*, 49: 33–55.

McCrone, D. (1998), *The Sociology of Nationalism*, London: Routledge.

McCrone, D. (2001), *Understanding Scotland: The Sociology of a Nation*, 2nd edn, London: Routledge.

McIntosh, I., Sim, D. and Robertson, D. (2004), '"We hate the English, except for you, cos you're our Pal": identification of the "English" in Scotland', *Sociology*, 38: 43–59.

Paterson, L., Brown, A., Curtice, J., Hinds, K., McCrone, D., Park, A., Sproston, K. and Surridge, P. (2001), *New Scotland, New Politics?*, Edinburgh: Polygon.

Rosie, M. and Bond, R. (2003), 'Identity matters: the personal and political significance of feeling Scottish', in C. Bromley, J. Curtice, K. Hinds and A. Park (eds), *Devolution – Scottish Answers to Scottish Questions?*, Edinburgh: Edinburgh University Press.

Watson, M. (2003), *Being English in Scotland*, Edinburgh: Edinburgh University Press.

CHAPTER 10

Islamophobia and Anglophobia in Post-Devolution Scotland

Asifa Hussain and William Miller

INTRODUCTION

Devolution was undeniably a move in a nationalist direction, even if it was intended to inoculate Scots against more extreme nationalism. Indeed, opponents had long argued that it was a step onto a 'slippery slope' that would encourage rather than discourage nationalism. In an increasingly self-conscious post-devolution Scotland, English immigrants might feel ill-at-ease like the Protestants in the Irish Republic after partition (Fedorowich 1999), or Russians in post-Soviet Central Asia or the Baltic states (Sendich and Payin 1994; Brubaker 1996: 148–78) – an unwelcome 'post-imperial' minority. During the 1990s, SNG (Siol nan Gaidheal – 'Seed of the Gael') pledged to 'unstintingly campaign against English imperialism' and spawned both Scottish Watch and the more clearly titled Settler Watch to 'expose and oppose' English 'incomers' (Hearn 2000: 65–70). And an increasingly self-conscious Scotland, increasingly focused on its own history, culture and traditions, might regard other minorities as even more culturally alien than the 'auld enemy' – especially, after '9/11', Muslims. At elite level, both advocates of devolution and the more independence-minded nationalists consistently proclaimed their commitment to a non-ethnic, inclusive, 'civic' concept of nationalism (Henderson 1999: 138). Labour 'First Minister' Jack McConnell has declared that Scotland needs more immigrants, asylum-seekers and ethnic minorities (McConnell 2003). Still more important is that leading nationalists have not so far attempted to increase their support by attacking minorities. John Swinney as SNP leader accused Labour of 'racism' in its ill-treatment of Muslim asylum-seekers (Dinwoodie et al. 2003), repeatedly describing it as a 'national shame' (Horsburgh 2003) or a 'national disgrace' (Dinwoodie 2003) – despite the fact that the 2003 Scottish Social Attitudes survey shows that a large majority of Scots are in favour of detaining asylum-seekers: 62 per cent agree that 'asylum-seekers should be kept in detention centres while their cases are being considered', and only 26 per cent disagree. There was no short-term political advantage in Swinney's accusation – though such statements help to define the SNP as a civic rather than an ethnic nationalist party, and in the longer term that may help to position the party in the mainstream of Scottish politics rather than on the extremist fringe.

This inclusive approach extends to the English as well. Current SNP leader Alex Salmond, for example, has regularly claimed to be an 'Anglophile'. To take just one from his many public statements: 'I have often pronounced myself one of the most anglophile of all Scottish Members . . . We present our case for Scotland in a positive way. We do not spend our time being antagonistic about other nations' (Salmond 1997).

Kellas (1998: 65) distinguishes between 'ethnic' nationalism, which he describes as 'in essence exclusive', stressing the ethnic group and common descent, and the civic nationalism of those such as McConnell, Swinney and Salmond, which, he says, claims to be 'inclusive in the sense that anyone can adopt the culture and join the nation'. This distinction between civic and ethnic nationalism has been drawn so often that it has become 'almost a cliché in the literature' (Kymlicka 2001: 243), often equated with Gellner's (1994: 99) distinction between 'benign' and 'nasty' nationalism. Yet there are problems with the apparently simple civic-versus-ethnic distinction. First, minorities may be either unwilling or even unable to 'adopt the culture' or 'join the nation'. Our own research suggests that the Muslim minority in Scotland is unwilling to adopt the culture (though willing to join the nation), while the English minority is psychologically unable to join the nation (though willing to adopt the culture).

Second, civic nationalism can easily degenerate into ethnic nationalism. For Gellner (1994: 1–2), 'nationalist sentiment' is at root a 'feeling of anger'; for Breuilly (1993: 5–7), although nationalism can be asserted in a 'universalist [i.e. civic] spirit', it has 'not often been so sweetly reasonable'. For Vincent (1997: 294), 'nationalism will always resist being assimilated into liberalism . . . and easily collapses into . . . shallow expressions of blood, soil and xenophobia'; for Pulzer (1988: 287; see also Porter 2000), 'nationalism degenerates . . . often inspired in its first stage by the urge to emancipate, it finds its logical conclusion in a paroxysm of destructiveness'.

Third, and perhaps the greatest problem – so easy to overlook but so difficult to resolve – is that liberal notions of tolerance and equality, while welcome, may be grossly insufficient: 'one might enjoy all the rights of citizenship and be a formally equal member of the community, and yet feel an outsider who does not belong' (Parekh 2000: 237). Minorities seek acceptance, reassurance and warmth, not simply cold, liberal, equal justice. Part of the problem is the significance of 'political symbols, images, ceremonies, collective self-understanding and views of national identity' (Parekh 2000: 203; see also Modood and Werbner 1997: 263) for that feeling of acceptance and belonging. An increasing emphasis on Scottish history, enthusiasm for films like *Braveheart* (Edensor 1997: 147), claims that the Scottish Parliament is not new but an old parliament that merely 'adjourned on 25 March 1707' and is now 'reconvened' (*Scottish Parliament Debate*, 1999), or even John Swinney's own call to use Scotland's 'patron saint' to promote the new Scotland (Swinney, 2002), are necessarily exclusionist for those whose ethnic culture and identity makes it impossible for them to identify with historic Scotland – as distinct from contemporary Scotland.

Last, even if political elites take greater care to ensure that political symbols are inclusive, and successfully avoid unfortunate lapses such as over-enthusiasm for Christian saints or military victories over the English, minorities can be made 'to feel outsiders who do not belong' by the way they are treated by ordinary people in everyday life. If minorities feel that they are regarded by the general public as a burden on the country's resources, as social untouchables or as a disloyal element, they are likely to feel excluded. Street-level prejudice can be just as alienating as elite-level discrimination. The purpose of this chapter is to investigate street-level prejudice towards two key minorities in post-devolution Scotland, Muslims and English immigrants. It will show how far the inclusive civic nationalism of political elites reaches down to the street, how well it can cope with minorities that cannot 'adopt the culture' or 'join the nation', and whether it extends equally to both these minorities.

These minorities constitute the largest 'visible' and 'invisible' minorities in post-devolution Scotland. According to the 2001 Scottish census, English immigrants constitute 8 per cent of Scotland's population, rising to 12 per cent across the whole of the capital city, Edinburgh, and to 18 per cent across all of rural/small-town southern Scotland. By contrast, Muslims (mainly, by self-description, ethnic Pakistanis) constitute just over 1 per cent of Scotland's population, but they are more 'visible' – by dress code as well as skin colour. Their visibility is enhanced by their concentration in the cities, especially Glasgow, and by generally increasing awareness of Muslim minorities since '9/11' and the invasion of Iraq. Our own research shows that their primary identification is 'Muslim' rather than any territorial identity – Scottish, British or even Pakistani.

For direct measurements of Islamophobia and Anglophobia among 'ordinary' or 'majority' Scots, we need to focus on something less than the entire population resident in Scotland. In particular, it would be absurd to include English immigrants themselves in any calculation of Anglophobia. They are so numerous as well as so distinctive that including English immigrants and their partners – together about 12 per cent of the resident population – would grossly underestimate Anglophobia. So, to measure Islamophobia and Anglophobia in Scotland, we focus on the attitudes of 'majority Scots' – defined to exclude Muslims (only 1 per cent of the population), English immigrants (8 per cent) and those whose partners are English immigrants (another 4 per cent). Just 1,158 of the 1,508 respondents in the 2003 Scottish Social Attitudes survey sample fit this tight definition of 'majority Scots'. The difference between 'majority Scots' and the population of Scotland (including English immigrants and their partners) is evident from a tabulation of Moreno identities – that is, whether they feel more Scottish or more British, as shown in Table 10.1.

Table 10.1 The identities of 'majority Scots' and others

	'Majority Scots'	Others	All
	%	%	%
Scottish, not British	36	15	31
More Scottish than British	38	17	34
Equally Scottish and British	21	24	22
More British than Scottish	2	11	4
British, not Scottish	1	13	4
Other identity	1	14	4
None of these	*	5	1
Sample size	1,158	350	1,508

* = less than 0.5 per cent.

It should be unnecessary to point out that this procedure is a methodological requirement only, driven by the need for clarity. We do not ourselves equate 'majority Scots' with 'real Scots' or 'true Scots', for example – though many 'majority Scots' do make that equation, recognising only people 'like themselves' as being 'truly' Scottish.

EQUALITY

'Majority Scots' are overwhelmingly committed to the liberal concept of ethnic equality – for English immigrants as well as Muslims. About 80 per cent support the extension of anti-discrimination laws from race and gender to both religion and sub-UK origin – specifically to cover discrimination against Muslims or against English immigrants.

Majority Scots are not opposed to having both Muslim and English immigrant MSPs in the Scottish Parliament but are not enthusiastic either (see Table 10.2). Over half do not think that it matters – a view that in fact is similar to that held by English immigrants themselves but certainly not by Muslims. Those majority Scots who do have a view divide in favour of Muslim MSPs by over two to one but are evenly divided about English immigrant MSPs. (At the time of the survey, there was in fact a dispro-portionately large number of English immigrant MSPs in the Scottish Parliament, but not any Muslims.)

Table 10.2 **Majority Scots' views on anti-discrimination laws and minority MSPs**

	Views in respect of	
	Muslims	English
	%	%
Should be a law against discrimination		
Definitely should	65	64
Probably should	16	15
Probably should not	8	9
Definitely should not	6	8
View on having MSPs		
Should be	31	22
Does not matter either way	52	57
Should not be	14	19
Sample size	1,158	1,158

But we are concerned with something that goes beyond liberal equalities – with recognition and respect or rejection and suspicion, with warmth and acceptance rather than cold justice.

RECOGNITION

There are some reasons to expect that Anglophobia among 'majority Scots' might be less extensive or less virulent than Islamophobia. Muslims are not cut off from the Scottish majority, but they are somewhat less closely connected by ties of friendship and far less by ties of family. Since English immigrants are far more numerous than Muslims in Scotland – roughly ten times as numerous according to the 2001 census – that alone might explain why most 'majority Scots' know someone who is English but only half know a Muslim.

Indeed, as Table 10.3 shows, twice as many 'know' an English person as 'know' a Muslim. But *four* times as many have an English 'friend' as a Pakistani friend, and twenty times as many have English family connections. A remarkable 40 per cent of 'majority Scots' (who by our strict definition exclude those with English immigrant partners) have an English relative, while only 2 per cent have a Pakistani relative. (Among all those born and resident in Scotland, 44 per cent have either an English partner or other English relatives.)

Table 10.3   Majority Scots' links with minorities

	Who is	
	Muslim	English
	%	%
Know someone	49	93
Have partner	*	2
Have someone in family	2	40
Have friend	15	60
Know someone else	32	38
Know 'not very much/nothing at all' about Muslims in Scotland	86	n/a
Sample size	1,158	1,158

Note: Those with English immigrant partners are excluded by definition from 'majority Scots', but a few described their partner as 'English' nonetheless.
* Only two respondents described their partner as Muslim.
n/a = not applicable.

But while friendship and family might tie majority Scots more closely to the English than to Muslims, their perceptions of what it takes to be a 'true Scot' tie them more closely to Scottish Muslims than to English immigrants. The criteria used to determine whether someone else is a 'true Brit' or a 'true Scot' vary from person to person, but among those most frequently cited are birthplace, parentage and race (McCrone et al. 1998; Paterson et al. 2001: 117–19). Majority Scots stress the importance of birthplace: 57 per cent feel that to be 'truly Scottish' it is essential to be born in Scotland, while only 33 per cent disagree (see Table 10.4). But they put little weight on race: only 16 per cent feel that it is essential to be white, while 69 per cent disagree. Although neither ethnic Pakistanis nor English immigrants are mentioned explicitly in these questions, Pakistanis are not 'white' and English immigrants are by definition not Scottish by birth (although almost half the Pakistanis are). Since Scots put so much more stress on birthplace than on skin colour, it follows that majority Scots could more easily recognise ethnic

Pakistanis as Scots than recognise English immigrants as Scots – and we have no reason to think that majority Scots would object to that inference from their answers. (See Chapter 9 for a discussion of the importance of accent, another marker which would make it easier for Scots to recognise ethnic Pakistanis than English immigrants as truly Scottish.)

Failure to qualify as a 'true Scot' has implications in the eyes of at least some majority Scots. SNP policy is to give full citizenship and a Scottish passport to all who live in Scotland on the day of independence. But 29 per cent of majority Scots would deny 'a Scottish passport and full Scottish citizenship' to those who they felt were not 'truly Scottish'.

Table 10.4 Majority Scots' views on what it takes to be 'truly Scottish'

	%
To be truly Scottish, it is necessary to be born in Scotland	
Agree strongly	15
Agree	42
Disagree	27
Disagree strongly	5
To be truly Scottish, it is necessary to be white	
Agree strongly	4
Agree	12
Disagree	50
Disagree strongly	19
Only 'true Scots' should get a Scottish passport and full Scottish citizenship	29
Sample size	*1,158*

Even cultural similarity might not count in favour of the English. We asked on a seven-point scale whether it was 'better for a country if almost everyone shares the same customs, religions and traditions' or 'better for a country if there is a variety of different customs, religions and traditions'. Majority Scots come down overwhelmingly on the side of cultural variety. As many as 66 per cent opt for one of the points in the scale that signify support for cultural variety against only 16 per cent who prefer uniformity. Indeed, the single most popular choice (backed by 26 per cent) is the most extreme point at the 'variety' end of the scale.

Measuring and comparing phobias

We can measure the extent of street-level phobias by using five strictly comparable indicators of Islamophobia and Anglophobia. Since the wording of these questions is critical, we reproduce it in detail. We began:

People from lots of different backgrounds live in Scotland. I would now like to ask you some questions about two of these groups – English people and Muslims. By Muslims I mean people who follow the Islamic faith, many of whom in Scotland are Pakistani.

To measure Islamophobia, we then asked respondents to place themselves on various five- or seven-point scales:

M1: Muslims who come to live in Scotland (1) take jobs, housing and healthcare from other people in Scotland or (7) contribute a lot in terms of hard work and much-needed skills (seven-point numerical scale)

M2: Muslims in Scotland (1) are really committed to Scotland or (7) could never be really committed to Scotland (seven-point numerical scale)

M3: How much do you agree or disagree: Scottish Muslims are more loyal to other Muslims around the world than they are to other people in this country? (five-point scale from strongly agree to strongly disagree)

M4: How much do you agree or disagree: Scotland would begin to lose its identity if more Muslims came to live in Scotland? (five-point scale from strongly agree to strongly disagree)

M5: How would you feel if a close relative of yours married or formed a long-term relationship with a Muslim? (five-point scale from very happy to very unhappy)

Interleaved between these questions were corresponding questions about English immigrants, generally substituting 'English people' for 'Muslims', but in the third question substituting 'loyal to England' for 'loyal to other Muslims around the world', and in the fifth referring to 'with an English person now living in Scotland'. While the question-wording never uses the brief and accurate but unfamiliar phrase 'English immigrants', it always uses a phrase that indicates that the question refers to English immigrants rather than the English in England. That is particularly important in the fifth question, which emphasises forming a relationship with an English person in Scotland, thereby ensuring that the question addresses people's attitudes towards the relationship per se rather than the possibility that it might mean the relative moving away.

These two sets of the five questions provide a comparative index of Islamophobia and Anglophobia. Islamophobia or Anglophobia is indicated by feeling on balance that Muslims/English 'take jobs, housing and healthcare from other people', that they 'could never be really committed to Britain/Scotland', that they 'are more loyal to other Muslims around the world/in England' than they are to 'this country', that 'Scotland would begin to lose its identity' if more came to live in Scotland, and that they would 'feel unhappy if a close relative married or formed a long-term relationship with a Muslim/English person now living in Scotland'.

In addition, we have one indicator that applies specifically to Muslims after '9/11' and is not generalisable to other anti-minority phobias:

> M6: *How much do you agree or disagree: Muslims living in Britain have done a great deal to condemn Islamic terrorism? (five-point scale from strongly agree to strongly disagree)*

The Islamophobic response to this question is of course disagreement.

Economic resentment

As Table 10.5 indicates, relatively few majority Scots actually express economic resentment of minorities taking jobs, housing and healthcare. Only 21 per cent feel that Muslims take jobs, housing and healthcare from people in Scotland, while just 13 per cent express the same view about English immigrants. By contrast, 50 per cent take a clearly positive view of Muslims and 60 per cent about English immigrants. So economic resentment is low in general, but is particularly low with regard to English immigrants.

Table 10.5 Economic resentment among majority Scots

	View about	
	Muslims	English
	%	%
Muslims/English people who come to Scotland . . .		
take jobs, housing, healthcare	8	3
	4	3
	9	7
(mid-point)	24	23
	25	29
	16	21
contribute a lot in terms of hard work and skills	9	10
Sample size	*1,158*	*1,158*

Commitment and loyalty

More doubt the minorities' commitment to Scotland: 34 per cent take a negative view of Muslims' commitment to Scotland and 30 per cent about

English immigrants' commitment (see Table 10.6). By contrast, only 30 per cent take a clearly positive view of Muslims and 38 per cent about English immigrants' commitment. So, on balance, majority Scots have a marginally positive view of English immigrants' commitment and a marginally negative view of Muslims' commitment. They also take a marginally – but no more than marginally – negative view of British Muslims in regard to condemning Islamic terrorism.

Most of all, however, majority Scots suspect that the minorities' primary loyalties lie outside Scotland – with 'other Muslims around the world' or with 'England': four times as many majority Scots take a negative view of the minorities' loyalty to Scotland as take a positive view. And, by this measure, majority Scots doubt the loyalty of English immigrants more than they doubt the loyalty of Muslims.

Table 10.6 Majority Scots' perceptions of the commitment and loyalty of minorities

	Perceptions of	
	Muslims	English
	%	%
Muslims/English people living in Scotland . . .		
are really committed to Scotland	4	6
	11	16
	15	16
(mid-point)	26	28
	15	14
	8	8
could never be really committed to Scotland	11	8
Muslims living in Britain have done a great deal to condemn Islamic terrorism		
Agree strongly	3	n/a
Agree	23	n/a
Disagree	25	n/a
Disagree strongly	7	n/a
Muslims/English people are more loyal to other Muslims/to England than to Scotland		
Agree strongly	10	11
Agree	33	51
Disagree	11	14
Disagree strongly	*	*
Sample size	1,158	1,158

n/a = not applicable.
* = less than 0.5 per cent.

Fears for national identity

As Table 10.7 shows, majority Scots are apprehensive that 'Scotland would begin to lose its identity if more English/Muslim people came to live in Scotland'. But, despite the huge imbalance in the numbers of English immigrants and Muslims already living in Scotland, majority Scots are rather less apprehensive about the impact on Scotland's national identity of a further influx of English immigrants than they are about an increase in the number of Muslims: 42 per cent take a negative view of Muslims coming to Scotland, but only 34 per cent of more English immigrants. By contrast, 37 per cent take a positive view of Muslims coming to Scotland, and 46 per cent of more English immigrants. So, on balance, majority Scots have a moderately positive view of further English immigration and a marginally negative view towards more Muslims coming to Scotland.

Table 10.7 Majority Scots' fears for national identity

	View about	
	Muslims	English
	%	%
Scotland would begin to lose its identity if more Muslims/English people came to live in Scotland		
Agree strongly	11	7
Agree	31	27
Disagree	33	41
Disagree strongly	4	5
Sample size	1,158	1,158

Social exclusion

There is scant evidence of support for social exclusion in the workplace: only 4 per cent say that they would be unhappy to work beside a suitably qualified person from a different racial or ethnic background. And 29 per cent say that they would be not merely 'happy' but 'very happy' to do so. Equally, so far as relationships are concerned (see Table 10.8), while most Scots doubt the loyalty of English immigrants to Scotland and many regard them as a threat to Scotland's own national identity, only a mere 3 per cent of majority Scots say that they would be at all 'unhappy' to have a close relative form a long-term relationship with an English immigrant. Social exclusion is not a part of Anglophobia, just as indeed it is not of sectarianism in Scotland. (Three per cent of Catholics would be unhappy about acquiring a Protestant relative, while 5 per cent of those brought up in the Church of Scotland would be unhappy about acquiring a Catholic relative.)

Table 10.8 Majority Scots' views on relationships

| | View about | | | |
	Muslim	English	Catholic	Protestant
	%	%	%	%
If a close relative formed a long-term relationship with Catholic/Protestant/ Muslim/English person now living in Scotland, I would feel				
Very happy	17	23	30	31
Happy	28	43	35	38
Unhappy	15	2	3	1
Very unhappy	7	1	1	*
Sample size	1,158	1,158	1,158	1,158

* = less than 0.5 per cent.

But there is much more evidence of social exclusion in regard to relationships with Muslims. As many as 22 per cent of majority Scots would be 'unhappy' if a 'close relative' married or formed a long-term relationship with a Muslim. The degree of social exclusion should not be overstated, however: 45 per cent said that they would be at least happy to acquire a Muslim relative, including 17 per cent who would be 'very happy'.

PERCEPTIONS OF CONFLICT

Large numbers of majority Scots regard conflicts between Scots and English, Muslims and non-Muslims, or Protestants and Catholics as at least 'fairly serious'. But, by any measure, they rate conflict with the English as far less serious than the sectarian conflict between Catholics and Protestants. They are less clear in their assessment of the conflict between Muslims and non-Muslims in Scotland, however. Relatively few rate Muslim/non-Muslim conflict as 'very serious', but at the same time relatively few rate it as 'not very serious', and – in contrast to the sectarian and Scots/English conflicts – there is a significant number who simply 'do not know'.

On the other hand majority Scots are very clear that Muslim/non-Muslim conflict in England is far more serious than in Scotland, and that the conflict 'around the world' is, in turn, far more serious still than in England. As Table 10.9 shows, the numbers of majority Scots who rate it as 'very serious' rise from a mere 3 per cent with regard to Scotland, to 12 per cent with regard to England, and to 28 per cent with regard to the rest of the world.

Table 10.9 Majority Scots' perceptions of inter-ethnic conflicts

	Between Protestants and Catholics	Between Scots and English	Between Muslims and non-Muslims		
			in Scotland	in England	around the world
	%	%	%	%	%
Very serious	10	5	3	12	28
Fairly serious	31	20	32	43	44
Not very serious	51	66	46	21	12
No conflict	8	8	4	1	1
Don't know	1	1	15	22	15
Sample size	1,158	1,158	1,158	1,158	1,158

Perceptions of conflict are not quite the same as phobias, though they may be closely related as either cause or effect. But this pattern of perceptions of conflict would at least be consistent with greater Islamophobia than Anglophobia within Scotland, and with greater Islamophobia in England than in Scotland.

OVERALL INDICES OF ISLAMOPHOBIA AND ANGLOPHOBIA

Overall indices of Islamophobia and Anglophobia are crude but useful measures for comparing the two phobias and for simplifying the discussion that follows of how they vary across different social and political groups among majority Scots. To construct these summary indices, we use the five fully comparable questions asked about both Muslims and English immigrants that we introduced earlier. For each question, we exclude those with no opinion or with neutral opinions and calculate the percentage who take the Islamophobic/Anglophobic side as a percentage of the total who take one side or the other.

That provides very simple, easily interpretable and fully comparable measures of the two phobias:

Index of Islamophobia = the average, across the five questions, of the
percentages who hold negative rather than positive views of Muslims.
Index of Anglophobia = the average, across the five questions, of the
percentages who hold negative rather than positive views of English
immigrants.

Excluding those with no opinion or mixed opinions, an average of
49 per cent across the five questions hold negative rather than positive
views of Muslims (Islamophobia), and an average of 38 per cent hold
negative rather than positive views of English immigrants (Anglophobia).
So, on these strictly comparable indicators, Islamophobia in Scotland runs
just 11 per cent ahead of Anglophobia. (A similar calculation using British
Social Attitudes survey data on the same five questions in England shows
that Islamophobia in England runs 14 per cent ahead of Islamophobia in
Scotland. See Hussain and Miller 2004).

How Islamophobia and Anglophobia vary

Generally narrow, limited and parochial backgrounds are likely to foster
narrow, limited, inward-looking and parochial attitudes. Too much focus
on the familiar may stimulate a fear of the foreign, the different, the 'other'.
Nationalism need not entail xenophobia, but it has often done so. And
xenophobia tends to be indiscriminate, targeting anyone and everyone who
is 'not like us'. Consequently, all anti-minority phobias may vary together,
and in particular the same factors that make people relatively Islamophobic
are likely to make them Anglophobic.

But, while the English might be judged less culturally different from
majority Scots than Muslims, England has a far larger role than Pakistan or
Islam in defining Scottish identity itself. So, cultural parochialism –
indicated by age and generation, low education and lack of minority
knowledge or friendship, along with religion perhaps – might be expected
to have a greater impact on Islamophobia than on Anglophobia. Yet, at the
same time, historical or political nationalism – indicated by exclusively
Scottish identities or SNP voting – might be expected to have a greater
impact on Anglophobia than on Islamophobia.

The impacts of age and generation, education, knowledge and contact
with minorities are universal. There is nothing uniquely Scottish about
them. We would expect to find similar patterns in many societies. But the
impact of Scottish nationalism on Anglophobia and Islamophobia is
uniquely Scottish and is important for the insight it gives us into the
character of both Scottish national identity and political nationalism in

Scotland. It provides the critical test of the claim that twenty-first-century Scottish nationalism – unlike many other nationalisms – is civic, inclusive and benign.

Age and generation

Conceptually, it is important to distinguish between the impact of age and the impact of generation (sometimes termed 'cohort'), though in a single-wave cross-sectional survey age and generation are both measured by asking respondents how old they are. Despite the measurement problem, we can at least bear the conceptual distinction in mind and look at the shape of the relationship between years of age and phobias. If there is a steady tendency for older people to be more phobic, we might speculate that this was the consequence of aging. But, if there were a sharp difference that coincided with significantly different periods in which different people had grown up, we might speculate that this was a consequent of the different experiences of different cohorts or generations. Statistics alone cannot determine which is the correct explanation – the impact of aging or the impact of significantly different experiences. But we do not have to rely on statistics alone. We can, should, indeed must bring outside knowledge to bear on the raw survey statistics.

Age and generation have very little impact on Anglophobia. Only one of the five indicators of Anglophobia – doubts about the English immigrants' commitment to Scotland – varies consistently across the age cohorts. That contrasts with the much greater impact of age and especially of generation on Islamophobia in Scotland (see Table 10.10).

There are certainly some indisputable generation effects. Older people are far less likely than the young to claim some knowledge of Muslims or to have a Muslim friend. It is beyond reason to suppose that this is because older people have forgotten what they once knew about Muslims or have lost the friendships they once had with them. Instead, these patterns reflect the fact that they grew up in a society where there were far fewer Muslims and far less interaction between Muslims and non-Muslims: it is the imprint of history.

Overall, older people are 20 per cent more Islamophobic, but only 6 per cent more Anglophobic, than the young. But the pattern is more complex than that, in two ways. First, older people are actually *less* likely (15 per cent less) than the young to fear that Muslims might take jobs, healthcare and housing from other Scots. But older people have greater doubts about Muslims' commitment to Scotland. They are much more apprehensive (21 per cent more) that Scotland would begin to lose its

Table 10.10 Impact of age and generation on Anglophobia and Islamophobia

			Age group			Impact
	18–34	35–44	45–54	55–64	65+	
	%	%	%	%	%	
Agree that Muslims take jobs, housing and healthcare from others in Scotland	37	29	26	32	22	−15
Unhappy at relative forming relationship with Muslim	16	23	19	48	64	+48
Anglophobia average	35	39	37	39	41	+6
Islamophobia average	42	46	45	55	62	+20
Know nothing about Muslims	26	20	22	32	44	+18
Have a Muslim friend	24	18	19	8	4	+20
At least 'fairly serious' conflict between Muslims and non-Muslims in Scotland	50	44	38	36	37	+13
Sample size	255	237	193	206	264	

In each case, figures are based only on those respondents who give either an Islamophobic/Anglophobic or an Islamophile/Anglophile response. The 'impact' shows the difference between those aged 65 and over and those aged under 35.

identity if there were an influx of Muslims, and they are much more likely (24 per cent more) to feel that 'true Scots' must be white. And, by the huge margin of 48 per cent, older people are much more unhappy at the thought of acquiring a Muslim relative. Secondly, the variation with age is not smooth and continuous. On the three indicators which display the greatest variation, there is a sharp 'step effect' at around age 55, implying a generational effect rather than an age effect.

The pattern points to a cultural difference between the generations that affects cultural or racial cosmopolitanism (especially intermarriage) but is partially offset by older people feeling less fear of competition for jobs, probably by reason of age (as they leave the job market) rather than generation.

This tentative conclusion gains some corroboration from the pattern of age-variation in friendship, knowledge and perceived conflict. Older people have much less knowledge of, or friendship with, minorities. That is especially true for friendship with Muslims. And, again, there is a sharp generational cleavage at age 55 – especially with respect to Muslims. But, at the same time, older people are less likely to perceive serious conflict with either minority – and again especially with respect to Muslims.

These patterns fit the model of a culture-based generational cleavage at age 55, offset by less fear of economic competition and conflict among older people, by reason of age rather than generation.

Education

Friendship with, and knowledge of, minorities varies more sharply with education than with anything else. As can be seen in Table 10.11, compared to those with no qualifications, graduates are 37 per cent more likely to have an English friend and over five times more likely to have a Muslim friend (32 per cent compared to only 6 per cent). And those without qualifications are 25 per cent more Anglophobic than graduates as well as 34 per cent more Islamophobic. Both phobias run at over twice the level among the unqualified as among graduates.

The impact is large; and, with one reservation, the level of phobia decreases the higher the level of educational attainment. The sole exception to this generalisation is that those with 'higher education below degree level' display greater levels of both Islamophobia and Anglophobia than those with Higher Grade (or equivalent) school qualifications.

The impact is also large on every individual indicator of Islamophobia and Anglophobia, with just one exception: attitudes of social exclusion towards English immigrants remain very low at all levels of education. The

Table 10.11 Impact of education on Anglophobia and Islamophobia

	Highest educational qualification						Impact
	Degree	Higher education below degree	Higher Grade	Standard Grades 1–3	Standard Grades 4–7	None	
	%	%	%	%	%	%	
Anglophobia average	22	35	30	42	45	47	+25
Islamophobia average	28	44	38	54	57	62	+34
Have an English friend	78	71	66	66	56	41	+37
Have a Muslim friend	32	21	20	12	8	6	+26
Unhappy to acquire an English relative	3	2	1	6	8	7	+4
Unhappy to acquire a Muslim relative	17	24	11	31	38	56	+39
Sample size	131	170	169	145	189	342	

In each case, figures are based only on those respondents who give either an Islamophobic/Anglophobic or an Islamophile/Anglophile response. The 'Impact' shows the difference between those with a degree and those with no educational qualifications.

contrast with attitudes of social exclusion towards Muslims is striking. Among graduates, only 3 per cent would be unhappy to acquire an English relative and only 17 per cent unhappy to acquire a Muslim relative. Among those with the least education, the numbers unhappy to acquire an English relative remain very low (at 7 per cent), but the numbers unhappy to acquire a Muslim relative rise to 56 per cent.

Contacts with and knowledge of minorities

As we might expect from the above, having a minority friend makes a difference to the attitudes of majority Scots towards minorities. Having a Muslim friend reduces Islamophobia by 21 per cent, and having an English friend reduces Anglophobia by 11 per cent. Much less obviously, however, having a friend in either minority reduces phobia towards both. Those with an English friend are 12 per cent less Islamophobic, while those with a Muslim one are 11 per cent less Anglophobic. That is partly because those who have a friend in one minority are much more likely also to have a friend in the other: 21 per cent of those with English friends also have Muslim friends; by contrast, only 6 per cent of those without English friends have Muslim friends. Conversely, 85 per cent of those with Muslim friends also have English friends, while only 56 per cent of those without Muslim friends have English friends.

But knowledge is far more important than friendship. There are so few Muslims in Scotland that many majority Scots can be sympathetic towards such a small minority without actually having a personal friend within it. It is those who lack knowledge – as well as friendship – who are prey to the most intense phobias.

Most Scots know something about the English, but many – by their own account – do not know much about Muslims. Compared to those who have a Muslim friend, those who say they 'know nothing at all' about Muslims are 34 per cent more Islamophobic. But they are also 25 per cent more Islamophobic than those who, irrespective of whether they have Muslim friends, know at least 'quite a lot' about Muslims. Most of the variation in Islamophobia occurs across levels of knowledge rather than friendship.

Religion

Most majority Scots divide into just three religious categories – Presbyterians (overwhelmingly Church of Scotland), Catholics and the largest category, the irreligious. Overall, they differ very little on Anglophobia, though both Catholics (by 17 per cent) and Presbyterians (by 11 per cent) are more inclined than the irreligious to doubt English immigrants' commitment to Scotland. Catholics are also the least likely to have an English friend.

But those of different religious persuasions differ more on Islamophobia – especially on whether Scotland 'would begin to lose its identity' if more Muslims came, and on social exclusion. On these two matters, Presbyterians are the most Islamophobic, Catholics less so. As Table 10.12 shows, Presbyterians are 23 per cent more concerned than the irreligious about the impact of Muslim immigration on Scotland's identity and 29 per cent more unhappy at the prospect of acquiring a Muslim relative. From the sixteenth-century to the nineteenth, Scotland was defined primarily by its Presbyterianism rather than by geography (see, for example, Findlay 2005). Although the simple equation of Scotland with Presbyterianism was finally destroyed by Irish Catholic immigration, Presbyterians apparently retain a stronger concept of there being a unified national culture than do Catholics, who necessarily had to pioneer multiculturalism in Scotland.

At the same time, however, on other matters – on perceptions of loyalty and commitment to contemporary Scotland, and on jobs – Catholics are the most Islamophobic, Presbyterians less so. As a result, overall, both Catholics and Presbyterians are both around 13 per cent more Islamophobic than the irreligious. The impact of religion is thus quite powerful within certain restricted issue-domains, but overall it has far less impact than education.

Table 10.12 Impact of religion on majority Scots' Anglophobia and Islamophobia

	Religion			Impact
	Presbyterian	Catholic	None	
	%	%	%	
Anglophobia average	40	41	37	+4
Islamophobia average	56	54	42	+14
Agree that Scotland would begin to lose its identity if more Muslims came	65	54	42	+23
Unhappy to acquire an English relative	6	3	4	+3
Unhappy to acquire a Muslim relative	47	33	18	+29
Have an English friend	57	51	64	+13
Have a Muslim friend	9	17	18	+9
Sample size	439	131	490	

In each case, figures are based only on those respondents who give either an Islamophobic/ Anglophobic or an Islamophile/Anglophile response. The 'Impact' shows the largest difference between any pair of columns in that row.

Social nationalism: sub-state identities

As Table 10.13 shows, compared to those who identify equally with Britain and Scotland, those who identify themselves as Scottish but not British are 13 per cent more Anglophobic but scarcely any more (only 4 per cent more) Islamophobic. The impact of national identity is thus relatively weak. However, in contrast to the impact of education, which has significantly more impact on Islamophobia than on Anglophobia, it evidently has a greater impact on Anglophobia than on Islamophobia.

It appears that those with a Scottish identity are focused on the historic enemy, the 'significant other' that helps define Scottish identity, rather than on a minority that differs more in terms of race, religion or culture from the majority Scots. The pattern of attitudes towards social exclusion is particularly striking. Unsurprisingly, those who say that they are Scottish and not British are 5 per cent more unhappy at the prospect of acquiring an English relative. In contrast, they are actually 2 per cent less unhappy than those who feel equally Scottish and British at the prospect of acquiring a Muslim relative. The figure of 2 per cent is scarcely significant statistically – but that is the point: it is a case of 'the dog that did not bark'.

There is a further contrast of some significance for our understanding of the impact of national identity: among the 'majority English' in England (defined as majority 'white', non-Muslim), an exclusively English national identity increases Islamophobia in general, and social exclusion towards Muslims in particular, by 20 per cent (Hussain and Miller 2004). Those who have discovered similar contrasts between the impact of English nationalism in England and Scottish nationalism in Scotland on attitudes towards asylum-seekers, 'ethnic minorities', blacks or Asians have been tempted to characterise English nationalism as more ethnic or 'nasty', and Scottish nationalism as more civic and 'benign'. If we had focused only on Islamophobia, which proves to be almost uncorrelated with Scottish nationalism, we too would have concluded that Scottish nationalism is remarkably uncorrelated with anti-minority phobias. But it does correlate with Anglophobia. Moreover, the existence of Anglophobia may help to explain why Scottish nationalism is so uncorrelated with Islamophobia. Muslims in Scotland may benefit from being 'not-English' and thus, in the eyes of majority Scots, a little bit more 'like us' than they would be in the absence of Anglophobia. They do at least speak English with a Scottish accent.

Table 10.13 Impact of national identity on majority Scots' Anglophobia and Islamophobia

	National Identity			Impact
	Equally Scottish and British	More Scottish than British	Scottish, not British	
	%	%	%	
Anglophobia average	33	35	46	+ 13
Islamophobia average	50	46	54	+ 4
Unhappy to acquire an English relative	3	3	8	+ 5
Unhappy to acquire a Muslim relative	38	28	36	− 2
Sample size	*247*	*431*	*437*	

In each case, figures are based only on those respondents who give either an Islamophobic/ Anglophobic or an Islamophile/Anglophile response. The 'Impact' shows the difference between those who say they are 'Scottish, not British' and those who say they are 'Equally Scottish and British'. Those who say they are 'More British than Scottish' or 'British, not Scottish' are excluded from the table.

Political nationalism: partisanship

The voting choices of majority Scots at the 2001 general election provide us with an indicator of political nationalism. Table 10.14 demonstrates that both Anglophobia and Islamophobia are lowest among Liberal Democrat voters in Scotland. But, while Islamophobia is highest among Conservative voters, Anglophobia is highest among SNP voters. Anglophobia among SNP voters is 10 per cent higher than among Conservatives (and 16 per cent higher than among Liberal Democrats). Conversely, Islamophobia is 7 per cent higher among Conservatives than among SNP voters (and 20 per cent higher than among Liberal Democrats). (Non-voters come second only to SNP voters on Anglophobia, and second only to Conservatives on Islamophobia.)

Patterns of personal friendship tell the same story: Conservatives are 11 per cent more likely than SNP voters to have an English friend, but 3 per cent less likely than SNP voters to have a Muslim friend. And Liberal Democrats are the most likely to have both English and Muslim friends. Similarly, SNP voters would be the least happy to acquire an English relative: 12 per cent would be unhappy. And Conservative voters would be the least happy to acquire a Muslim relative: 47 per cent would be unhappy. By contrast, only 2 per cent of Liberal Democrats would be unhappy to acquire an English relative and 24 per cent unhappy to acquire a Muslim relative.

Many English people in Scotland vote Conservative, of course, and few vote SNP. So, it is important to stress that our analysis of the link between party support and Anglophobia is based – like all our other analyses of Anglophobia and Islamophobia – entirely on 'majority Scots', defined to exclude both English immigrants and their partners. So, our finding shows that it is Conservatives from among the 'majority Scots' (born in Scotland and with Scottish-born partners, if any) who are less Anglophobic than other majority Scots.

Table 10.14 Impact of vote choice on Anglophobia and Islamophobia

Vote at 2001 general election

	Conservative	Labour	Liberal Democrat	SNP	Did not vote
	%	%	%	%	%
Anglophobia average	33	38	27	43	40
Islamophobia average	55	48	35	48	51
Have an English friend	66	53	75	55	66
Have a Muslim friend	11	11	26	14	23
Unhappy to acquire an English relative	1	4	2	12	4
Unhappy to acquire a Muslim relative	47	32	24	36	25
Sample size	*138*	*432*	*83*	*163*	*255*

In each case, figures are based only on those respondents who give either an Islamophobic/Anglophobic or an Islamophile/Anglophile response.

A MULTIVARIATE ANALYSIS

We can usefully summarise and confirm our findings with a multivariate analysis. For that, we have constructed five-point scales for each of the elements of our indices of Islamophobia and Anglophobia. Some were already five-point agree/disagree scales (agree strongly, agree, neither, disagree, disagree strongly). Others were seven-point semantic differential scales running, for example, from 'Muslims are really committed to Scotland' to 'Muslims could never be really committed to Scotland', with the intermediate points unlabelled. In these latter cases, we merged the most extreme points with the adjacent categories to convert them into five-point scales. Numerical values running from minus two to plus two were assigned to each scale, with plus two being the most phobic. Those with mixed opinions, or no opinion, were placed at zero, the centre-point of the scale. Then, by averaging these scores across the five questions, we acquire composite Islamophobic and Anglophobic scales that run from minus two to plus two.

Correlations between the components of each composite scale proved to be uniformly high. The individual items contributing to the Islamophobia scale correlate on average at over 0.70 with the composite Islamophobia scale; and items contributing to the Anglophobia scale correlate on average at over 0.64 with the composite Anglophobia scale.

More interestingly, the two composite scales correlate at 0.65 with each other. We have already seen that the categories of people who are relatively Islamophobic tend also to be relatively Anglophobic. Now we know that this is true for individuals as well as categories: individual people who are relatively Islamophobic are likely to be relatively Anglophobic as well – and the correlation, at 0.65, is remarkably strong.

We use regression to see which of the influences we have considered actually explain phobias best, and which are redundant once more powerful explanations are taken into account. To do this, we predict levels of Islamophobia and Anglophobia from the following:

1. *age* both as a seven-point scale from young to old, and as a dichotomous generation-marker contrasting those above and below age 55.
2. *education* as a three-point scale distinguishing those with a degree, those with lower school qualifications (or none) and those with either higher school qualifications or higher education below university degree level.
3. *minority contacts* measured by three variables: a four-point scale of knowledge about Muslims, and two indicators of whether or not the respondent had a Muslim friend and/or an English friend.
4. *religion* measured by three separate indicators of whether the respondent was or was not Presbyterian, Catholic or irreligious.
5. *national identity* measured by a five-point scale that runs from exclusively Scottish to exclusively British.
6. *vote choice* measured by four separate indicators of whether or not the respondent voted Conservative, Labour or SNP in 2001 or abstained.

As we can see in Table 10.15, the multiple regressions confirm that the most important influence on both phobias is education. But, even taking that into account, other factors have their own independent and additional impact. Islamophobia is greater among those who know little or nothing about Islam. It is lower among those who have a Muslim friend and among those who are irreligious. But most significant is the factor that does *not* exert any substantial impact: Scottish nationalism. By contrast, Scottish identity comes close to rivalling low education as an influence towards Anglophobia. Beyond that, having an English friend reduces Anglophobia by about as much as having a Muslim friend reduces Islamophobia. And lack of knowledge about Islam probably indicates a broader rejection of the 'other', for it has as much impact on Anglophobia as on Islamophobia.

Table 10.15   A multivariate analysis of Islamophobia and Anglophobia in Scotland

Independent variables	Beta coefficient for dependent variable	
	Islamophobia	Anglophobia
Degree	−0.26	−0.25
Not religious	−0.13	*
Knows little or nothing about Muslims	0.11	0.10
Has a Muslim friend	−0.10	*
Scottish, not British	*	0.17
Has an English friend	*	−0.13
R^2	15	17

* Beta coefficient less than 0.10. Those variables that had beta coefficients of less than 0.10 in both analyses are not shown. All entries shown are significant at the 1 per cent level.

Regression is better at demolishing hypotheses than generating them. In addition to showing that Scottish identity has no important impact on Islamophobia, it also shows (by their absence from Table 10.15) that age and generation do *not* have an independent impact once education, personal contacts and Scottish identity have been taken into account. And nor does political nationalism, once Scottish identity has been taken into account.

CONCLUSIONS

Our comparison of Anglophobia and Islamophobia in Scotland suggests four broad conclusions.

Less Anglophobia. Among majority Scots (tightly defined to exclude both English immigrants and their partners), Anglophobia runs at a lower level than Islamophobia. On five strictly comparable indicators, Anglophobia runs 11 per cent behind Islamophobia - at 38 per cent compared to 49 per cent.

But not much less Anglophobia. In Scotland, the level of Anglophobia, though less, is comparable with that of Islamophobia. The difference between Islamophobia in Scotland and England is greater than the difference between the levels of Anglophobia and Islamophobia within Scotland.

Moreover, the difference between Anglophobia and Islamophobia in Scotland varies sharply across our five indicators. There is a large difference on social exclusion: few (only 5 per cent) 'would feel unhappy if a close relative married or formed a long-term relationship with an English person now living in Scotland' but far more (32 per cent) if the relationship was 'with a Muslim'. There is somewhat less difference on economic resentment: almost a fifth (18 per cent) of majority Scots feel that English immigrants 'take jobs, housing and healthcare from other people in Scotland' rather than 'contributing a lot' to Scotland, but almost a third (30 per cent) feel that Muslims do that. Similarly, on fears for national identity, two-fifths (42 per cent) feel that 'Scotland would begin to lose its identity' if more English immigrants came to live in Scotland, and half (52 per cent) if more Muslims came.

However, on two indicators of commitment and loyalty, the differences are small and inconsistent. On commitment to Scotland, Anglophobia is only a little less than Islamophobia: 44 per cent feel that the English immigrants 'could never be really committed to Scotland', but 53 per cent feel that Muslims 'could never be really committed to Scotland'. Meanwhile, on loyalty, Anglophobia slightly exceeds Islamophobia: 81 per cent feel that English immigrants 'are more loyal to England', and only 79 per cent feel that Muslims 'are more loyal to other Muslims around the world' than they are to Scotland. The difference is too small to be statistically significant, but it shows beyond statistical doubt that 'majority Scots' do not draw any great distinction between the loyalty of English immigrants and Muslims.

Phobias generally go together. Anything that encourages one phobia tends to encourage the other – though not necessarily to the same degree. Having either an English friend or a Muslim friend reduces both Anglophobia and Islamophobia – especially the specific phobia corresponding to the friend, of course; but, beyond that, friendship has more impact on Islamophobia than on Anglophobia. Both Anglophobia and Islamophobia increase with age and generation (that is, older age and generations) – though Islamophobia more than Anglophobia. Higher education reduces both Anglophobia and Islamophobia – though Islamophobia more than Anglophobia. Liberal Democrat voters are at once the least Anglophobic and the least Islamophobic.

But narrow parochialism and nationalism have significantly different impacts on different phobias. Narrow backgrounds and attitudes have more impact on Islamophobia, but nationalism has more impact on Anglophobia. An exclusively Scottish identity increases phobias. But, in sharp contrast to low education, being older, or a lack of minority friendships, which might all be interpreted as indicators of narrow parochialism, having an exclusively Scottish national identity has much more impact on Anglophobia (13 per cent) than on Islamophobia (only 4 per cent) – though it has much less impact on Anglophobia than English national identity has on Islamophobia in England (20 per cent).

Similarly, while SNP voters are the most Anglophobic (16 per cent more so than Lib Dems), Conservative voters are the most Islamophobic in Scotland (12 per cent more so than Lib Dems) – though Conservative voters in England are even more Islamophobic (14 per cent more so than even Scottish Conservative voters).

So, is Scottish nationalism, unlike English nationalism, 'benign' rather than 'nasty', as so many writers suggest? Towards Muslims, the answer must be an unequivocal 'yes'. But, towards English immigrants, perhaps not. Scottish nationalism, unlike English nationalism, does not make people significantly more Islamophobic. But, at street level, if not at Alex Salmond's SNP leadership level, it does make them more Anglophobic.

ACKNOWLEDGEMENT

This research was supported by grants to the authors from the ESRC (Economic and Social Research Council, grant no. L219252118) and the Nuffield Foundation (grant no. OPD/00213/G).

REFERENCES

Breuilly, J. (1993), *Nationalism and the State*, 2nd edn, Manchester: Manchester University Press.

Brubaker, R. (1996), *Nationalism Reframed: Nationhood and the National Question in the New Europe*, Cambridge: Cambridge University Press.

Dinwoodie, R. (2003), 'Evicted asylum seekers denied final appeal: lack of access a disgrace, SNP claims', *The Herald*, 10 October, p. 10.

Dinwoodie, R., Settle, M. and Puttick, H. (2003), 'Swinney attacks "racist" Labour policies', *The Herald*, 8 September, p. 1.

Edensor, T. (1997), 'Reading Braveheart: representing and contesting Scottish identity', *Scottish Affairs*, 21: 135–58.

Fedorowich, K. (1999), 'Reconstruction and resettlement: the politicization of Irish migration to Australia and Canada 1919–29', *English Historical Review*, 114: 1143–78.

Findlay, R. (2005), 'Scotland and the monarchy', in W. L. Miller (ed.), *Proceedings of the British Academy 128: Anglo-Scottish Relations since 1900*, Oxford: Oxford University Press.

Gellner, E. (1994), *Nations and Nationalism*, Oxford: Blackwell.

Hearn, J. (2000), *Claiming Scotland: National Identity and Liberal Culture*, Edinburgh: Polygon.

Henderson, A. (1999), 'Political constructions of national identity in Scotland and Quebec', *Scottish Affairs*, 29: 121–38.

Horsburgh, F. (2003), 'SNP fails to split coalition over asylum seekers stuck in (detention) regime', *The Herald*, 12 September, p. 7.

Hussain, A. and Miller, W. L. (2004), 'How and why Islamophobia is tied to English nationalism but not to Scottish nationalism', *Ethnic Studies Review*, 27: 78–101.

Kellas, J. (1998), *The Politics of Nationalism and Ethnicity*, 2nd edn, Basingstoke: Macmillan.

Kymlicka, W. (2001), *Politics in the Vernacular: Nationalism, Multiculturalism and Citizenship*, Oxford: Oxford University Press.

McConnell, J. (2003), speaking at the City Challenge Conference, Edinburgh, 25 Feb 2003. Reported at length in *The Scotsman* 26 Feb 2003, p. 9, 'McConnell bids to attract more refugees to Scotland' and supplement pp. 2–3, 'Your country needs you' above a picture of visible ethnic minorities; *The Independent*, 26 Feb 2003, p. 7, 'Scots seek immigrants to reverse brain drain'; *The Guardian*, 26 Feb 2003, p. 6, 'Scotland launches drive to draw in foreign workers'; *The Herald*, 26 Feb 2003, p. 2, 'Immigration is McConnell's solution to population fall'.

McCrone, D., Stewart R., Kiely, R. and Bechhofer, F. (1998), 'Who are we? Problematising national identity', *Sociological Review*, 46: 629–52.

Modood, T. and Werbner, P. (eds) (1997), *The Politics of Multiculturalism in the New Europe: Racism, Identity and Community*, London: Zed.

Parekh, B. (2000), *Rethinking Multiculturalism: Cultural Diversity and Political Theory*, Basingstoke: Macmillan.

Paterson, L., Brown, A., Curtice, J., Hinds, K., McCrone, D., Park, A., Sproston, K. and Surridge, P. (2001), *New Scotland, New Politics?*, Edinburgh: Polygon.

Porter, B. (2000), *When Nationalism Began to Hate: Imagining Modern Politics in Nineteenth-Century Poland*, New York: Oxford University Press.

Pulzer, P. (1988), *The Rise of Political Anti-Semitism in Germany and Austria*, London: Peter Halban.

Salmond, A. (1997), *Hansard*, 30 July, vol. 299, col. 396.

Scottish Parliament (1999), *Official Report*, 9 June, vol. 1, col. 5.

Sendich, M. and Payin, E. (1994), *The New Russian Diaspora: Russian Minorities in the Former Soviet Republics*. Armonk, NY: Sharpe.

Swinney, J. (2002), 'Patron saint should promote Scotland', *The Scotsman*, 19 November, p. 8.

Vincent, A. (1997), 'Liberal nationalism: an irresponsible compound?', *Political Studies*, 45: 275–95.

CHAPTER 11

Conclusion

The contributions to this book have covered a wide terrain. They have examined how well the Scottish public think they are being governed now that devolution is in place. They have considered how the public have behaved when electing their MSPs. And they have analysed the incidence and nature of national identity in post-devolution Scotland. In so doing, they have examined and evaluated many of the key claims that were made about what devolution would deliver for Scotland. Now we consider how well the devolution project appears to emerge from the scrutiny to which it has been subjected.

In the Introduction, we outlined two key claims made on behalf of devolution. The first was that, by demonstrating the ability of the Union to accommodate Scotland's distinctiveness, the Union might actually be strengthened. Cognitive support for remaining in the Union would increase, while more people would feel an affective sense of Britishness. The second claim was that, by bringing the government of Scotland closer to those whom it seeks to serve, and in so doing making it both more accountable and more accessible, people in Scotland would feel that they were being better governed. As a result, it was hoped that they would feel more 'engaged' in their country's democratic process. We will examine how far these objectives appear to have been fulfilled in turn.

Perhaps the simplest measure of the strength of public support for the Union is the number of people who say that they would prefer Scotland to become independent. If fewer people say that they would like Scotland to be independent, then public support for the Union can be said to be stronger. If more people say that they would like Scotland to be independent, then support for the Union would appear to be weaker. In truth, neither development has occurred. Immediately after the 1997 UK general election, 26 per cent said that they favoured independence. Soon after the 2003 Scottish Parliament election, again 26 per cent expressed a preference for independence. It would seem that devolution has neither strengthened nor weakened public support for the Union.

There are, however, some ways in which the Union does look stronger. The prospect of independence appears to have become more remote in the public's mind; the proportion thinking that the advent of devolution makes independence more likely has diminished by as much as a third since 1999. Although nearly a half of Scots still feel that Scotland receives less than its fair share of public spending (despite a continuing elite-level debate about the alleged generosity of the level of public spending in Scotland), no longer is there a predominant perception that England gets more out of the Union economically than Scotland does. To that degree, at least, envy of Scotland's southern neighbour seems to have declined. Meanwhile, around half think that creating the Scottish Parliament has actually strengthened Scotland's voice in the United Kingdom. Indeed, this is the achievement for which Scots appear most willing to give the Scottish Parliament credit.

But, in other ways, it would seem that devolution has achieved relatively little. First, the proportion of people willing to acknowledge a British identity has not increased. Indeed, on one of our measures, Moreno national identity, the proportion claiming some degree of British identity has consistently been lower since 1999 than it was previously. British national identity certainly continues to play second fiddle to Scottish national identity, even if many feel able to acknowledge it in addition to their Scottish identity. Second, there has actually been an increase since 1999 in the proportion of people who say that the government of Britain as a whole is in need of improvement. Finally, just under one in five Scots say that they support the principal political opponents of the Union, the SNP, a figure little different from what it was a decade earlier even if support for the SNP appears to be more fragile than that enjoyed by Labour.

Yet, perhaps all of this is somewhat to miss the point. Devolution may not have contributed a great deal to increased explicit public support for the Union, but it does at least seem to have secured legitimacy for itself. A majority of Scots continue to prefer devolution rather than independence or the status quo ante. Around two in three trust the Scottish Parliament to look after Scotland's interests 'just about always' or 'most of the time', an accolade that only around one in five are prepared to extend to the UK government. Similar proportions also feel that the parliament rather than the UK government should have the most influence over what happens in Scotland. It seems that, whatever the controversy or disappointment that may surround decisions made by the parliament, they are thought to have the crucial virtue of being decisions made at home rather than imported from England.

If that analysis is correct, then devolution (and by implication a continued willingness to remain in the Union) should continue to secure public support so long as it seems to fulfil the need felt by many in Scotland that their country should have its own recognisably distinct national political institutions. What perhaps remains in question is whether the current devolution settlement can meet that need in the long term. For, as we have seen on a variety of measures, Westminster still emerges as the more powerful body in the public's mind than does Holyrood, the very opposite of what they think *should* be the case. At the same time, nearly three in five think that the parliament should have more powers. Perhaps the current devolution settlement will need to be adjusted somewhat before it represents a sufficient response to the demand that Scotland should have its own political institutions.

Still, it would seem that, in responding to that demand, devolution has avoided the apparent danger that it would promote a 'narrow' or 'nasty' ethnic nationalism. Scottish national identity does apparently have more of a 'civic' than an 'ethnic' character. It is an identity that many of those who have moved to Scotland feel able to adopt once they have lived in the country for a while. It is an identity to which those from a non-white background are regarded as having a legitimate claim if they exhibit markers of the country's culture, such as a Scottish accent. True, there is some evidence that those who hold a Scottish identity while rejecting a British one are rather more likely to exhibit some dislike of immigrants from England, while it would certainly be a mistake to argue that all Scots are necessarily accepting of all those who decide to settle in their country. But much of the antipathy that does exist seems to be associated with other characteristics, such as a low level of educational attainment, rather than with a strong adherence to a Scottish national identity.

All in all, it might be felt that, so far as the first set of claims is concerned, the balance sheet of devolution's achievements is a positive one. But what of the second set of claims, that devolution should improve the accountability and accessibility of government and make people in Scotland feel better about the way they are being governed? How much of this agenda appears to have been achieved?

Much of our evidence suggests that it has not. For the most part, people feel that having a Scottish Parliament has not improved how they are governed or the quality of the public services that they receive. Despite the hopes that devolution would make government more accessible, only around two in five think that having the Scottish Parliament is giving ordinary people more say. More people feel now that their politicians soon lose touch with them or that parties are only interested in people's votes rather than their opinions than was the case when the parliament was first created. Meanwhile, only around one in four feel that having a Scottish Parliament is improving the quality of education. At the same time, nearly a half feel that the health service has actually got worse during the first four years of devolution, while only one in five feel that it has become better.

Moreover, when Scots are disappointed with the performance of those newly responsible for their nation's affairs, they do not appear to reflect this in the ballot box. Those who in 2003 thought that the Scottish Executive was responsible for what they thought had been a decline in the public services in Scotland over the previous four years were not particularly disinclined to vote Labour (or Liberal Democrat) in that year's Scottish Parliament election. This makes it difficult to argue that the introduction of Scottish Parliament elections has ensured that the government of Scotland is accountable to the electorate. Equally, what people thought of the various policy proposals put forward by the parties in the 2003 election does not seem to have made much difference to how they voted. Or, rather, if they did react to these proposals or to the leaders promoting them, it was reflected in a decision not to vote at all. Those who in truth have never been particularly interested in politics and require some stimulus to go to the polls appear to have stayed at home in large numbers simply because they found the choices put before them to be too dull to be worth the effort. At the same time, voters' enthusiasm for voting was not enhanced by the fact that they were being asked to vote under an electoral system which most did not understand very well and which seems to have lost some of its popularity between 1999 and 2003.

On the other hand, some of the worst fears about the impact of devolution on the quality of Scottish democracy do not appear to have been realised. Elections to the Scottish Parliament may not have particularly high turnouts, but they cannot be dismissed as unimportant 'second-order' affairs in which those who do vote do so primarily on the basis of what is happening at Westminster. Even a reserved matter as divisive as the war in Iraq only had a small impact on the way that people voted in 2003. Equally, it cannot be argued that people felt able to vote for smaller parties in large numbers because they thought that the election did not matter very much; perceptions of the importance of the election seem to have made little difference to people's willingness to vote for a smaller party in 2003. True, many of those who voted for a smaller party on the list vote seem to have been backing a second choice, but in so doing they were clearly giving expression to a relatively distinctive and perhaps relatively well-informed set of values.

Meanwhile, responsibility for the disappointments of the early years of devolution is not necessarily thought to lie with Holyrood itself. As we indicated above, there are widespread doubts about how much influence the Holyrood parliament actually has. Fewer than one in five think that the Scottish Parliament has most influence over what happens in Scotland; nearly two-thirds think that Westminster does. Even when people are asked specifically about such devolved matters as health and education, more feel that Westminster is responsible for recent trends in Scotland than feel that the devolved institutions are. Moreover, it is those who are critical of what has been achieved in health and education who are most likely to feel that the responsibility – and thus the blame – lies with Westminster. It is perhaps unsurprising that the creation of the Scottish Parliament has not persuaded people that they are being better governed if that body is thought in practice to be relatively uninfluential.

Our evidence does not suggest either that disappointment with the achievements of devolution – including the saga of the parliament's new building – explains why people did not vote in the 2003 elections or indeed that it did much to undermine confidence in the principle of devolution. Equally, while people may have become more cynical about politicians and political parties, an even bigger increase in cynicism occurred in England over the same period, suggesting that responsibility for the increase does not necessarily lie with the Scottish Parliament. Indeed, it is even possible that it helped to stem an adverse tide whose origins lie with politicians in London.

Nevertheless, while it can hardly be convincingly argued that devolution has weakened the public's relationships with its rulers, the devolution project has evidently not found it easy to strengthen the involvement of the general public in Scotland's political process. In providing Scotland with her own distinctive national political institutions without doing harm at least to support for the Union, the devolution project can be said, so far at least, to have delivered. But getting the public actively engaged in the working of that mechanism has proved to be a rather more elusive objective.

Technical Appendix

TECHNICAL ASPECTS OF THE SURVEYS

Most data in this book are drawn from the 2003 Scottish Social Attitudes Survey and its predecessors conducted by the Scottish Centre for Social Research, a part of the National Centre for Social Research. The 2003 survey was the fifth in an annual series, which started in 1999 with the Scottish Parliamentary Election Survey (Paterson et al. 2001). The series is parallel to the long-established British Social Attitudes Survey (Park et al. 2004). In addition, data have also been drawn from the Scottish Election Surveys of 1979, 1992 and 1997, together with the 1997 Scottish Referendum Survey. The datasets of all these surveys are publicly available through the UK Data Archive at the University of Essex.

DETAILS OF THE 2003 SCOTTISH SOCIAL ATTITUDES SURVEY

The survey was funded from a number of sources. Two modules, one on elections and devolution and one on constitutional change, were funded through a grant (number L219252033) from the Economic and Social Research Council as part of its Devolution and Constitutional Change research programme. Further questions on identity and devolution were funded by the Leverhulme Trust as part of its Nations and Regions research programme. The Independent Commission on Proportional Representation (ICPR 2004) funded a module of questions on attitudes to electoral systems, while a module on attitudes towards English people and Muslims in Scotland was funded by the Nuffield Foundation. A further module on access to services that was funded by the Scottish Executive is not reported here. None of these bodies is responsible for the interpretations of the data provided in this book.

The survey comprised a face-to-face interview with 1,508 respondents and a self-completion questionnaire that was completed by 1,324

(88 per cent) of those who completed the face-to-face interview. Copies of the two questionnaires are available from the website of the Scottish Centre for Social Research (www.scotcen.org.uk).

Sample design

The 2003 Scottish Social Attitudes Survey was designed to yield a representative sample of adults aged 18 or over in Scotland. People were eligible for inclusion in the survey if they were aged 18 when the interviewer first made contact with them. The sampling frame for the survey was the Postcode Address File (PAF), a list of addresses (or postal delivery points) compiled by the Post Office.

For practical reasons, the sample was confined to those living in private households. People living in institutions (such as nursing homes or hospitals, though not in private households at such institutions) were excluded, as were households whose addresses were not on the Postcode Address File. The sampling method involved a multi-stage design, with three separate stages of selection, namely of sectors, addresses and individuals:

1. Postcode sectors were selected from a list of all postal sectors in Scotland, with probability proportional to the number of addresses in each sector. In 2003, eighty-four postcode sectors were selected. Prior to selection, the sectors were stratified by region, population density, and percentage of household heads recorded as employers/ managers (taken from the 2001 census). The list was also stratified using the Scottish Household Survey (SHS) six-fold classification of urban and rural areas (for further details, see below), in part so that sectors in rural and remote areas could be over-sampled.

2. Thirty-one addresses were selected from each sector located within one of the three most urban categories in the SHS urban/rural classification (four largest cities, other urban areas, and accessible small towns), while sixty-two addresses were selected from each sector located within one of the three most rural categories (remote small towns, accessible rural areas and remote rural areas). The total size of the issued samples is shown in Table A.1 below.

   In some places, more than one accommodation space shares an address. The Multiple Occupancy Indicator (MOI) on the Postcode Address File shows whether this is known to be the case. If the MOI indicated more than one accommodation space at a given address, the chance of the given address being selected from the list of addresses was increased to match the total number of accommodation spaces.

As would be expected, the majority of MOIs had a value of one (96 per cent of those where an interview was obtained). The value for the remainder, which ranged between three and fifteen, was incorporated into the weighting procedures (described below). In total, the sample comprised 3,007 addresses.

3. Interviewers called at each selected address, identified its eligibility and, where an address was eligible, listed all residents eligible for inclusion in the sample – that is, all persons currently aged 18 or over residing at the selected address. The interviewer then selected one respondent using a computer-generated random selection procedure.

Table A.1   Response rate to 2003 survey

	Number	%
Addresses issued	3,007	
Vacant, derelict and other out of scope[1]	358	12
In scope	2,649	
Interview achieved	1,508	57
Self-completion returned	1,324	50
Interview not achieved	1,141	43
Refused[2]	830	31
Non-contacted[3]	146	6
Unknown eligibility[4]	53	2
Other non-response	112	4

Notes to table
1. This included empty or derelict addresses, holiday homes, businesses and institutions.
2. Refusals include refusals prior to selection of an individual, refusals to the office, refusal by the selected person, 'proxy' refusals made by someone on behalf of the respondent, and broken appointments after which a respondent could not be recontacted.
3. Non-contacts comprise households where no-one was contacted after at least four calls and those where the selected person could not be contacted.
4. 'Unknown eligibility' includes cases where the address could not be located, where it could not be determined if an address was a residence and where it could not be determined if an address was occupied or not.

Weighting

The data were weighted to take account of the fact that not all the units covered in the survey had the same probability of selection. The weighting reflected the relative selection probabilities of the individual at the three main stages of selection: address, household and individual.

First, because addresses were selected using the Multiple Occupancy Indicator (MOI), weights had to be applied to compensate for the greater probability of an address with an MOI of more than one being selected, compared to an address with an MOI of one. Second, the data were weighted to compensate for the fact that dwelling units at an address which contained a large number of dwelling units were less likely to be selected for inclusion in the survey than ones which did not share an address. (We used this procedure because in most cases these two stages will cancel each other out, resulting in more efficient weights.) Third, the data were weighted to compensate for the lower selection probabilities of adults living in large households compared with those living in small households. Finally, weighting was applied to correct the over-sampling of addresses in rural and remote areas. All weights fell within a range between 0.049 and 2.948. The weighted sample was scaled so that the number of weighted productive cases exactly equalled the number of unweighted productive cases. All the percentages presented in this book are based on weighted data, but the sample sizes in the tables are unweighted.

Fieldwork

Interviewing was carried out between May and October 2003, with 80 per cent of the interviews being completed by the end of August. An advance letter advising people living at selected addresses that an interviewer would call was distributed before the interviewers called.

Fieldwork was conducted by interviewers drawn from the National Centre's regular panel of interviewers and undertaken using face-to-face computer-assisted interviewing. (Computer-assisted interviewing uses lap-top computers that display on the computer screen the questions inter-viewers should ask and that provide a means for recording respondents' answers.) Interviewers attended a one-day briefing conference to familiarise them with the questionnaires and procedures for selecting addresses and individuals to interview.

The average interview length was fifty-eight minutes. The interviewers achieved an overall response rate of 57 per cent. Details are shown in Table A.1.

All respondents were asked to fill in a self-completion questionnaire that, whenever possible, was collected by the interviewer, but in some cases was posted to the National Centre. Up to three postal reminders were sent to obtain the maximum number of self-completion supplements.

A total of 184 respondents (12 per cent of those interviewed) did not return their self-completion questionnaire. It was judged that it was not necessary to apply additional weights to correct for this non-response.

Other surveys used in this book

Previous Scottish Social Attitudes surveys

The sample design of the previous Scottish Social Attitudes surveys conducted annually between 2000 and 2002 was similar to that of the 2003 survey except that rural and remote areas were not over-sampled prior to the 2002 survey. These three surveys were funded by a variety of sources, though in most cases the cost of collecting the data used in this book was funded by either the Economic and Social Research Council (ESRC) or the Leverhulme Trust. Further details about these surveys can be found in Curtice et al. (2001), Bromley et al. (2003) and Bromley and Curtice (2003). The achieved sample sizes of these surveys were as follows:

2000 1,663 (response rate 65 per cent), of whom 1,506 also returned the self-completion questionnaire
2001 1,605 (response rate 60 per cent), of whom 1,383 also returned the self-completion questionnaire
2002 1,665 (response rate 62 per cent), of whom 1,507 also returned the self-completion questionnaire

Scottish Election Surveys

A Scottish Parliamentary Election/Scottish Social Attitudes survey was carried out in 1999, and full details of its sample design and survey methods – which were very similar to those described above for the 2003 survey – can be found in Paterson et al. (2001). It was funded by the ESRC. Previous Scottish Election Surveys were conducted as part of the British Election Survey (BES) series immediately after the October 1974, 1979, 1992 and 1997 UK general elections. The samples for each of these studies were chosen using random selection modified by stratification and clustering. Until 1992, the sampling frame used was the electoral register (ER); in 1997 it was the Postcode Address File (PAF). Weights can be applied to make the 1997 survey (PAF) comparable with the previous (ER) samples. The achieved sample sizes were:

1979 729 (response rate 61 per cent)
1992 957 (response rate 74 per cent)
1997 882 (response rate 62 per cent)

Weighting of the data was carried out in each year to take account of unequal selection probabilities.

Scottish Referendum Survey

The Scottish Referendum Survey (alongside a comparative Welsh Referendum Survey) was undertaken in September–October 1997, funded by the ESRC. Fieldwork was carried out by the National Centre for Social Research, and interviewing began immediately after the referendum on 11 September 1997.

The sample was designed to be representative of the adult population who were living in private households in Scotland and eligible to vote in the referendum. It was drawn from the Postcode Address File and involved stratification and clustering. Weighting of the data was subsequently carried out to correct for variable selection probabilities.

The survey involved a face-to-face interview, administered using a traditional paper questionnaire, and a self-completion questionnaire. The number of interviews carried out was 676, a response rate of 68 per cent. Self-completion questionnaires were obtained from 657 respondents (97 per cent of those interviewed).

British Social Attitudes survey

The BSA survey, on which the Scottish Social Attitudes survey is modelled, has been running annually since 1983. It aims to yield a representative sample of adults aged 18 and over living in Britain. Since 1993, the sampling frame has been the Postcode Address File. The sample is selected by methods similar to those used for the Scottish Social Attitudes surveys. The sample size has generally been between 3,000 and 3,500, with about 300–350 of the interviews being conducted in Scotland. The purpose of the surveys is to go beyond the work of opinion polls to collect information about underlying changes in people's attitudes and values. Further information on each year's British Social Attitudes survey is contained in the relevant annual report on it: see, for example, Park et al. (2004).

CLASSIFICATIONS USED IN ANALYSIS

Standard Occupational Classification

Respondents are classified according to their own occupation, not that of the 'head of household'. Each respondent was asked about either their current or their last job, so that only those respondents who had never worked were not coded. Additionally, if the respondent was not working but their spouse or partner *was* working, their spouse or partner was similarly classified.

In the 2003 survey, occupation was coded using the new Standard Occupational Classification 2000 (SOC 2000), which has now replaced the Standard Occupational Classification 1990 (SOC 90). The main socio-economic grouping that can be derived from SOC 2000 is the National Statistics Socio-Economic Classification (NS-SEC).

National Statistics Socio-Economic Classification (NS-SEC)

A combination of the SOC 2000 code and the respondent's employment status in their current or last job is used to generate the following seven NS-SEC analytic classes:

- Employers in large organisations, higher managerial and professional
- Lower professional and managerial; higher technical and supervisory
- Intermediate occupations
- Small employers and own-account workers
- Lower supervisory and technical occupations
- Semi-routine occupations
- Routine occupations

The remaining respondents are grouped as 'never had a job' or 'not classifiable'. For some analyses, it may be more appropriate to classify respondents according to their current socio-economic status, which takes into account only their present economic position. In this case, in addition to the seven classes listed above, the remaining respondents not currently in paid work fall into one of the following categories: 'not classifiable', 'retired', 'looking after the home', 'unemployed', or 'others not in paid occupations'.

Industry

All respondents whose occupation could be coded were allocated a Standard Industrial Classification 1992 (SIC 92) code. Two-digit class codes are used. As with social class, SIC may be generated on the basis of the respondent's current occupation only, or on his or her most recently classifiable occupation.

Urban/rural classification

The urban/rural character of the area in which a respondent lived was measured using the urban/rural scale adopted by the Scottish Household Survey (Hope et al. 2000). This scale places each postcode sector in Scotland into one of six categories as shown in Table A.2.

Table A.2 **Scottish Household Survey (SHS) six-fold classification of urban and rural areas**

Area type	Postcode sectors in
1 The four cities	Settlements over 125,000 population (Aberdeen, Dundee, Glasgow and Edinburgh)
2 Other urban	Other settlements over 10,000 population
3 Small, accessible towns	Settlements 3–10,000 population *and* within a 30-minute drive of a settlement of 10,000 or more
4 Small, remote towns	Settlements 3–10,000 population *and* more than a 30-minute drive of a settlement of 10,000 or more
5 Accessible rural	Settlements less than 3,000 population *and* within a 30-minute drive of a settlement of 10,000 or more
6 Remote rural	Settlements less than 3,000 population *and* more than a 30-minute drive of a settlement of 10,000 or more

Party identification

Respondents were classified as identifying with a particular political party if they considered themselves supporters of that party, or as closer to it than to others, or more likely to support a party in the event of a general election.

National identity

One question asked in the survey that taps national identity is known as the Moreno scale (Moreno 1988). It measures the relative strength of Scottish and British national identity by asking the following question:

Which, if any, of the following best describes how you see yourself?
Scottish, not British
More Scottish than British
Equally Scottish and British
More British than Scottish
British, not Scottish
None of these

A second question asked in the survey simply asks respondents to select one or more identities from a list. They are asked:

Please say which, if any, of the words on this card describes the way you think of yourself. Please choose as many or as few as apply.
British, English, European, Irish, Northern Irish, Scottish, Welsh, Ulster, Other answer.

Those who select more than one of these are then further asked the following:

If you had to choose, which one best describes the way you think of yourself?

Attitude scales

The 2003 Scottish Social Attitudes survey included two Likert-type attitude scales designed to measure where respondents stood on certain underlying value dimensions (Heath et al. 1994). These were a left–right (or socialist–laissez-faire) scale and a liberal–authoritarian scale. Two versions of these scales have been in use since the 1986 BSA and 1987 BES. One version is usually included in BSA surveys whereas the other has been used in the election study series. The 1999, 2001 and 2003 Scottish Social Attitudes surveys carried the BES versions of the left–right scales (for details, see below), whereas the 2000 and 2002 surveys asked the BSA version. Meanwhile, the 1999 Scottish Social Attitudes survey asked the BES version of the libertarian–authoritarian scales, whereas all subsequent surveys included the BSA version (see below). For details of the 2000 left–right scale, see Curtice et al. (2001); for details of the 1999 libertarian–authoritarian scale, see Paterson et al. (2001). A respondent's score on the two scales is calculated by combining into an additive index their answers to a set of individual survey items that between them measure different aspects of the underlying value in question. This approach rests on the assumption that there is an underlying – 'latent' – attitudinal or value dimension that characterises the answers to all of the questions included in the scale (DeVellis 1991; Spector 1992). If this is the case, then the scale scores are likely to be a more reliable indication of where a respondent stands on the underlying dimension than would the answers to any single question.

The items that comprise the two scales included on the 2003 survey are as follows:

Left–right (socialist–laissez-faire) scale
Ordinary working people get their fair share of the nation's wealth
There is one law for the rich and one for the poor
There is no need for strong trade unions to protect employees' working conditions and wages
Private enterprise is the best way to solve Britain's economic problems
Major public services and industries ought to be in state ownership
It is the government's responsibility to provide a job for everyone who wants one

Libertarian–authoritarian scale
Young people today don't have enough respect for Britain's traditional values
People who break the law should be given stiffer sentences
For some crimes, the death penalty is the most appropriate sentence
Schools should teach children to obey authority
The law should always be obeyed, even if a particular law is wrong
Censorship of films and magazines is necessary to uphold moral standards

Low values on the scales represent the socialist and liberal positions respectively.

DATA INTERPRETATION

Statistical significance

All of the data in the book are derived from samples of the population. This means that they are subject to sampling error. However, it is possible to calculate the confidence intervals for any value from a given sample; these intervals specify the range within which we can have a certain level of confidence that the true value in the whole population lies. Table A.3 gives an indication of the confidence intervals that apply to different percentages for different sample sizes. The intervals shown are 95 per cent confidence intervals, meaning that we can be 95 per cent sure that the true answer lies within the range shown. For example, for a percentage result of 50 per cent based on a sample of 500, there is a 95 per cent chance that the true result lies within +/− 4 per cent (thus, between 46 per cent and 54 per cent).

These confidence intervals assume a simple random sample and do not make any adjustment for the effects of clustering the sample into a number of sample points. Although such an adjustment would increase the confidence limits slightly, in most cases these would not differ notably from those shown in Table A.3 (Paterson 2000: Appendix). It should be noted that certain types of variables (those most associated with the area a person lives in) are more affected by clustering than others. For example, Labour identifiers and local-authority tenants tend to be concentrated in certain areas and so, when the effects of the sample's clustered design are taken into account, the confidence intervals around such variables are greater than is the case for many other attitudinal variables (see Park et al. 2004 for examples of these kinds of design effects).

Table A.3 Confidence intervals for survey findings

Sample size	Approximate 95 per cent confidence limits for a percentage result of:		
	10 per cent or 90 per cent +/−	30 per cent or 70 per cent +/−	50 per cent +/−
50	8	13	14
100	6	9	10
250	4	6	6
500	3	4	4
1,000	2	3	3
2,000	1	2	2

Tests of statistical significance take account of the confidence intervals attached to survey findings. They can be carried out using modelling techniques (such as those described below), or by hand. Whenever comments on differences between sub-groups of the sample are made in this book, these differences have been tested and found to be statistically significant at the 95 per cent level or above. Similarly, although standard deviations are mostly not presented alongside mean figures in this book, these have been calculated and used to verify the statistical significance of the differences between mean figures which are commented on.

Statistical modelling

For many of the more complex analyses in the book, we have used logistic or linear regression models to assess whether there is reliable evidence that particular variables are associated with each other.

Regression analysis aims to summarise the relationship between a 'dependent' variable and one or more 'independent' explanatory variables. It shows how well we can estimate a respondent's score on the dependent variable from knowledge of their scores on the independent variables. The technique takes into account the relationship between the different independent variables (for example, between education and income, or social class and housing tenure). Regression is often undertaken to support a claim that the phenomena measured by the independent variables cause the phenomenon measured by the dependent variable. However, the causal ordering, if any, between the variables cannot be verified or falsified by the technique. Causality can only be inferred through special experimental designs or through assumptions made by the analyst. All regression analysis assumes that the relationship between the dependent and each of the independent variables takes a particular form. In *linear regression*, a common form of regression analysis, it is assumed that the relationship can be adequately summarised by a straight line. This means that a one-point increase in the value of an independent variable is assumed to have the same impact on the value of the dependent variable on average, irrespective of the previous values of those variables.

Strictly speaking, the technique assumes that both the dependent and the independent variables are measured on an interval-level scale, although it may sometimes still be applied even where this is not the case. For example, one can use an ordinal variable (for example, a Likert scale) as a *dependent* variable if one is willing to assume that there is an underlying interval-level scale and that the difference between the observed ordinal scale and the underlying interval scale is due to random measurement error. Categorical or nominal data can be used as *independent* variables by converting them into dummy or binary variables; these are variables where the only valid scores are 0 and 1, with 1 signifying membership of a particular category and 0 otherwise.

The assumptions of linear regression can cause particular difficulties where the *dependent* variable is binary. The assumption that the relationship between the dependent and the independent variables is a straight line means that it can produce estimated values for the dependent variable of less than 0 or greater than 1. In this case, it may be more appropriate to assume that the relationship between the dependent and the independent variables takes the form of an S-curve, where the impact on the dependent variable of a one-point increase in an independent variable becomes progressively less the closer the value of the dependent variable approaches 0 or 1. *Logistic regression* is an alternative form of regression which fits such an S-curve rather than a straight line. The technique can also be adapted to analyse multinomial non-interval-level dependent variables, that is, variables that classify respondents into more than two categories.

Full technical details of regression can be found in many textbooks on social statistics, for example Bryman and Cramer (1997).

References

Bromley, C. and Curtice, J. (2003), *Attitudes to Discrimination in Scotland*, Edinburgh: Scottish Executive.

Bromley, C., Curtice, J., Hinds, K. and Park, A. (2003), *Devolution – Scottish Answers to Scottish Questions?*, Edinburgh: Edinburgh University Press.

Bryman, A. and Cramer, D. (1997), *Quantitative Data Analysis*, London: Routledge.

Curtice, J., McCrone, D., Park, A. and Paterson, L. (eds) (2001), *New Scotland, New Society?*, Edinburgh: Polygon.

DeVellis, R. F. (1991), *Scale Development: Theory and Applications*, Newbury Park, CA: Sage.

Heath, A., Evans, G. and Martin, J. (1994), 'The measurement of core beliefs and values', *British Journal of Political Science*, 24: 115–31.

Hope, S., Braunholtz, S., Playfair, A., Dudleston, A., Ingram, D., Martin, C. and Sawyer, B. (2000), *Scotland's People: Results from the 1999 Scottish Household Survey, Volume 1*, Edinburgh: Scottish Executive.

Independent Commission on Proportional Representation (2004), *Changed Voting, Changed Politics: Lessons of Britain's Experience of PR since 1997*, London: Constitution Unit.

Moreno, L. (1988), 'Scotland and Catalonia: the path to home rule', in D. McCrone and A. Brown (eds), *The Scottish Government Yearbook 1988*, Edinburgh: Unit for the Study of Government in Scotland.

Park, A., Curtice, J., Thomson, K., Bromley, C. and Phillips, M. (eds) (2004), *British Social Attitudes: The 21st Report*, London: Sage.

Paterson, L. (2000), 'The social class of Catholics in Scotland', *Journal of the Royal Statistical Society* (Series A Statistics in Society), 163: 363–79.

Paterson, L., Brown, A., Curtice, J., Hinds, K., McCrone, D., Park, A., Sproston, K. and Surridge, P. (2001), *New Scotland, New Politics?*, Edinburgh: Edinburgh University Press.

Spector, P. E. (1992), *Summated Rating Scale Construction: An Introduction*, Newbury Park, CA: Sage.

Index